Camper's Guide to

Texas

Parks, Lakes, and Forests

Where to Go and How to Get There

FIFTH EDITION

Mickey Little

Taylor Trade Publishing
Lanham • New York • Boulder • Toronto • Oxford

CAMPER'S GUIDE TO
TEXAS
PARKS, LAKES, AND FORESTS
Where to Go and How to Get There
FIFTH EDITION

Copyright © 2006 by Mickey Little
First Taylor Trade Publishing edition 2006

This Taylor Trade Publishing paperback edition of
Camper's Guide to Texas Parks, Lakes, and Forests, 5th ed.,
is an original publication. It is published by arrangement with
the author.

All photographs are by the author unless otherwise indicated.

Published by Taylor Trade Publishing
An imprint of The Rowman & Littlefield Publishing Group, Inc.
4501 Forbes Boulevard, Suite 200, Lanham, Maryland 20706

Distributed by NATIONAL BOOK NETWORK

Library of Congress Cataloging-in-Publication Data
Little, Mildred J.
  Camper's guide to Texas parks, lakes, and forests : where to go and
how to get there / Mickey Little.—5th ed.
     p. cm.
  Includes bibiliographical references and index.
  ISBN 1-58979-204-1 (pbk. : alk. paper)
1. Camp sites, facilities, etc.–Texas–Directories. 2. Parks–Texas–
Recreational use–Guidebooks. 3. Lakes–Texas–Recreational use–
Guidebooks. 4. Forest reserves–Texas–Recreational use–
Guidebooks. 5. Texas–Guidebooks. I. Title: Camper's guide to
Texas. II. Title.
GV191.42.T4L58 2006
917.6406'864—dc22

                                                  2005019781

The paper used in this publication meets the minimum requirements of
American National Standard for Information Sciences—Permanence of
Paper for Printed Library Materials, ANSI/NISO Z39.48-1992.

Manufactured in the United States of America.

CONTENTS

PREFACE

This fifth edition of the *Camper's Guide* is substantially updated with address and phone number changes, revision of facility charts, addition of new trails, map revisions, and a website listing for agencies offering camping facilities. New entries include one state park (Lake Tawakoni); three LCRA parks (Canyon of the Eagles, Lake Fayette, and Pace Bend); and recreation areas on two of the National Grasslands (Caddo and LBJ).

The newest trend in trails is to construct or adapt existing trails so they are multi-use and can accomodate either mountain bikes and/or horses. Since the last edition, numerous parks have added mountain bike trails as well as equestrian trails. The updated "Facility & Activities" chart will depict those additions.

While every effort has been made to ensure accuracy of the information in this guide, neither I nor the publisher assumes liability arising from the use of this material. Because park facilities and policies and reservation procedures are subject to change, campers may want to verify the accuracy of important details before beginning a trip. May this fifth edition of the *Camper's Guide* contribute to your quest for many happy camping days in the Lone Star State!

Mickey Little
Johnson City, TX

ACKNOWLEDGMENTS

I am indebted to and wish to thank the following individuals and agencies for information in the form of maps, brochures, books, articles, telephone conversations, and personal interviews, without which this revision would not have been possible.

Colorado River Municipal Water District
Franklin County Water District
Gay Ippolito, National Forests & Grasslands in Texas
Guadalupe-Blanco River Authority
Lavaca-Navidad River Authority
Lower Colorado River Authority
Michael Owen, U.S. Army Corps of Engineers, Fort Worth District
National Forests & Grasslands in Texas
National Park Service
Sabine River Authority
Texas Department of Transportation, Travel Division
Texas Parks and Wildlife Department
Trinity River Authority
U.S. Army Corps of Engineers, Fort Worth District

Mickey Little
Johnson City, TX

INTRODUCTION

One of the greatest things about camping in Texas is that you can choose exactly what appeals to you—rugged mountains, placid lakes, thorny deserts, flowing rivers, sandy beaches, and lots more in between. The number of campgrounds located at our Texas parks, lakes, and forests appears to be almost countless. The purpose of this *Camper's Guide* is to suggest places to go and provide directions to get there. You will discover information about the popular, well-known campgrounds, as well as the lesser used ones—where you will find everything, except crowds!

These public campgrounds, provided and operated by federal, state, county, or city agencies, afford varied options for outdoor recreation. You can hike, swim, canoe, sail, fish, water ski, backpack, bicycle, or ride a horse. You can pursue your favorite hobby as a bird watcher, shell collector, photographer, geologist, botanist, or naturalist. You may choose to rough it at a primitive campsite or to enjoy all of the comforts of home in a recreational vehicle. You can spend a day, a weekend, or an entire vacation doing what you like best, no matter how active, or inactive, it is.

This fifth edition of *Camper's Guide to Texas Parks, Lakes, and Forests* is substantially updated with address and phone number changes, revision of the facility charts, map revisions and addition of new trails. Previous owners of a *Camper's Guide* will immediately notice the increased number of trails called multi-use trails. These trails can accommodate mountain bike, horses or hikers. "Resources for Further Information," located in Appendix 2, now includes the websites for the various agencies to enable you to go online for more detailed information. Six new entries include Lake Tawakoni (the one new state park); Canyon of the Eagles, Lake Fayette, and Pace Bend (all administered by the Lower Colorado River Authority); and, recreation areas located on the Caddo National Grasslands and LBJ National Grasslands.

Garner State Park is one of the most popular camping spots in Texas. The clear, spring-fed waters of the Frio River have a special attraction to the young and old alike.

Let's look more closely at the state of Texas and what it has to offer to the camping enthusiast. In elevation, the surface of the state varies from sea level along the coast of the Gulf of Mexico to 8,749 feet at the summit of Guadalupe Peak. Terrain varies from the subtropic Rio Grande Valley to the Great

Plains in the far north, from the lush pine forests of East Texas to the mountainous Trans-Pecos region of West Texas. In straight-line distance, Texas extends 801 miles from north to south and 773 miles from east to west. The tidewater coastline extends 624 miles.

The weather is generally characterized by mild temperatures. Average annual rainfall varies sharply, from more than 59 inches along the Sabine River to less than 8 inches in the extreme west. Included in Texas' 26 million acres of woodland are 4 national forests with 675,855 acres. The most important forest area of the state is the East Texas pine-hardwood region, known as the "Piney Woods." It extends over 43 counties.

Texas has 91 mountains a mile or more high, all of them in the Trans-Pecos region. Guadalupe Peak, at 8,749 feet, is the state's highest mountain. The longest river in the state is the Rio Grande, which forms the international boundary between Texas and Mexico and extends 1,270 miles along Texas. The next longest river is the Red River, which extends 726 miles.

Of the 50 states, Texas ranks second only to Alaska in the volume of its inland water—more than 6,000 square miles of lakes and streams. Toledo Bend Reservoir, on the Sabine River between Texas and Louisiana, is the largest reservoir in Texas or on its borders, with 185,000 surface acres at normal operating level. The largest body of water wholly within the state is Sam Rayburn Reservoir, with a normal surface area of 114,500 acres.

Texas is fortunate, indeed, to have so many agencies vitally interested in providing and maintaining such excellent camping facilities for the public. The Texas Parks and Wildlife Department presently operates over 82 parks that have camping facilities, and more are being added each year. Their continuing goal is to provide a park within a two-hour drive of every major metropolitan area in Texas.

Numerous parks with camping facilities are located along the shorelines of 24 lakes under the jurisdiction of the U.S. Army Corps of Engineers and at 18 other lakes under the jurisdiction of various river authorities, water districts, counties, and municipalities. Provisions for outdoor recreation development and administration vary greatly with each agency.

There are 4 national forests in Texas—Angelina, Davy Crockett, Sabine, and Sam Houston. They are open to the public for a wide variety of uses and pleasures. Presently, there are 13 recreation areas with camping facilities; maps are included for 10 of the campgrounds. These are designed and managed for families or small groups wanting "elbow room" in a natural forest setting. Backpacking and primitive camping are permitted anywhere in the national forests unless posted otherwise.

Six parks administered by the National Park Service of the U.S. Department of the Interior provide camping facilities: Amistad National Recreation Area, Big Bend National Park, Big Thicket National Preserve, Guadalupe Mountains National Park, Lake Meredith National Recreation Area, and Padre Island National Seashore. Because of the uniqueness of the national parks, a somewhat different format has been used to highlight points of interest and general information.

The Texas Department of Transportation operates travel information centers for the convenience of the traveling public. Visitors are provided with a wealth of information and free statewide travel brochures. The *Texas Official Travel Map* and the *Texas State Travel Guide* are also available at

Wow! What a lovely campsite near the water. A dream come true!

LOCATIONS OF TRAVEL INFORMATION CENTERS

Amarillo	I-40, east	806/335-1441
Anthony	I-10 (from New Mexico)	915/886-3468
Austin	State Capitol Complex	512/463-8586
Denison	US 75/69 (from Oklahoma)	903/463-2860
Gainesville	I-35 (from Oklahoma)	940/665-2301
Langtry	US 90 (Loop 25)	432/291-3340
Laredo	I-35 (from Mexico)	956/417-4728
Orange	I-10 (from Louisiana)	409/883-9416
Texarkana	I-30 (from Arkansas)	903/794-2114
Harlingen	Junction of US 77 & US 83	956/428-4477
Waskom	I-20 (from Louisiana)	903/687-2547
Wichita Falls	I-44, US 287, Exit 1C	940/723-7931

the centers. The travel information centers are open daily 8 am to 5 pm except New Year's Day, Thanksgiving, Christmas, and the day before Christmas. In addition, travel information, literature, and emergency road condition information may be obtained by calling 1-800-452-9292.

Texas pioneered the concept of highway rest areas along roadways, an idea that has been adopted nationally. More than 1,000 rest areas, picnic areas, and scenic turnouts invite travelers to pause and relax. Areas are equipped with shaded arbors, tables, benches, and cooking grills. One-day stops are permitted, limited to a maximum of 24 hours; no tent or other structure may be erected in such areas.

There are rules and regulations encountered at all public campgrounds, whether administered by a state or national agency. Please remember that policies, fees, regulations, and available facilities change from time to time. It's easy for campers to stay informed: request updated information from the parks you visit, read the material posted or distributed at the parks, and read newspaper articles reporting policy changes. And while we're on the subject of staying informed, take time to get acquainted with the remaining pages of this introduction; the information will guide you in planning your next camping trip. There's a lot to see in Texas . . . and what better way to see it than by camping!

STATE FACTS

State Name: From "Tejas," Indian word meaning "friendly"

State Motto: Friendship

State Nickname: Lone Star State

State Bird: Mockingbird

State Flower: Bluebonnet

State Tree: Pecan

State Grass: Sideoats Grama

State Gem: Topaz

State Stone: Petrified Palmwood

State Dish: Chili

State Song: "Texas, Our Texas"

State Seashell: Lightning Whelk

State Fish: Guadalupe Bass

State Insect: Monarch Butterfly

State Large Mammal: Texas Longhorn

State Small Mammal: Armadillo

State Flying Mammal: Mexican Free-Tailed Bat

State Pepper: Jalapeño

State Plant: Prickly Pear Cactus

HOW TO USE THE CAMPER'S GUIDE

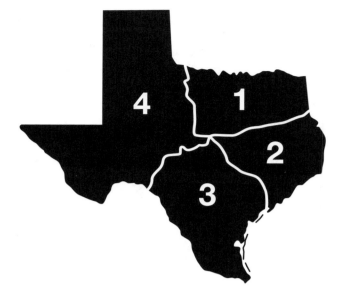

The state has been divided into four geographic regions as shown in the illustration. The parks, lakes, and forests within each region are arranged alphabetically. All campgrounds, parks, lakes, and forests are cross-listed by name and city in the index.

All information reported in this *Camper's Guide* has been supplied by the respective operating agency, through literature distributed by them, verbal communication, or secondary sources deemed reliable.

Most parks are easily found with the aid of a good road map; after you reach the general vicinity of a park, signs along the way will guide you. The maps in this guide show the location of facilities within a park and should be of considerable help. These maps are often available to you at the park headquarters, but they can also aid you in planning a trip to an unfamiliar park. Those of you who have attempted to meet up with friends at a predetermined spot at a large campground can readily appreciate the value of possessing such a map.

The maps showing the location of the numerous parks around a lake should also be of tremendous help to campers; perhaps, this information will help to better distribute visitors to these parks. The size of each lake, either in miles of shoreline or in surface acres, is given to serve as a point of reference when comparing lakes that may be unfamiliar. The major roads to each park are shown, but remember that many back roads exist. You may eventually choose to obtain a more detailed local map from the reservoir manager; addresses are provided.

The facilities available at a campground are always changing, but a change in status usually means the addition of a service rather than a discontinuation. In other words, a camper often finds better and more facilities than those listed in the latest brochure.

The average camper usually doesn't need help deciding what activities to engage in. Obviously, water-related sports are the most popular activities at a lake setting. Other possible activities have been listed to indicate the availability of nature/hiking trails, mountain bike trails, horseback trails, swimming pools, etc. In many parks, interpretive programs, including nature walks, guided tours, and evening talks, are conducted by park personnel.

Checklists for general camping equipment, cooking equipment, and hiking/backpacking are included on pages 12–13 to guide you in planning your camping trips. Careful and adequate planning can mean the difference between an enjoyable trip and a miserable trip.

This fifth edition also contains a summary of the key facilities and accommodations at state parks on pages 188–189. At a glance, you can tell which parks have screened cabins, shelters, walk-in campsites, swimming pools, equestrian/bicycle trails, golf courses, etc.

May this *Camper's Guide* serve you well in the years ahead, whether you are a beginner or a seasoned camper. Take time to camp, to become *truly* acquainted with nature . . . and with yourself and your family! Don't put off until tomorrow what can be enjoyed today! Something special is waiting for you! Go Camping!

Many parks have an abundance of tame deer to enjoy; look, but don't feed.

STATE PARKS

More than 80 state parks in Texas provide camping opportunities. Facilities range from primitive camping only at Big Bend Ranch, Colorado Bend, Devils River, and Matagorda Island to campsites with full hookups at 20 parks. These parks are operated by the State Parks Division of the Texas Parks and Wildlife Department. The recreational opportunities and the scenic beauty of each state park are as varied as Texas itself. In addition to the developed campsites, many of the parks have walk-in campsites, as well as primitive camping areas for backpackers and/or horses and their riders. In addition, many state parks offer cabins, screened shelters, and group trailer areas. Several state parks offer other types of accommodations such as cottages and mini-cabins. For the reader's convenience, a listing has been compiled that displays various activities and facilities available at the state parks. See page 188 for "Facilities at a Glance for State Parks."

FEES

On May 1, 1996, the Texas State Parks system changed from vehicular entry pricing to per-person pricing. These fees range from $1 to $5 with most parks charging $2 per person. Children under 13 are admitted free. Entrance fees are not collected at some historic parks, but a tour fee may be charged at a historic site. The Texas State Parks Pass grants unlimited park entrance to the holder and everyone in the permitted vehicle.

In addition to the entrance fees, parks also charge for the use of facilities, such as camping sites, screened shelters, and cabins. An activity use fee is charged for special activities such as tours and rock climbing, or activities that occur after closing hours, such as night fishing or stargazing. Some parks give a discounted entrance price to those visitors who camp overnight. Some parks have seasonal or other special rates. For details on fees, contact the Park Information Center at 1-800-792-1112.

ANNUAL PASSPORTS/PERMITS

Texas State Parks Pass—is a vehicle pass that grants:

▲ Unlimited visits to all 120 Texas state parks and historic sites for you and your guests, with no daily entrance fees for one year.

▲ Discount coupons for camping, lodging, park store merchandise, and recreational equipment rentals.

▲ Special promotions offered on a park-by-park basis.

▲ Special subscription rate to the *Texas Parks and Wildlife* magazine.

▲ The "Getaway Planner" e-newsletter, customized to fit your recreational and cultural interests.

▲ Member's decal to display your support of Texas State Parks.

Texas State Parklands Passport—This passport entitles persons who reached 65 years of age before September 1, 1995, and military veterans with a 60% or greater disability rating to free state park entrance. Texas residents who turned 65 on or after this date are eligible for discounted entry fees, while non-residents who turned 65 on or after this date pay the regular price.

RESERVATION SYSTEM

Reservations can be made for campsites, cabins, shelters, and group facilities and for some tours and activities; they can be reserved up to 11 months in

The majority of state parks provide picnic facilities; many parks even provide friends to welcome you.

advance. Reservations must be made at least 2 days in advance of your planned stay. During the two-day window (today and tomorrow), call the park directly. If sites are available, a reservation can be made with a credit card (Discover, MasterCard, or Visa). The credit card will be charged the first night's stay. Reservations made in the two-day window at the park are not refundable. Sites may not be reserved by site number, but requests are considered at check-in time. Facilities that have not been reserved are available on a first-come, first-served basis upon arrival at the park.

For state park reservations, call the Central Reservation Center (CRC) in Austin. The CRC is staffed from 9 am to 8 pm, Monday through Friday, and from 9 am to 12 noon on Saturday; it is closed on Sunday and major holidays. The CRC accepts Visa, MasterCard, and Discover for payment of the reservation deposit. You can make/cancel resevations 24 hours a day, 7 days a week and check site availability through the Internet at:

www.tpwd.state.tx.us/park/admin/res/

or through e-mail. Also, if you use a touch tone phone, you can check status or cancel reservations 24 hours a day, 7 days a week.

TEXAS STATE PARK RESERVATION BASICS

Telephone Reservations and Cancellations Only

512/389-8900

Fax Reservations

512/389-8959

Internet Reservations

www.tpwd.state.tx.us

E-Mail Reservations

e-mail.reservations@tpwd.state.tx.us

Park Information

800/792-1112

Tent camping is still quite popular. Thirty-four state parks offer walk-in campsites; some sites have a table, grill, or fire ring, while others are more primitive.

NATIONAL PARKS

Six of the 13 national parks in Texas provide camping opportunities. Facilities range from backcountry camping at Big Thicket National Preserve to a concession-operated trailer park with full hookups at Big Bend National Park. Entrance fees are collected at Big Bend National and Guadalupe Mountains Parks and at Padre Island National Seashore, but not at the other 3 parks. Camping fees are charged at 3 of the parks: Big Bend, Padre Island and Guadalupe Mountains National Park. Camping at all of the national parks in Texas is on a first-come, first-served basis with the exception of Big Bend. Between November 15 and April 15, a limited number of sites in Rio Grande Village and in the Basin can be reserved. However, reservations can be made at most group campgrounds. Brief information on each park is provided in the following sections.

Amistad National Recreation Area encompasses the shoreline of the Texas portion of Amistad Reservoir up to the high-water elevation of 1,144 feet. The reservoir, 12 miles north of Del Rio on US 90, impounds water from the Devils River, the Pecos River, and the Rio Grande. All 4 campgrounds are primitive; chemical toilets are provided and potable water is available only at Governor's Landing. Back-country camping by boat is permitted along the shore below the high-water mark, except in restricted areas; a permit is required. (See pages 113–114.)

Big Bend National Park is edged on 3 sides by the "big bend" of the Rio Grande, the international boundary between Mexico and Texas. The park has 3 campgrounds; drinking water is available, but there is no electricity. There is also a concessionaire-operated trailer park at Rio Grande Village; full hookup capability is required. Backcountry campsites are designated; a permit is required. (See pages 159–161.)

Big Thicket National Preserve, composed of 12 units of various sizes and spread over 50 square miles, is located in southeastern Texas. Several backcountry camping zones have been designated in isolated portions on some preserve units and on the sandbars of the Neches River. Campsites are hike-in or boat-in; a backcountry permit is required. From October 1 to January 15, camping is suspended in all areas open to hunting with the exception that a portion of the Turkey Creek Unit is open year-round. (See pages 73–75.)

Guadalupe Mountains National Park, located 55 miles southwest of Carlsbad, New Mexico, lies astride the most scenic and rugged portion of the Guadalupe Mountains; Guadalupe Peak, the highest point in Texas is within the park. There are 2 campgrounds; both have drinking water and flush toilets. A camping fee is charged at Pine Springs and at Dog Canyon Campgrounds. Backcountry camping is allowed at designated sites only; permits are required. (See pages 172–173.)

Lake Meredith National Recreation Area is located 30 miles northeast of Amarillo. Alibates Flint Quarries National Monument adjoins the national recreation area. There are 13 designated areas for camping; the number of campsites available varies when the lake level fluctuates. Drinking water and flush toilets are provided at 2 campgrounds; other camping areas have chemical toilets but no potable water. (See page 179.)

Padre Island National Seashore is one of the longest stretches of primitive, undeveloped ocean beach in the United States. Access to this 70-mile long barrier island park is from the north end near Corpus Christi. A fee is charged at Malaquite Beach, a developed campground; it has flush toilets and cold showers. Primitive camping is allowed at designated sites along Laguna Madre and all along the Gulf beach except in the Malaquite Beach area. (See pages 151–152.)

If you like the challenge of hiking and camping in the high country, consider a trip to the Guadalupe Mountains National Park.

NATIONAL FORESTS

Texas has 4 national forests within its borders: Angelina, Davy Crockett, Sabine, and Sam Houston. They were established in 1934 and cover 675,855 acres in east Texas. In 1984, 5 wilderness areas were established within the national forests. They are Big Slough, Indian Mounds, Turkey Hill, Upland Island, and Little Lake Creek. The forests are administered by the Forest Service of the U.S. Department of Agriculture under multiple-use management to protect and obtain the greatest benefit from all forest resources: recreation, timber, range, fish, wildlife, soil, water, and minerals. Management is directed by the forest supervisor, located in Lufkin. Maps of the 4 national forests and the 5 wilderness areas are available from the forest supervisor's office (see Resources, page 190, for address).

The 4 national forests provide a variety of outdoor recreation opportunities. There are 13 developed recreation areas: Angelina has 4; Sabine has 2; Davy Crockett has 3; and Sam Houston has 4. Camping is offered on a first-come, first-served basis in developed recreation areas with one exception—campsites at Double Lake Recreation Area in the Sam Houston National Forest may be reserved through the National Recreation Reservation Service. (See p. 6 for details on NRRS.) Some areas charge a daily use fee for swimming, picnicking, and use of group picnic shelters. The group picnic shelters usually need to be reserved. Fees are not charged at Bouton Lake and Neches Bluff. Fee rates and instructions for payment are located on the self-service pay station at the entrance to the recreation area. Holders of a Golden Age Passport pay half of the prescribed fee, even if the facility is operated by a private concessionaire.

Campground facilities generally include tent pads, picnic tables, parking spurs for trailers, lantern-holding posts, fireplaces, potable water, and toilets. Some areas also have cold water showers, swimming beaches, boat ramps, amphitheaters, interpretive trails, and concession services. Electrical and water hookups are available at Ratcliff and Red Hills recreation areas.

Backpacking is permitted anywhere in the national forests in Texas. Brochures are available for most of the established hiking trails. The major trails include the 129-mile Lone Star Trail on the Sam Houston National Forest, the 20-mile 4-C Hiking Trail on the Davy Crockett National Forest, the 28-mile Trail Between the Lakes on the Sabine National Forest, and the 5½-mile Sawmill Hiking Trail on the Angelina National Forest. The Big Creek Scenic Area on the Sam Houston National Forest has 3 loop trails ranging from ¾ mile to 2 miles in length, and a 5-mile trail that connects this area to the Double Lake Recreation Area.

Primitive camping is allowed anywhere in the forest area, except during deer hunting season or unless posted otherwise. All campers are encouraged to practice "no trace" camping, leaving an area in the same natural condition in which it was found. A permit is not needed for a campfire; however, all visitors are responsible for their fire and damage from any resulting wildfire. Campfires should be left "dead out." Permits are not needed for backpacking or primitive camping.

Visitors should become acquainted with the rules and regulations governing the use of forest lands; they are are available from any forest service office and are usually posted on the entrance station bulletin board. Several general rules are:

▲ Length of stay is 14 consecutive days.
▲ Campsite must be occupied the first night you arrive. It should not be left unoccupied for more than 24 hours at a time.
▲ Animals (other than a seeing eye dog), should be under physical restrictive control (either crated, caged, or on a leash not longer than 6 feet).
▲ Quiet hours are between 10 pm and 6 am.
▲ Motorbikes and motorcycles are to be used only to enter or leave the recreation area.
▲ Operators of ATVs and ORVs should familarize themselves with all regulations that apply to their use on forest lands.
▲ In developed recreation sites, fires must be built within the fire ring or grill.
▲ Motorboaters must observe the 5 mph speed limit when within 150 feet of bathers, other boats, and boat landings.
▲ Hunting and fishing are permitted in accordance with state laws established by the Texas Parks and Wildlife Department.

LAKES

Dams have been constructed on numerous rivers in Texas for a variety of reasons. The purposes usually cited for impounding water include flood control, power generation, conservation, irrigation, and water supply for nearby municipalities. These lakes have also created a wide variety of water-related outdoor recreational opportunities, such as fishing, boating, waterskiing, sailing, swimming, hiking, picnicking, and camping.

Twenty-four lakes in Texas operated by the U.S. Army Corps of Engineers have numerous parks located along their shorelines that provide camping facilities. Most of these parks are operated by the Corps of Engineers, but other agencies, both state and local, often lease project land to provide specialized camping facilities.

Other Texas lakes are under the jurisdiction of various river or water districts, counties, and municipalities. Lakes, other than Corps of Engineers' lakes, receiving full page coverage in this guidebook are under the jurisdiction of the Guadalupe-Blanco River Authority, Colorado River Municipal Water District, Franklin County Water District, City of San Angelo, Sabine River Authority, Trinity River Authority, and the Lower Colorado River Authority. Provisions for outdoor recreation development and administration

vary greatly with each agency. Most of these agencies provide outstanding recreation areas.

However, it should be noted that the Lower Colorado River Authority (LCRA), with its chain of 7 lakes, has various parcels of land designated for park development, but in 8 instances the area remains as primitive recreation areas. Although their stated function is merely "to not prevent free use," it is noted that most of these primitive areas do charge a small entry fee.

In 1993, Congress gave the U.S. Army Corps of Engineers authority to collect day-use fees. Fees are charged at many Corps-operated boat ramps, at designated developed swimming beaches, and at entrances to developed recreation areas. An annual pass to cover day-use fees is available; it allows for the use of any Corps-operated boat launching ramp or swimming beach at any project for that calendar year. In addition, fees are collected for use of facilities, such as campsites and group shelters. Holders of Golden Age and Golden Access Passports receive a 50% discount on both daily and annual pass fees. Reservations can be made at selected facilities through NNRS. (For information, see Resources in Appendix 2.)

Some LCRA parks and recreation areas are free to the public while others may charge an entry fee. Most entry fees are per vehicle but entry to some LCRA sites may be per person. An annual pass (called the LCRA Recreation Area Annual Vehicle Permit) is available to cover day-use fees for any project for that calendar year. The LCRA offers a Lone Star Senior Pass free to anyone 65 years of age or older. The Golden Age and Golden Access Passports are also recognized at the LCRA sites. Reservations for several of the LCRA parks are available through the CRS (Central Reservation System) of the Texas Parks and Wildlife Department. (For information, see Resources in Appendix 2.)

Refer to the facility chart for each lake for information regarding the availability of specific camping facilities. Remember that the water level in some reservoirs can change dramatically. High water levels can close down beaches, boat ramps, and some camping areas; low water levels can close down boat ramps and make water-related activities dangerous. If in doubt, be sure to call ahead before making the trip.

At popular lakes, waiting in line at the boat ramp is probably inevitable.

Federal Recreation Passport Program

Entering or using facilities or services in some national parks, national forests, wildlife refuges, or Corps of Engineers recreation areas requires payment of entrance fees, user fees, or special recreation permit fees.

There are several congressionally authorized entrance fee passes which are applicable to the parks, forests, wildlife refuges, and lakes in Texas that charge entrance fees. They are the National Parks Pass, the Golden Eagle Passport, the Corps of Engineers Annual Day Use Pass, and the two lifetime passes—the Golden Age Passport and the Golden Access Passport.

National Parks Pass*—is good for one year from date of purchase and is an entrance pass to national park sites that charge entrance fees. It admits the pass owner and any accompanying passengers in a private vehicle. In those areas where a per-person fee is charged, the pass admits the pass owner, spouse, parents, and children.

Golden Eagle Passport*—is good for one year from date of purchase and is an entrance pass to national parks, wildlife refuges, and national forest recreation areas that charge entrance fees. It admits the pass owner and any accompanying passengers in a private vehicle. In those areas where a per person fee is charged, the pass admits the pass owner, spouse, parents, and children.

Golden Age Passport—is for a one-time fee of $10, a lifetime entrance/discount pass to national parks, wildlife refuges, national forests, and Corps of Engineers recreation areas that charge entrance and user fees. The passport is for citizens or permanent residents of the United States who are 62 years or older; it admits the pass owner and any accompanying passengers in a private vehicle. In those areas where a per-person fee is charged, the pass admits

the pass owner, spouse, and children. Another benefit is a 50% discount at campgrounds, developed boat launches and swimming sites and for specialized interpretive services. The passport must be obtained in person, with proof of age.

Golden Access Passport—is a free lifetime entrance/discount pass to national parks, wildlife refuges, national forests, and Corps of Engineers recreation areas that charge entrance fees and user

If you enjoy the magnificent scenery at Big Bend National Park and make several trips there each year, consider purchasing the Golden Eagle Passport. It is an entrance pass for the pass holder and anyone in the vehicle.

*Cost of each pass is not included since it is subject to change.

fees. The passport is for citizens or permanent residents of the United States who are legally blind or permanently disabled; it admits the pass owner and any accompanying passengers in a private vehicle. In those areas where a per-person fee is charged, the pass admits the pass owner, spouse and children. Another benefit is a 50% discount at campgrounds, developed boat launches and swimming sites and for specialized interpretive service. The passport must be obtained in person, with proof of medically determined permanent disability, or eligibility for receiving benefits under federal law.

Corps of Engineers Annual Day Use Pass*—is for day-use facilities at any Corps of Engineers site during the calendar year in which it is purchased. The pass admits the pass owner and any accompanying passengers (up to a total of 8 people) in a private vehicle.

MAP SYMBOLS

 AMPHITHEATER

 BIKE TRAIL

 BOAT RAMP

 CABINS

 CONCESSION

 DUMP STATION

 EQUESTRIAN SITES

 FISHING PIER

 FULL HOOKUPS

 GROUP BARRACKS/ CAMP/LODGE/REC HALL/ETC.

 GROUP PICNIC SHELTER

 GROUP PICNIC AREA

 HIKING TRAIL

 HORSE TRAIL

 MARINA

 NATURE/ INTERPRETIVE TRAIL

 PARK OFFICE

 PARKING

 PICNIC AREA

 PICNIC SHELTER

PRIMITIVE GROUP SITES

 PRIMITIVE SITES

 RANGER STATION

 RESTROOMS

 SCREENED SHELTERS

 SWIMMING

 TENT SITES

 TOILETS FOR PRIMITIVE SITES

WATER/ ELECTRICITY

CAMPING EQUIPMENT CHECKLIST

The following checklists are designed to guide you in planning your next camping trip. Your needs will vary according to the type, length, and destination of your trip, as well as personal preferences, number of persons included, season of the year, and budget limitations.

Obviously, all items on the checklists aren't needed on any one trip. Since using checklists helps you think more methodically in planning, these extensive lists should serve merely as a reminder of items you may need.

When using these checklists to plan a trip, the item may be checked (√) if it needs to be taken. Upon returning, if the item was considered unnecessary, a slash could be used: ⍉. If a needed item was forgotten, a zero could be used (0); if the item has been depleted and needs to be replenished, an encircling of the check could be used: ⓥ. This is of particular importance if you camp regularly and keep a camping box packed with staples that can be ready to go on a moment's notice.

Cooking equipment needs are quite dependent on the menu—whether you plan to cook and eat three balanced meals a day or whether you plan to eat non-cooked meals or snacks the entire

trip. Many campers find it helpful to jot down the proposed menu for each meal on a 4″ × 6″ index card to help determine the grocery list as well as the equipment needed to prepare the meal. By planning this way, you'll avoid taking equipment you'll never use and you won't forget important items.

Typical Menu with Grocery and Equipment Needs

MEAL: Saturday breakfast		Number of Persons: 5
MENU	GROCERY LIST	EQUIPMENT
orange juice	Tang	camp stove
bacon	10 slices bacon	gasoline, funnel
eggs (scrambled)	8 eggs	folding oven
biscuits	1 can biscuits	frying pan
	peach jelly	baking pan
	honey	pitcher
	margarine	mixing bowl
	salt	cooking fork, spoon
	pepper	

Shelter/Sleeping:
_____ Air mattresses
_____ Air mattress pump
_____ Cots, folding
_____ Cot pads
_____ Ground cloth
_____ Hammock
_____ Mosquito netting
_____ Sleeping bag or bedroll
_____ Tarps (plastic & canvas)
_____ Tent
_____ Tent stakes, poles, guy ropes
_____ Tent repair kit
_____ Whisk broom

Extra Comfort:
_____ Camp stool
_____ Catalytic heater
_____ Folding chairs
_____ Folding table
_____ Fuel for lantern & heater
_____ Funnel
_____ Lantern
_____ Mantels for lantern
_____ Toilet bags
_____ Toilet chemicals
_____ Toilet, portable
_____ Wash basin

Clothing/Personal Gear:
_____ Bathing suit
_____ Boots, hiking & rain
_____ Cap/hat
_____ Facial tissues
_____ Flashlight (small), batteries
_____ Jacket/windbreaker
_____ Jeans/trousers
_____ Pajamas
_____ Pocket knife

_____ Poncho
_____ Prescription drugs
_____ Rain suit
_____ Sheath knife
_____ Shirts
_____ Shoes
_____ Shorts
_____ Socks
_____ Sweatshirt/sweater
_____ Thongs (for showering)
_____ Toilet articles (comb, soap, shaving equipment, toothbrush, toothpaste, mirror, etc.)
_____ Toilet paper
_____ Towels
_____ Underwear
_____ Washcloth

Safety/Health:
_____ First-aid kit
_____ First-aid manual
_____ Fire extinguisher
_____ Insect bite remedy
_____ Insect repellant
_____ Insect spray/bomb
_____ Poison ivy lotion
_____ Safety pins
_____ Sewing repair kit
_____ Scissors
_____ Snakebite kit
_____ Sunburn lotion
_____ Suntan cream
_____ Water purifier

Optional:
_____ Binoculars
_____ Camera, film, tripod, light meter
_____ Canteen

_____ Compass
_____ Fishing tackle
_____ Frisbee, horseshoes, washers, etc.
_____ Games for car travel & rainy day
_____ Hobby equipment
_____ Identification books: birds, flowers, rocks, stars, trees, etc.
_____ Knapsack/day pack for hikes
_____ Magnifying glass
_____ Map of area
_____ Notebook & pencil
_____ Sunglasses

Miscellaneous:
_____ Bucket/pail
_____ Candles
_____ Clothesline
_____ Clothespins
_____ Electrical extension cord
_____ Flashlight (large), batteries
_____ Hammer
_____ Hand axe/hatchet
_____ Nails
_____ Newspapers
_____ Pliers
_____ Rope
_____ Saw, bow or folding
_____ Sharpening stone/file
_____ Shovel
_____ Tape, masking or plastic
_____ Twine/cord
_____ Wire
_____ Work gloves

COOKING EQUIPMENT CHECKLIST

Food Preparation/ Serving/Storing:

_____ Aluminum foil
_____ Bags (large & small, plastic & paper)
_____ Bottle/juice can opener
_____ Bowls, nested with lids for mixing, serving & storing
_____ Can opener
_____ Colander
_____ Fork, long-handled
_____ Ice chest
_____ Ice pick
_____ Knife, large
_____ Knife, paring
_____ Ladle for soups & stews
_____ Measuring cup
_____ Measuring spoon
_____ Pancake turner
_____ Potato & carrot peeler
_____ Recipes
_____ Rotary beater
_____ Spatula
_____ Spoon, large
_____ Tongs
_____ Towels, paper
_____ Water jug
_____ Wax paper/plastic wrap

Cooking:

_____ Baking pans
_____ Charcoal
_____ Charcoal grill (hibachi or small collapsible type)
_____ Charcoal lighter
_____ Coffee pot
_____ Cook kit, nested/pots & pans with lids
_____ Fuel for stove (gasoline/ kerosene/liquid propane)
_____ Griddle
_____ Hot pads/asbestos gloves
_____ Matches
Ovens for baking:
_____ Cast iron dutch oven
_____ Folding oven for fuel stoves
_____ Reflector oven
_____ Tote oven
_____ Skewers
_____ Skillet with cover
_____ Stove, portable
_____ Toaster (folding camp type)
_____ Wire grill for open fire

Eating:

_____ Bowls for cereal, salad, soup
_____ Cups, paper
_____ Forks
_____ Glasses, plastic
_____ Knives
_____ Napkins, paper
_____ Pitcher, plastic
_____ Plates (plastic, aluminum, paper)
_____ Spoons
_____ Tablecloth, plastic
_____ _____
_____ _____

Clean-Up:

_____ Detergent (Bio-degradable soap)
_____ Dishpan
_____ Dishrag
_____ Dish towels
_____ Scouring pad
_____ Scouring powder
_____ Sponge

HIKING/BACKPACKING CHECKLIST

This list is not meant to be all inclusive or necessary for each trip. It is a guide in choosing the proper gear. Although this list was prepared for the hiker/backpacker, it is quite appropriate for anyone using the backcountry, whether they are traveling by foot, canoe, bicycle, or horse. Parentheses indicate those optional items that you may not want to carry depending upon the length of the trip, weather conditions, personal preferences, or necessity.

Ten Essentials for Any Trip:

___ Map
___ Compass
___ First-aid kit
___ Pocket knife
___ Signaling device
___ Extra clothing
___ Extra food
___ Small flashlight/extra bulb & batteries
___ Fire starter/ candle/waterproof matches
___ Sunglasses

Day Trip (add to the above):

___ Comfortable boots or walking shoes
___ Rain parka or 60/40 parka

___ Day pack
___ Water bottle/canteen
___ Cup
___ Water purification tablets
___ Insect repellant
___ Sun lotion
___ Chapstick
___ Food
___ Brimmed hat
___ (Guidebook)
___ Toilet paper & trowel
___ (Camera & film)
___ (Binoculars)
___ (Book)
___ Wallet & I.D.
___ Car key & coins for phone
___ Moleskin for blisters
___ Whistle

Overnight or Longer Trips (add the following):

___ Backpack
___ Sleeping bag
___ Foam pad
___ (Tent)
___ (Bivouac cover)
___ (Ground cloth/ poncho)
___ Stove
___ Extra fuel
___ Cooking pot(s)
___ Pot scrubber
___ Spoon (knife & fork)
___ (Extra cup/bowl)
___ Extra socks
___ Extra shirt(s)
___ Extra pants/shorts
___ Extra underwear
___ Wool shirt/sweater
___ (Camp shoes)

___ Bandana
___ (Gloves)
___ (Extra water container)
___ Nylon cord
___ Extra matches
___ Soap
___ Toothbrush/powder/ floss
___ Mirror
___ Medicines
___ (Snakebite kit)
___ (Notebook & pencil)
___ Licenses & permits
___ (Playing cards)
___ (Ziplock bags)
___ (Rip stop repair tape)
___ Repair kit—wire, rivets, pins, buttons, thread, needle, boot strings

REGION 1

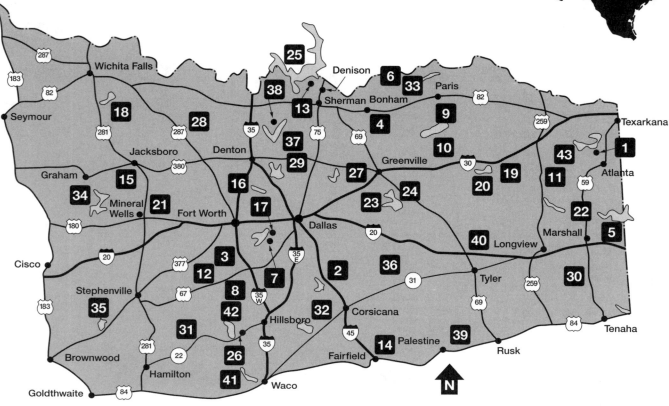

1—ATLANTA STATE PARK, 15

2—BARDWELL LAKE, 16

3—BENBROOK LAKE, 17

4—BONHAM STATE PARK, 18

5—CADDO LAKE STATE PARK, 19

6—CADDO NATIONAL GRASSLANDS, 20

7—CEDAR HILL STATE PARK, 21

8—CLEBURNE STATE PARK, 22

9—COOPER LAKE STATE PARK
    (DOCTORS CREEK UNIT), 23

10—COOPER LAKE STATE PARK
    (SOUTH SULPHUR UNIT), 24

11—DAINGERFIELD STATE PARK, 25

12—DINOSAUR VALLEY STATE PARK, 26

13—EISENHOWER STATE PARK, 27

14—FAIRFIELD LAKE STATE PARK, 28

15—FORT RICHARDSON STATE PARK &
    HISTORIC SITE, 29

16—GRAPEVINE LAKE, 30

17—JOE POOL LAKE & LOYD PARK, 31

18—LAKE ARROWHEAD STATE PARK, 33

19—LAKE BOB SANDLIN STATE PARK, 34

20—LAKE CYPRESS SPRINGS, 35

21—LAKE MINERAL WELLS STATE PARK AND
    TRAILWAY, 36

22—LAKE O' THE PINES, 37

23—LAKE TAWAKONI, 38

24—LAKE TAWAKONI STATE PARK, 39

25—LAKE TEXOMA, 40

26—LAKE WHITNEY STATE PARK, 42

27—LAVON LAKE, 43

28—LBJ NATIONAL GRASSLANDS, 45

29—LEWISVILLE LAKE, 47

30—MARTIN CREEK LAKE STATE PARK, 49

31—MERIDIAN STATE PARK, 50

32—NAVARRO MILLS LAKE, 51

33—PAT MAYSE LAKE, 52

34—POSSUM KINGDOM STATE PARK, 53

35—PROCTOR LAKE, 54

36—PURTIS CREEK STATE PARK, 55

37—RAY ROBERTS LAKE STATE PARK
    (ISLE DU BOIS UNIT), 56

38—RAY ROBERTS LAKE STATE PARK
    (JOHNSON BRANCH UNIT), 57

39—RUSK-PALESTINE STATE PARK, 58

40—TYLER STATE PARK, 60

41—WACO LAKE, 61

42—WHITNEY LAKE, 62

43—WRIGHT-PATMAN LAKE, 64

ATLANTA STATE PARK

FOR INFORMATION

Atlanta State Park
927 Park Rd. 42
Atlanta, TX 75551
903/796-6476

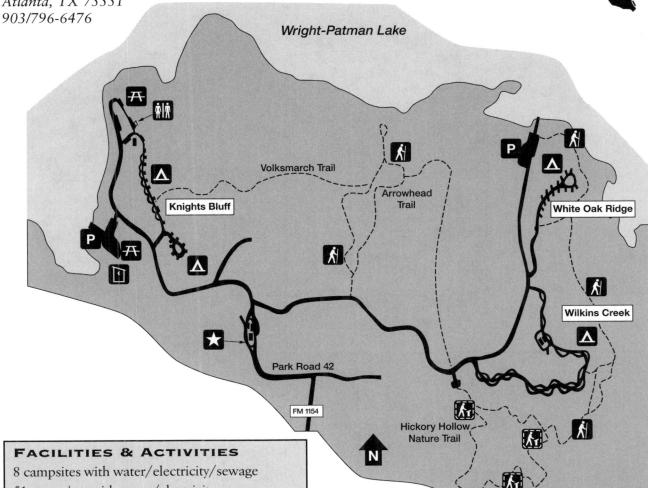

Wright-Patman Lake

Volksmarch Trail

Arrowhead Trail

Knights Bluff

P

White Oak Ridge

Wilkins Creek

Park Road 42

FM 1154

Hickory Hollow Nature Trail

N

FACILITIES & ACTIVITIES

8 campsites with water/electricity/sewage

51 campsites with water/electricity

restrooms/showers

trailer dump station

picnicking

group picnic pavilion

playground

beach swimming area

fishing/fish cleaning shelter

2 boat ramps

boating/waterskiing

2 hiking trails (1.2 & 3.5 miles)

1.2 miles of nature trails

amphitheater

park store at headquarters

LOCATION

Atlanta State Park, set in pine forests on the shores of 20,300-acre Wright-Patman Lake, is located about 11 miles northwest of Atlanta. The 1,475-acre park may be reached by driving 2 miles north of Atlanta on US 59 to Queen City, then west on FM 96 for 8 miles to FM 1154, then north for 2 miles to Park Road 42.

BARDWELL LAKE

FOR INFORMATION

Bardwell Lake
4000 Observation Drive
Ennis, TX 75119-1339
972/875-5711

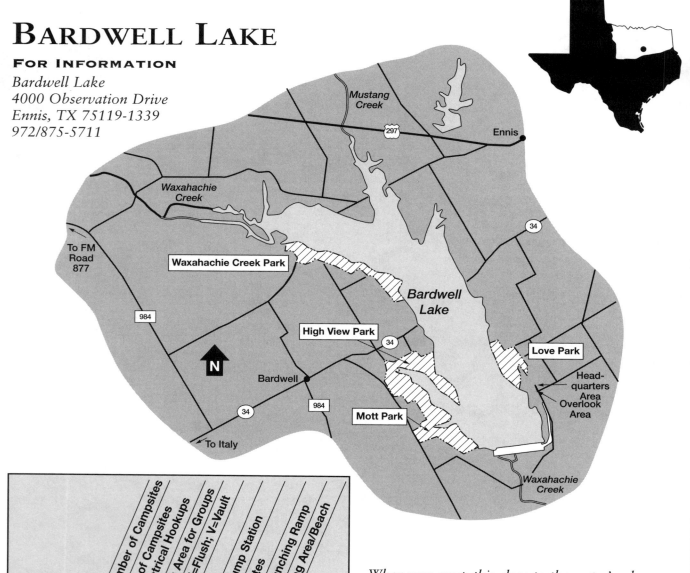

Parks	Total Number of Campsites	Number of Campsites with Electrical Hookups	Camping Area for Groups	Toilets: F=Flush; V=Vault	Showers	Trailer Dump Station	Picnic Sites	Boat Launching Ramp	Swimming Area/Beach
High View	39	39		F/V	•	•	•	•	
Love	20			V			•	•	
Mott	40	33	•	F/V	•	•	•	•	
Waxahachie Creek	72	65	•	F/V	•		•	•	

Notes:
High View Park has a marina.
Waxahachie Creek Park has 11 miles of equestrian trails and a nature trail.
Love, Mott & Waxahachie Creek have group picnic shelter.

LOCATION

Bardwell Lake is a 3,570-acre Corps of Engineers impoundment of Waxahachie Creek with a 25-mile shoreline. The lake is southwest of I-45 at Ennis; TX 34 from Ennis to Bardwell crosses the lake. Other nearby towns include Waxahachie, Italy, and Corsicana.

When you camp this close to the water's edge, you don't have far to go to "wet a line."

U.S. Army Corps of Engineers

BENBROOK LAKE

FOR INFORMATION

Benbrook Lake
P.O. Box 26619
Fort Worth, TX 76126-0619
817/292-2400

LOCATION

Benbrook Lake is a 3,770-acre Corps of Engineers impoundment of the Clear Fork of the Trinity River with a 40-mile shoreline. The lake is southwest of Fort Worth with access from US 377 near Benbrook. Other nearby towns include Cresson and Crowley.

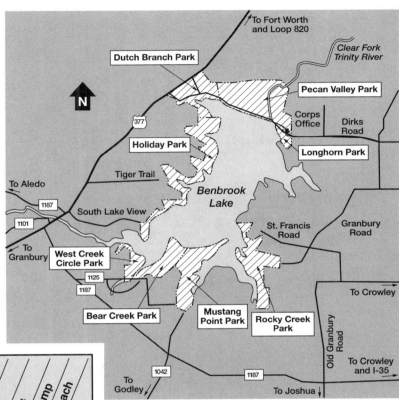

Campgrounds/ Parks	Total Number of Campsites	Number of Campsites with Electrical Hookups	Camping Area for Groups	Toilets: F=Flush; V=Vault	Showers	Trailer Dump Station	Picnic Sites	Group Picnic Areas	Boat Launching Ramp	Swimming Area/Beach
Bear Creek	40	40	•	F/V	•	•		•	•	
Dutch Branch				F/V			•	•		•
Holiday	105	71		F/V	•	•	•		•	
Longhorn				F			•	•	•	
Mustang Point	11		•	F/V		•	•	•	•	•
Pecan Valley				F/V			•			
Rocky Creek	21			V		•	•		•	
West Creek Circle	4			V						

Notes:
Bear Creek has 2 campsites with full hookups.
Mustang Point allows primitive camping in an open area.
West Creek Circle does not have water.
Dutch Branch & Rocky Creek have marinas.
Dutch Branch has a fitness trail. Holiday has a 7.3-mile equestrian trail & a 1.7-mile hiking trail.

A 7.3-mile horseback and nature trail is located on the west side of Benbrook Lake.

BONHAM STATE PARK

FOR INFORMATION

Bonham State Park
1363 State Park 24
Bonham, TX 75418
903/583-5022

Because the lake is small, boats must observe a 5 mph speed limit.

FACILITIES & ACTIVITIES

14 campsites with water/electricity
7 campsites with water/electricity (tents only)
restrooms/showers
trailer dump station
group barracks & dining hall
picnicking
group picnic pavilion
playground
beach swimming area
fishing/lighted fishing pier
boat ramp & dock
boating (5 mph speed limit)
11 miles of hiking/mountain bike trails

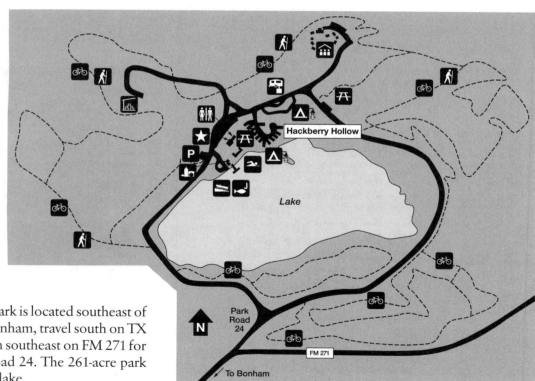

Hackberry Hollow

Lake

N

Park Road 24

FM 271

To Bonham

LOCATION

Bonham State Park is located southeast of Bonham. From Bonham, travel south on TX 78 for 2 miles, then southeast on FM 271 for 2 miles to Park Road 24. The 261-acre park includes a 65-acre lake.

CADDO LAKE STATE PARK

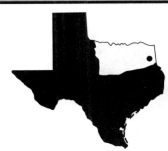
FOR INFORMATION

Caddo Lake State Park
245 Park Rd. 2
Karnack, TX 75661
903/679-3351

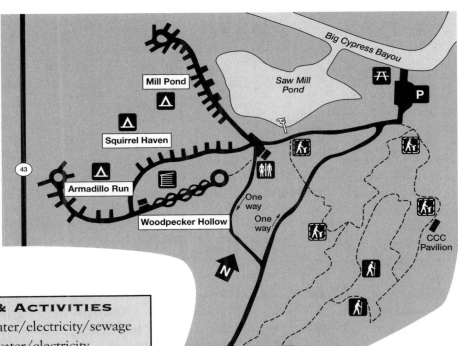

FACILITIES & ACTIVITIES

8 campsites with water/electricity/sewage

18 campsites with water/electricity

20 campsites with water only

restrooms/showers

trailer dump station

8 screened shelters

9 cabins

recreation hall (daytime use)

picnicking

playground

fishing/fishing pier

boat ramp

boating

pontoon boat tours Thurs.–Tues.
   (March–Nov.) (fee)

1½ miles of hiking trails

¾ miles of nature trails

amphitheater

interpretive center

park store at headquarters

canoe rentals/snacks at Saw Mill Pond
   (903/679-3743)

LOCATION

Caddo Lake State Park is located 15 miles northeast of Marshall; travel north on TX 43, then east on FM 2198 for .4 mile to Park Road 2. The 484-acre park fronts Big Cypress Bayou with access to Caddo Lake, a sprawling maze of bayous and sloughs covering 28,610 acres of cypress swamp.

CADDO NATIONAL GRASSLANDS

FOR INFORMATION

Caddo/LBJ National Grasslands
1400 N. US Hwy. 81/287
P.O. Box 507
Decatur, TX 76234
940/627-5475

LOCATION

The 17,874-acre Caddo National Grasslands is located near the Oklahoma border in Fannin County in three sections. It not only provides grazing land for cattle and habitat for wildlife, but offers a variety of recreation. The largest section, located north of Honey Grove and northeast of Bonham, has 3 recreation areas that offer a variety of facilities for camping, picnicking, boating, fishing, hiking, horseback riding, mountain biking, and other outdoor activities. All are open year-round.

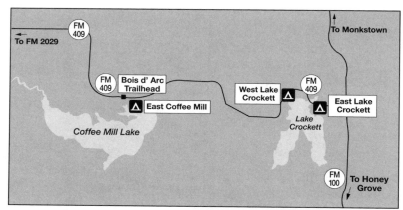

DIRECTIONS TO RECREATION AREAS

Bois d' Arc Trailhead—From Honey Grove, follow FM 100 north 12 miles to FM 409. Turn left and go 5.5 miles; turn left into trailhead.

Coffee Mill—From Honey Grove, follow FM 100 north 12 miles to FM 409. Turn left and go west 5 miles to camp entrance on the left.

East Lake Crockett—From Honey Grove, follow FM 100 north 12 miles to FM 409. Turn left and go west 1 mile to camp entrance on the left.

West Lake Crockett—From Honey Grove, follow FM 100 north 12 miles to FM 409. Turn left and go west 2 miles to the camp entrance on the left.

FACILITIES & ACTIVITIES

LAKE DAVY CROCKETT RECREATION AREA

12 RV & tent sites at West Lake
4 tent sites; no RVs at East Lake
drinking water
pit toilets
picnicking
no swimming
fishing/boating on 450-acre lake
fishing pier at East Lake
concrete boat ramp at East Lake
hiking at West Lake
user fee at West Lake
parking fee at East Lake

COFFEE MILL LAKE RECREATION AREA

tent camping; limited RV
drinking water
pit toilets
picnicking
no swimming
fishing/boating/skiing on 750-acre lake
concrete boat ramp
parking fee

BOIS D' ARC TRAILHEAD

12 campsites
11 pullthroughs
drinking water
pit toilets
horse washing
access to 20 miles of multi-use trails

CEDAR HILL STATE PARK

FOR INFORMATION

Cedar Hill State Park
1580 West FM 1382
Cedar Hill, TX 75104
972/291-6641

LOCATION

Cedar Hill State Park, located on Joe Pool Lake, is recognized as an urban area park due to its proximity to the Dallas-Fort Worth metroplex. It is located 10 miles southwest of Dallas, 4 miles southeast of Grand Prairie, and 3 miles west of Cedar Hill. The entrance to this 1,810-acre park is from FM 1382. From US 67, exit FM 1382 and travel northwest for 2½ miles. From I-20, exit FM 1382, and travel south for 4 miles south. The park is skirted by FM 1382 and Mansfield Road.

FACILITIES & ACTIVITIES

355 campsites with water/electricity
   45 premium campsites
30 primitive walk-in campsites (¼ mile)
restrooms/showers
trailer dump station
picnicking
2 group picnic pavilions
playground
beach swimming area
snack bar/paddleboat rental
perch pond for youngsters
fishing/fish cleaning shelter
5 fishing piers (2 are lighted)
2 boat ramps
boating/Jet Ski & boat rental
marina/concession
waterskiing
11 miles of nature/hiking/mountain bike trails
interpretive tour (fee)
park store

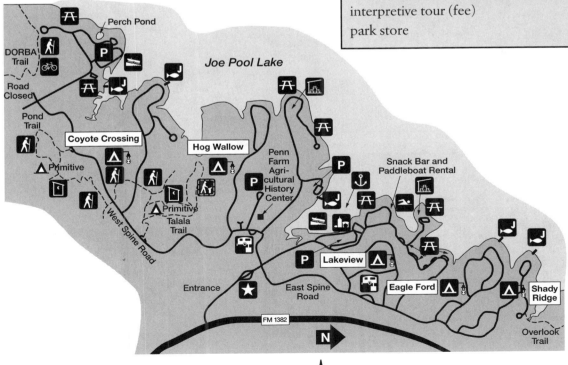

CLEBURNE STATE PARK

FOR INFORMATION

Cleburne State Park
5800 Park Road 21
Cleburne, TX 76033
817/645-4215

LOCATION

Cleburne State Park is located 10 miles southwest of Cleburne; from Cleburne, take US 67 southwest for about 4 miles, then left on Park Road 21 for 6 miles. This 529-acre park, named for Confederate hero General Pat Cleburne, includes a 116-acre lake of clear, clean water flowing from 3 natural springs beneath the surface of the lake.

FACILITIES & ACTIVITIES

27 campsites with water/electricity/sewage
31 campsites with water/electricity
sponsored youth group area
restrooms/showers
trailer dump station
6 screened shelters
2 group barracks with dining hall/kitchen
picnicking
playground
lake swimming
fishing
boat ramp/boating (5 mph speed limit)
canoe/paddleboat/small boat rental
nature/hiking trails
7 miles of bike trails
concessions (seasonal)

An abundance of lakes in Texas provides fishermen of all ages the opportunity to catch "the big one."

U.S. Army Corps of Engineers

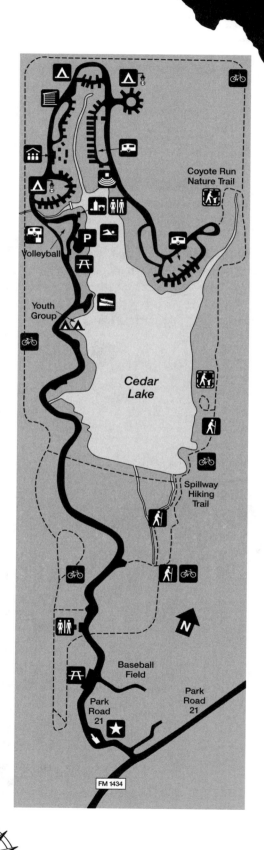

Coyote Run
Nature Trail

Volleyball

Youth
Group

Cedar
Lake

Spillway
Hiking
Trail

Baseball
Field

Park
Road
21

Park
Road
21

N

FM 1434

COOPER LAKE STATE PARK
DOCTORS CREEK UNIT

FOR INFORMATION

Cooper Lake State Park
Doctors Creek Unit
1664 FM 1529 South
Cooper, TX 75432
903/395-3100

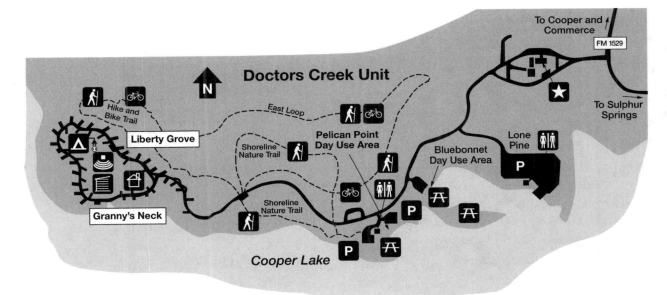

LOCATION

To reach the Doctors Creek Unit of Cooper Lake State Park, travel east on TX 154 from the town of Cooper for 1 mile, then turn right onto FM 1529 and travel 2 miles. Or, from I-30, take exit 122 on the west side of Sulphur Springs and travel north on TX 19 for 14 miles, then west on County Road 4795 for 2 miles to the Corps of Engineers Office; cross the lake dam and drive ½ mile to the park entrance.

A word of caution—when traveling north on TX 19/154, if you cross the South Sulphur River, you've gone too far and have missed the county road that crosses the dam. The 466-acre Doctors Creek Unit is on 19,305 surface-acre Cooper Lake on the Sulphur River.

FACILITIES & ACTIVITIES

42 campsites with water/electricity
restrooms/showers
trailer dump station
5 screened shelters
2 cottages
picnicking
group picnic pavilion
2 playgrounds
sand volleyball court
lake swimming
fishing
fish cleaning shelter
boat ramp
boating/waterskiing
nature trails
hike & bike trails
amphitheater

Cooper Lake State Park
South Sulphur Unit

Cooper Lake State Park
South Sulphur Unit
1690 FM 3505
Sulphur Springs, TX 75482
903/945-5256

Thirteen state parks offer campsites for equestrians; South Sulphur Unit has 15 with electricity.

Location

To reach the South Sulphur Unit of Cooper Lake State Park from Sulphur Springs, travel north on TX 19/154, then west on FM 71, then north on FM 3505 to the park entrance. The 2,310-acre South Sulphur Unit is on 19,305 surface-acre Cooper Lake on the Sulphur River.

Facilities & Activities

87 campsites with water/electricity
15 walk-in campsites with water
15 equestrian campsites with electricity
restrooms/showers
trailer dump station
19 screened shelters
14 cabins
2 cottages
picnicking
group picnic pavilion
playground
lake swimming
fishing/3 fish cleaning shelters
3 fishing piers
2 boat ramps
boating/waterskiing
10½ miles of equestrian trails
5 miles of hike/bike trails
park store at headquarters

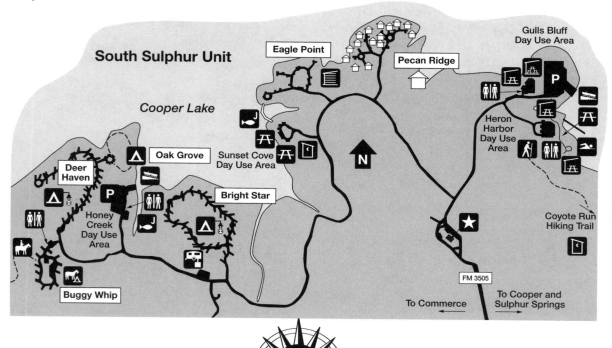

South Sulphur Unit
Cooper Lake
Eagle Point
Pecan Ridge
Gulls Bluff Day Use Area
Heron Harbor Day Use Area
Oak Grove
Sunset Cove Day Use Area
Deer Haven
Honey Creek Day Use Area
Bright Star
Buggy Whip
Coyote Run Hiking Trail
N
FM 3505
To Commerce
To Cooper and Sulphur Springs

DAINGERFIELD STATE PARK

FOR INFORMATION

Daingerfield State Park
455 Park Rd. 17
Daingerfield, TX 75638
903/645-2921

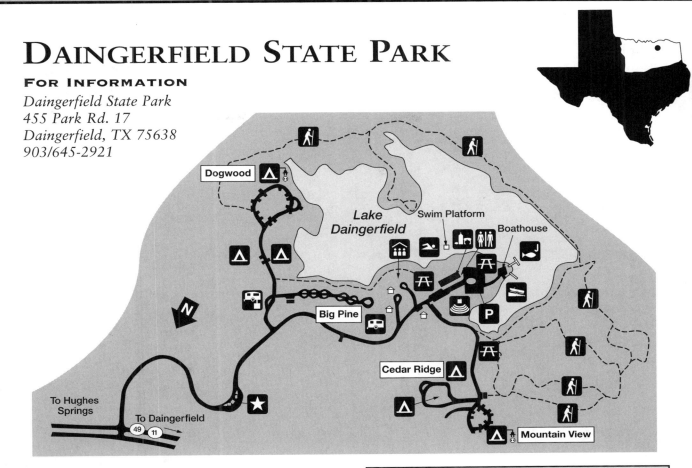

Dogwood

Lake
Daingerfield

Swim Platform
Boathouse

Big Pine

N

Cedar Ridge

To Hughes
Springs

To Daingerfield

49 11

Mountain View

LOCATION

From I-30 at Mt. Pleasant, Daingerfield State Park is reached by taking exit #160 and traveling south-east on TX 49 through Daingerfield to the park entrance on the right; distance is about 22 miles. From Longview, take SH 259 to Daingerfield, then right on TX 11/49 to the park entrance. Nestled inside the park's 551 pine-covered acres is an 80-acre spring-fed lake.

Trolling motors are ideal to use when the speed limit is 5 mph.

FACILITIES & ACTIVITIES

10 campsites with water/electricity/sewage
30 campsites with water/electricity
12 campsites with water only
restrooms/showers
trailer dump station
3 cabins
Bass Lodge (20 max.)
picnicking
group picnic area
playground
swimming beach & bathhouse
fishing
lighted fishing pier
boat ramp/boating (5 mph speed limit)
2½ miles of hiking trails
amphitheater
concessions (seasonal)

DINOSAUR VALLEY STATE PARK

FOR INFORMATION

Dinosaur Valley State Park
P.O. Box 396
Glen Rose, TX 76043
254/897-4588

LOCATION

From US 67 at Glen Rose, Dinosaur Valley State Park is reached by traveling west on FM 205/Park Road 59 for 4 miles, then north 1 mile to headquarters. This 1,525-acre park is located along the Paluxy River—widely known for the dinosaur tracks exposed at various places in its streambed. In recognition of its outstanding value as a natural feature, the park was designated as a National Natural Landmark by the National Park Service in 1969.

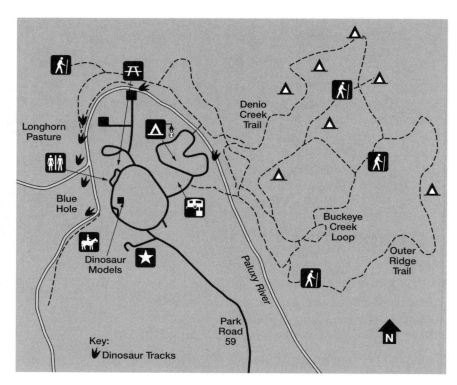

FACILITIES & ACTIVITIES

46 campsites with water/electricity	fishing
7 primitive camping areas for backpackers	10 miles of nature/hiking trails
restrooms/showers	9½ miles of mountain bike trails
trailer dump station	100-acre area for equestrian use
picnicking	amphitheater
group picnic pavilion	interpretive center
playground	dinosaur exhibits
river swimming	park store

EISENHOWER STATE PARK

FOR INFORMATION

Eisenhower State Park
50 Park Road 20
Denison, TX 75020-4878
903/465-1956

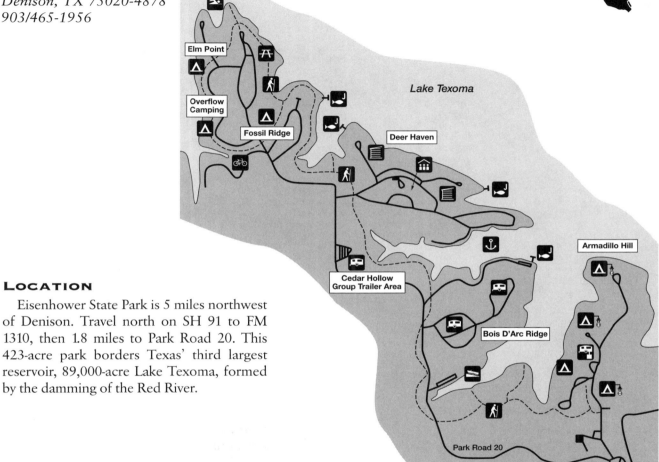

LOCATION

Eisenhower State Park is 5 miles northwest of Denison. Travel north on SH 91 to FM 1310, then 1.8 miles to Park Road 20. This 423-acre park borders Texas' third largest reservoir, 89,000-acre Lake Texoma, formed by the damming of the Red River.

FACILITIES & ACTIVITIES

50 campsites with water/electricity/sewage	group picnic pavilion
45 campsites with water/electricity	playgrounds
44 campsites with water only	beach swimming area
13 premium campsites	fishing/fish cleaning shelter
37-site group trailer area with water/electricity	lighted fishing pier
restrooms/showers	2 boat ramps
trailer dump station	boating/waterskiing
35 screened shelters	full service marina/concessions
recreation hall (day or overnight use)	4.2 miles of hiking trails
picnicking	8 miles of mountain bike trails

FAIRFIELD LAKE STATE PARK

FOR INFORMATION

Fairfield Lake State Park
123 State Park Rd. 64
Fairfield, TX 75840
903/389-4514

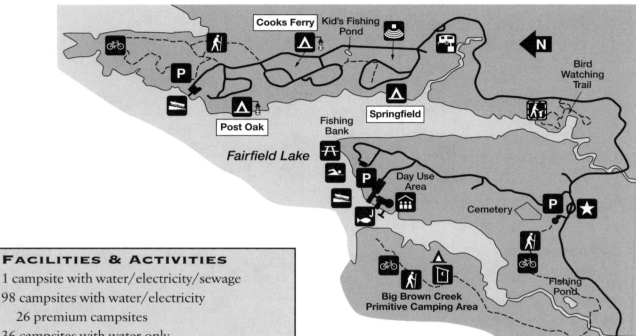

Cooks Ferry
Kid's Fishing Pond
N
Bird Watching Trail
Post Oak
Springfield
Fishing Bank
Fairfield Lake
Day Use Area
Cemetery
Big Brown Creek Primitive Camping Area
Fishing Pond

FACILITIES & ACTIVITIES

1 campsite with water/electricity/sewage
98 campsites with water/electricity
   26 premium campsites
36 campsites with water only
   10 premium campsites
restrooms/showers
trailer dump station
*backpacking campsites (2½-mile hike)
group dining hall/kitchen (day use only)
picnicking
playgrounds
beach swimming area
fishing/fish cleaning shelter
lighted fishing pier
2 boat ramps & docks
boating/waterskiing
6 miles of hiking & nature trails
9 miles of mountain bike trails
equestrian users on perimeter trail
amphitheater

*Closed Dec. through Feb.

LOCATION

Fairfield Lake State Park is located 6 miles northeast of Fairfield. From I-45, exit 197, take US 84 east to FM 488, north to FM 2570, and east to FM 3285. This 1,460-acre park, with its beautiful hardwood forest and rolling hills, is situated on the southern end of the 2,400-acre Fairfield Lake. Bald eagles are winter visitors.

Bald eagles aren't the only birds that enjoy Fairfield Lake.

FORT RICHARDSON STATE PARK & HISTORIC SITE

FOR INFORMATION

Fort Richardson State Park & Historic Site
228 State Park Rd. 61
Jacksboro, TX 76458
940/567-3506

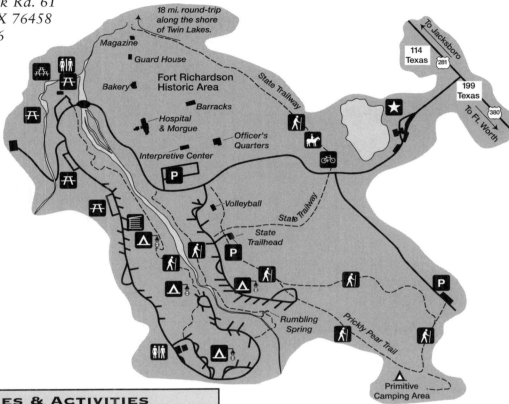

FACILITIES & ACTIVITIES

13 campsites with water/electrictiy/sewer

29 campsites with water/electricity

20 primitive hike-in campsites

restrooms/showers

trailer dump station

11 screened shelters

picnicking

group picnic pavilion

fishing

1.7 miles of hiking trails at State Park

½-mile nature trail

10-mile hike/bike/equestrian trail at State Trailway

7 original military structures

historic site tour/interpretive center

interpretive tour (fee)

park store

LOCATION

Fort Richardson State Park & Historic Site is in the Jacksboro city limits, 1 mile southeast of the square, with access from US 281. The remains of a federal fort, built in 1867 after the Civil War, include 2 replica barracks and 7 of the post's original structures; an interpretive center has exhibits about the history of the fort. The 402-acre park has an 8-acre lake.

GRAPEVINE LAKE

FOR INFORMATION

Grapevine Lake
110 Fairway Drive
Grapevine, TX 76051-3495
817/481-4541

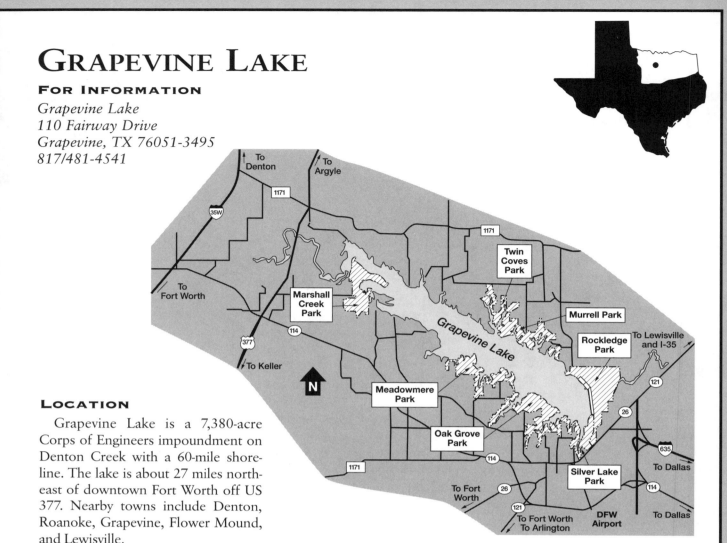

LOCATION

Grapevine Lake is a 7,380-acre Corps of Engineers impoundment on Denton Creek with a 60-mile shore-line. The lake is about 27 miles north-east of downtown Fort Worth off US 377. Nearby towns include Denton, Roanoke, Grapevine, Flower Mound, and Lewisville.

Do we have a friendly skier here, or has she merely forgotten her hand signals?

Parks	Total Number of Campsites	Number of Campsites with Electrical Hookups	Camping Area for Groups	Toilets: F=Flush; V=Vault	Showers	Trailer Dump Station	Picnic Sites	Group Picnic Areas	Boat Launching Ramp	Swimming Area/Beach
Marshall Creek				V			•		•	
Meadowmere				V			•		•	•
Murrell	36		•	V			•		•	
Oak Grove	18			F	•		•	•	•	
Rockledge				F/V			•	•		
Silver Lake	62	54		F/V	•	•	•			
Twin Coves	45	44		F/V	•	•	•		•	

Notes:
Oak Grove, Silver Lake, & Twin Coves have marinas.
Walnut Grove has a horse/hike trail.
All of the parks along the north shore have either hike/bike or horse/hike trails.

JOE POOL LAKE

FOR INFORMATION

Joe Pool Lake
P.O. Box 872
Cedar Hill, TX 75106-0872
972/299-2227

LOCATION

Joe Pool Lake is a 7,470-acre Corps of Engineers impoundment of Mountain Creek and Walnut Creek with a 60-mile shoreline. The lake is south of I-20 between Dallas and Forth Worth, east of US 287, and west of US 67 to Midlothian. Other nearby towns include Arlington, Grand Prairie, Duncanville, and Cedar Hill. There are 4 parks—Cedar Hill is a state park and the other 3 are run by the City of Grand Prairie.

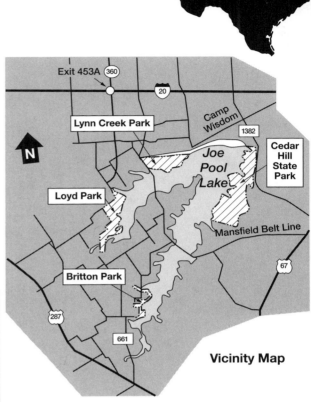

Vicinity Map

Other Parks	Total Number of Campsites	Number of Campsites with Electrical Hookups	Camping Area for Groups	Toilets: F=Flush; V=Vault	Showers	Trailer Dump Station	Picnic Sites	Group Picnic Areas	Boat Launching Ramp	Swimming Area/Beach
Britton				V					•	
Lynn Creek				F	•		•	•	•	•

Notes:
Lynn Creek has full service marina, boat rentals, Jet Ski and Hobie Cat beach and concession.

Three parks at Joe Pool Lake are run by the City of Grand Prairie, but only one of them—Loyd Park—offers camping facilities.

JOE POOL LAKE
LOYD PARK

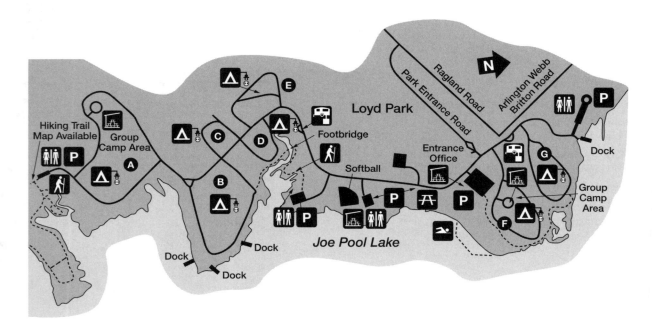

FOR INFORMATION

City of Grand Prairie–Lake Parks
3401 Ragland Road
Grand Prairie, TX 75052
817/467-2104

FACILITIES & ACTIVITIES

202 campsites with water & electricity*
2 group camp areas (10 sites each) with shelter*
flush toilets/showers
2 trailer dump stations
4 group picnic shelters
picnicking
2 playgrounds
swimming beach/bathhouse
boat ramp/4 boat docks
15 miles of hiking/mountain biking trails

---

*Reservations are taken by campsite number a min. of 2 weeks &
up to 1 year in advance; reservations must be made for a min. of
2 nights on weekends and 3 nights on holidays.

It pays to arrive early if you want a picnic shelter for your cook-out.

LAKE ARROWHEAD STATE PARK

FOR INFORMATION

Lake Arrowhead State Park
229 Park Rd. 63
Wichita Falls, TX 76301
940/528-2211

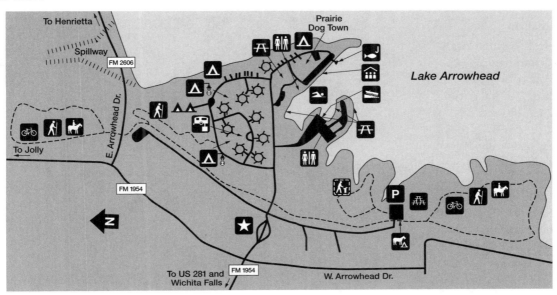

LOCATION

Lake Arrowhead State Park is located 16 miles southeast of Wichita Falls. From US 281, take FM 1954 east for 8 miles; from US 287, take FM 2393 south for 8 miles, turn left on FM 1954 and travel 3 miles to park entrance on left. The 524-acre park is on the northwest shore of Lake Arrowhead, adjacent to the west end of the 3-mile-long earthen dam and spillway. Built on the Little Wichita River, the lake has more than 100 miles of shoreline, and covers about 16,200 surface-acres; it is dotted with large steel oil derricks.

This youngster knows the importance of wearing a helmet.

FACILITIES & ACTIVITIES

48 campsites with water/electricity
19 campsites with water only
4 equestrian campsites with water & electricity, barn and pens
primitive area for groups
restrooms/showers
trailer dump station
picnicking
group dining hall
group picnic pavilion
playgrounds
18-hole disc golf course
swimming
fishing/2 fish cleaning shelters
2 fishing piers (1 lighted)
9 boat ramps
boating/waterskiing
5 miles of multi-use trails for hiking/mountain bike/equestrian
park store at headquarters
Prairie Dog Town

LAKE BOB SANDLIN STATE PARK

FOR INFORMATION

Lake Bob Sandlin State Park
341 State Park Rd. 2117
Pittsburg, TX 75686
903/572-5531

LOCATION

Lake Bob Sandlin State Park is located along the central portion of the north shore of Lake Bob Sandlin, a 9,460-acre reservoir on Cypress Creek, southwest of Mount Pleasant. The 640-acre park may be reached by FM 21, which bounds the west side of the park. From I-30, at Mt. Vernon, take the TX 37 exit and travel south .8 mile, turn left on FM 21, and go 10.2 miles to the park entrance.

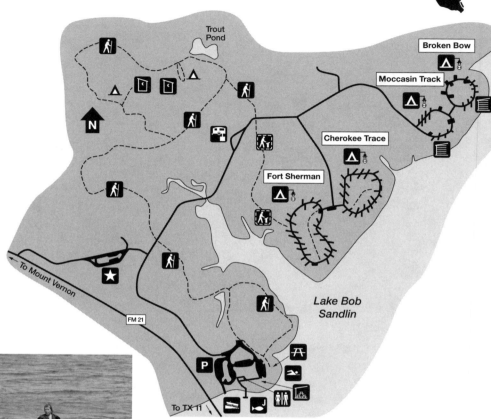

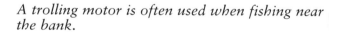

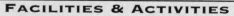

A trolling motor is often used when fishing near the bank.

FACILITIES & ACTIVITIES

75 campsites with water/electricity	playground
9 premium campsites	swimming
2 primitive walk-in camping areas (¼-mile)	fishing/fish cleaning shelter
restrooms/showers	lighted fishing pier
trailer dump station	boat ramp & dock
12 screened shelters	boating/waterskiing
8 enclosed shelters (cottages)	4½ miles of interpretive & hiking trails
picnicking	4½ miles of mountain bike trails
group picnic pavilion	park store at headquarters

LAKE CYPRESS SPRINGS

FOR INFORMATION

Lake Cypress Springs
P.O. Box 345
Mount Vernon, TX 75457
903/537-4536 (main office)
903/860-7799 (reservations)

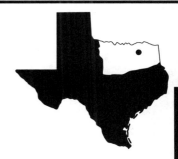

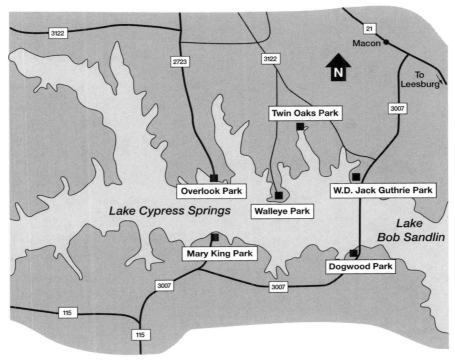

LOCATION

Lake Cypress Springs is a 3,400-acre impoundment on Big Cypress Creek; 6 public parks are operated by the Franklin County Water District. The lake is southeast of Mount Vernon and southwest of Mount Pleasant; from the south it is accessible from Winnsboro and Pittsburg.

Parks	Primitive Campsites	Number of Campsites with Water/Electricity	Camping Area for Groups	Toilets: F=Flush; V=Vault	Showers	Trailer Dump Station	Picnic Sites	Group Picnic Areas	Boat Launching Ramp	Lake Swimming
Dogwood	•			F					•	•
Mary King									•	
Overlook	•			F			•		•	•
Twin Oaks			•	F	•			•		•
Walleye		66		F	•	•	•	•	•	•
W.D. Jack Guthrie	•	39		F	•	•	•		•	•

Notes:
Twin Oaks is rented as a group camp only and has 15 campsites with water/electricity/sewage.
W.D. Jack Guthrie has tennis and volleyball courts, softball field, & basketball goals and a sandy beach.
Walleye has 5 screened shelters and pavilion.

Several of the parks at Lake Cypress Springs offer primitive campsites.

LAKE MINERAL WELLS STATE PARK AND TRAILWAY

FOR INFORMATION

Lake Mineral Wells State Park and Trailway
100 Park Road 71
Mineral Wells, TX 76067
940/328-1171

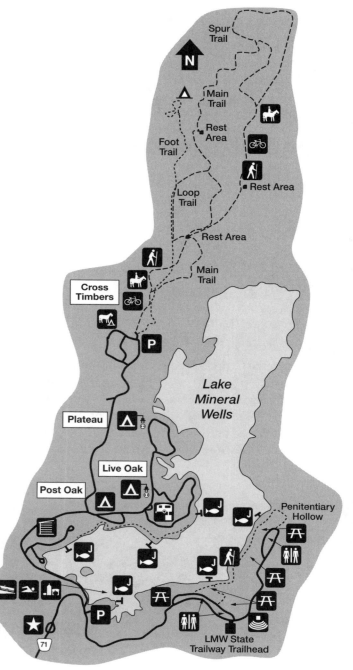

LOCATION

Lake Mineral Wells State Park and Trailway is located only a few miles from the center of town; it may be reached by traveling 3 miles east from the city of Mineral Wells on US 180, or by traveling 14 miles west from Weatherford on the same highway. The park contains 3,282 acres, and includes a 646-acre lake. The Penitentiary Hollow Climbing Area is one of Texas' few areas for rock climbing and rappeling.

FACILITIES & ACTIVITIES

77 campsites with water/electricity
    13 premium campsites
11 tent campsites with water only
20 campsites for backpackers (2½-mile trail)
20 equestrian campsites with water
restrooms/showers
trailer dump station
15 screened shelters
group dining hall/kitchen (day use)
picnicking
beach swimming area
fishing/fish cleaning facility
5 fishing piers (1 lighted)
boat ramp & dock/boating
boat/canoe/paddleboat rental
12 miles (round-trip) of multi-use trail for hiking, equestrian, and mountain biking
5-mile lake trail
2½-mile hiking/backpacking trail
Lake Mineral Wells State Trailway Trailhead
rock climbing/rappeling
Lone Star Amphitheater
concessions

LAKE O' THE PINES

FOR INFORMATION

Ferrells Bridge Dam/Lake O' the Pines
Jefferson, TX 75657-4635
903/665-2336

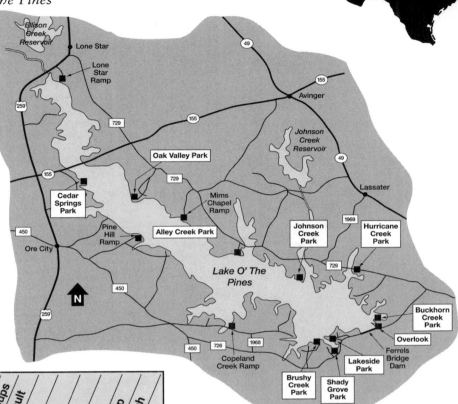

Parks	Total Number of Campsites	Number of Campsites with Electrical Hookups	Camping Area for Groups	Toilets: F=Flush; V=Vault	Showers	Trailer Dump Station	Picnic Sites	Group Picnic Areas	Boat Launching Ramp	Swimming Area/Beach
Alley Creek	91	31	•	F	•	•	•		•	•
Brushy Creek	101	61		F	•	•		•	•	•
Buckhorn Creek	101	60		F	•	•			•	
Cedar Springs	28			F					•	
Hurricane Creek	23			F					•	
Johnson Creek	98	75	•	F	•	•	•	•	•	•
Lakeside				F			•	•	•	•
Oak Valley									•	
Overlook				F			•		•	
Shady Grove				F			•	•	•	•

Notes:
Johnson Creek & Buckhorn Creek have marinas nearby.
A 4-mile hiking trail from Buckhorn to Brushy is under construction.

LOCATION

Lake O' the Pines is a 19,780-acre Corps of Engineers impoundment on Big Cypress Creek with a 144-mile shoreline. The lake is west of Jefferson via TX 49 and FM 729. Other nearby towns include Daingerfield, Gilmer, Lone Star, Ore City, and Avinger.

LAKE TAWAKONI

FOR INFORMATION

Lake Tawakoni
P.O. Box 310
Point, TX 75472-9998
903/598-2216

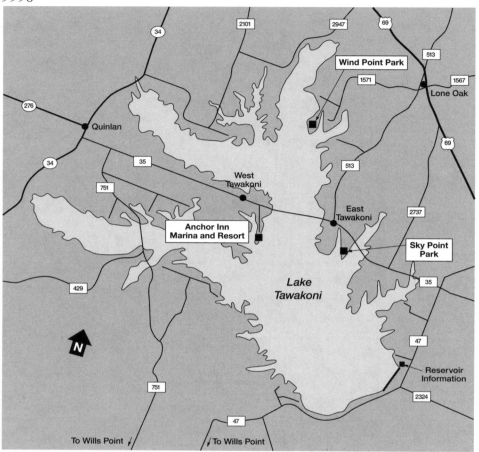

LOCATION

Lake Tawakoni is a 36,700-acre Sabine River Authority reservoir on the Sabine River with a 200-mile shoreline. The lake is to the south of US 69 between Greenville and Emory; TX 35 from Quinlin to Emory crosses the lake. Other nearby towns include Wills Point and Lone Oak.

Parks	Total Number of Campsites	Number of Campsites with Electrical Hookups	Camping Area for Groups	Toilets: F=Flush; V=Vault	Showers	Trailer Dump Station	Picnic Sites	Group Picnic Areas	Boat Launching Ramp	Swimming Area/Beach
Anchor Inn Marina & Resort	130	130	•	F	•	•	•	•	•	
Sky Point	53	28	•	F	•	•	•	•	•	
Wind Point	159	159	•	F	•	•	•	•	•	•

Notes:
All 3 parks are operated by concessionaires.
All 3 parks have campsites with full hookups: Anchor Inn has 100;
   Sky Point has 18; Wind Point has 69.
Wind Point has 15 screened shelters & 8 cabins.
Anchor Inn & Wind Point have trails.

LAKE TAWAKONI STATE PARK

FOR INFORMATION

Lake Tawakoni State Park
10822 FM 2475
Wills Point, TX 75169
903/560-7123

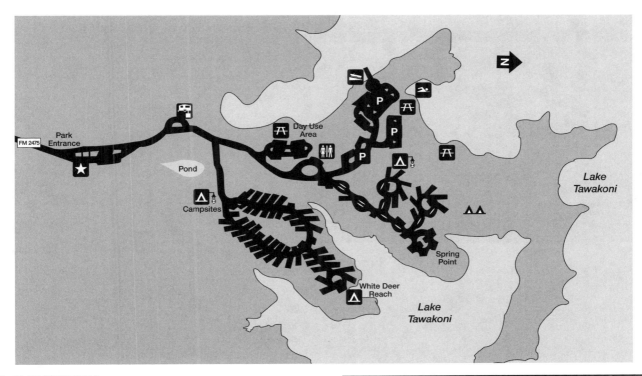

LOCATION

Lake Tawakoni State Park is located some 50 miles east of Dallas and 25 miles south of Greenville. From I-20, take SH 47 north through Wills Point to FM 2475 and continue for about 4 miles. The park covers 376 rolling, wooded acres on the south shore of Lake Tawakoni and has 5 miles of shoreline. This 36,700-acre Sabine River Authority reservoir was created in 1960 to provide water to the city of Dallas.

FACILITIES & ACTIVITIES

78 campsites with water/electricity
youth group camping area
restrooms
trailer dump station
restroom with showers in day use area
picnicking
volleyball court
lake swimming/beach
bank fishing
fishing at stocked ponds
boating/4-lane boat ramp
nature/hiking trails

This state park has a 4-lane boat ramp.

LAKE TEXOMA

FOR INFORMATION

Lake Texoma
351 Corps Road
Denison, TX 75020-6425
903/465-4990

With 580 miles of shoreline, seeing all of Lake Texoma from a Jet Ski is quite a challenge.

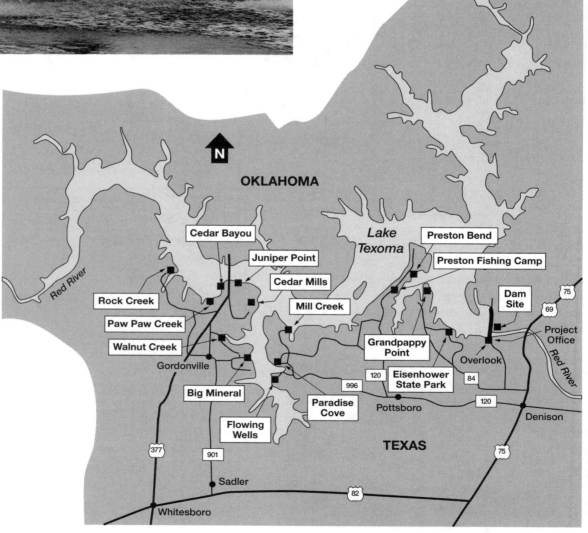

OKLAHOMA

Lake Texoma

Red River

Cedar Bayou

Juniper Point

Preston Bend

Preston Fishing Camp

Cedar Mills

Rock Creek

Mill Creek

Dam Site

Paw Paw Creek

Project Office

Walnut Creek

Red River

Gordonville

Grandpappy Point

Overlook

Big Mineral

Eisenhower State Park

Paradise Cove

Pottsboro

Denison

Flowing Wells

TEXAS

Sadler

Whitesboro

Parks	Total Number of Campsites	Number of Campsites with Electrical Hookups	Toilets: F=Flush; V=Vault	Showers	Trailer Dump Station	Picnic Sites	Group Picnic Areas	Boat Launching Ramp	Lake Swimming
*Big Mineral Camp	111	100	F/V	•	•	•	•	•	•
*Cedar Bayou Resort	39	15	F/V		•	•	•	•	•
*Cedar Mills Resort	38	25	F	•	•	•	•	•	•
Dam Site Texas	32	22	F/V	•	•	•	•	•	
Eisenhower State Park	139	95	F	•	•	•	•	•	•
Flowing Wells	23		F/V			•		•	
*Grandpappy Point Resort	84	•	F	•	•	•		•	
Juniper Point	70	44	F/V	•	•	•		•	
*Mill Creek Resort	10		F/V			•		•	•
Paradise Cove	50	50	F/V	•	•	•		•	•
*Paw Paw Creek Resort	108	108	V			•		•	•
Preston Bend Recreation Area	38	26	F/V	•	•	•	•	•	•
*Preston Fishing Camp	40	30	F	•	•	•	•	•	
*Rock Creek Camp	73	55	F/V			•	•	•	
*Walnut Creek Resort	44	22	F		•	•	•	•	

Notes:
*Denotes facilities operated by concessionaires.
Sites with full hookups: Big Mineral (23), Cedar Mills (25), Eisenhower (50), Paradise Cove (32), Paw Paw Creek (86), & Walnut Creek (6).
Cabins: Big Mineral (5), Cedar Bayou (3), Cedar Mills (18), Paradise Cove (11), Paw Paw (8), Preston Fishing Camp (19), Rock Creek (9), & Walnut Creek (9).
Eisenhower State Park has 35 screened shelters & camping area for groups.
Mill Creek has 8 motel units.
Marinas: Big Mineral, Cedar Bayou, Cedar Mills, Eisenhower, Flowing Wells, Grandpappy Point, Mill Creek, Paw Paw Creek, Preston Fishing, Rock Creek, and Walnut Creek.
Trails are at: Big Mineral, Cedar Bayou, Eisenhower, Juniper Point, Paw Paw Creek

LOCATION

Lake Texoma is an 89,000-acre Corps of Engineers impoundment on the Red River with a 580-mile shoreline. The lake extends westward along the Texas-Oklahoma border from Denison, with access from US 69/75 to the east, US 82 from the south, and US 377 to the west. Numerous camping facilities are located on both the Texas and Oklahoma sides of the lake; this guide includes only the agency parks on the Texas side.

U.S. Army Corps of Engineers

Lake Texoma claims to be one of the most popular Corps of Engineers lakes in the nation, logging more than 9 million visitors annually.

LAKE WHITNEY STATE PARK

FOR INFORMATION

Lake Whitney State Park
P.O. Box 1175
Whitney, TX 76692
254/694-3793

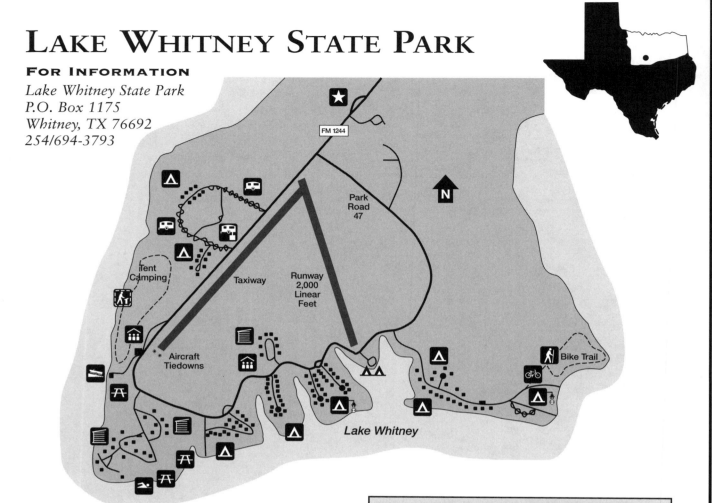

LOCATION

Lake Whitney State Park is located 3 miles west of Whitney on FM 1244. To reach Whitney from I-35, take the TX 22 exit to Hillsboro and travel west on TX 22. The 1,281-acre park fronts the east side of Whitney Lake, which extends 45 river miles along the Brazos River. This 23,560-acre lake is the fourth largest lake in Texas.

Yea! We're skiing double! Now can we try slalom?

FACILITIES & ACTIVITIES

20 campsites with water/electricity/sewage
46 campsites with water/electricity
71 campsites with water only
sponsored youth group primitive camping area
restrooms/showers
trailer dump station
21 screened shelters
screened group shelter/kitchen with 8 screened shelters nearby
recreation hall/kitchen (day or overnight use)
picnicking
beach swimming area
fishing/fish cleaning shelters
boat ramp
boating/waterskiing
1½ miles of hiking/nature trails
1-mile mountain bike trail
airstrip (no lights)

LAVON LAKE

FOR INFORMATION

Lavon Lake
3375 Skyview Drive
Wylie, TX 75098-7575
972/442-3141

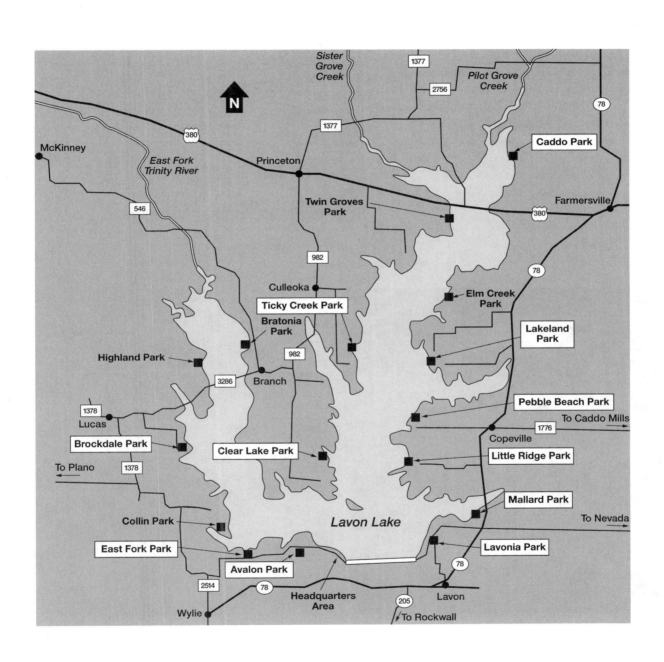

LAVON LAKE
(CONTINUED)

LOCATION

Lavon Lake is a 21,400-acre Corps of Engineers impoundment on the East Fork of the Trinity River with a 121-mile shoreline. The lake is northeast of Dallas, just north of TX 78 between Wylie and Lavon. Other nearby towns include Plano, McKinney, and Farmersville.

Parks	Total Number of Campsites	Number of Campsites with Electrical Hookups	Camping Area for Groups	Toilets: F=Flush; V=Vault	Showers	Trailer Dump Station	Picnic Sites	Group Picnic Areas	Boat Launching Ramp	Swimming Area/Beach
Avalon			•	F			•	•	•	
Brockdale			•	F					•	
Caddo				F			•		•	
Clear Lake	23	23	•	F	•	•	•		•	
East Fork	62	62	•	F	•	•	•		•	
Lakeland	32		•	F					•	
Lavonia	53	38		F	•	•	•		•	
Little Ridge	31			F			•		•	
Mallard				F	•		•		•	•
Pebble Beach				F			•		•	•
Ticky Creek	16			V			•		•	

Notes:
East Fork Park has a marina.
Brockdale & East Fork have hiking & equestrian trails.

Lavon Lake is proud of their new picnic shelters. They are quite attractive and very popular.

LBJ NATIONAL GRASSLANDS

FOR INFORMATION

Caddo/LBJ National Grasslands
1400 N. US Hwy. 81/287
P.O. Box 507
Decatur, TX 76234
940/627-5475

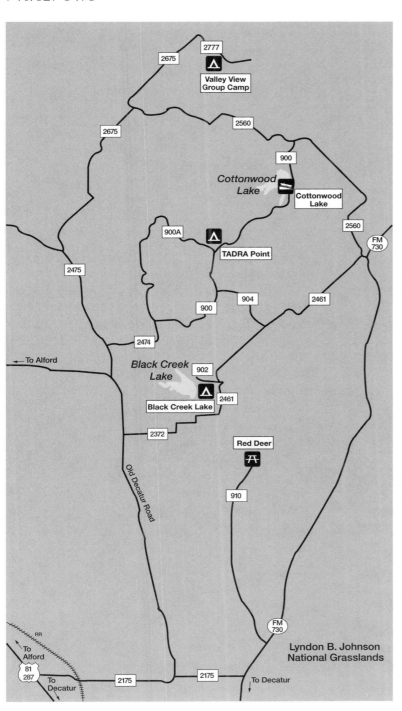

LOCATION

The 20,313-acre Lyndon B. Johnson (LBJ) National Grasslands is located north of Decatur. A little-known fact about the LBJ National Grasslands is that there are approximately 400 lakes and ponds, from ½ acre to 40 acres in size, which are open to public fishing. The recreation areas offer a variety of facilities for camping, picnicking, boating, fishing, hiking, horseback riding, mountain biking, and other outdoor activities. All are open year-round.

DIRECTIONS TO RECREATION AREAS

Black Creek—From Decatur, drive northwest on US 81/287 4½ miles, turn right on CR 2175 at the rest area, cross over RR tracks, go 1 mile and turn left on Old Decatur Road. Go 4 miles, and turn right on CR 2372; then, go 2 miles and turn left on CR 2461 for ½ mile. After crossing steel bridge, turn left (west) on FSR 902 to the recreation area.

Cottonwood Lake—From Decatur, drive north on FM 730 for 10 miles, and turn left on CR 2461. At the fork, turn right on CR 2560 and proceed 3 miles and turn left on FSR 900. Cottonwood Lake is on the right at ½ mile, and TADRA Point Trailhead is on the right at 2 miles.

Valley View Group Camp—From Decatur, drive north on FM 730 for 10 miles, and turn left on CR 2461; at the immediate fork, go right on CR 2560 for 6 miles, and then go right on CR 2675 for 2 miles. Turn right on CR 2777 and follow for 1 mile to Valley View on right.

FACILITIES & ACTIVITIES

BLACK CREEK LAKE RECREATION AREA

7 tent/small RV campsites

6 walk-in tent sites

no drinking water

pit toilets

picnicking

no swimming

fishing/boating on 30-acre lake

60-foot fishing bridge

concrete boat ramp

trailhead for 4-mile hiking trail to Cottonwood Lake

parking fee

COTTONWOOD LAKE RECREATION AREA

Fishing/boating on 40-acre lake

Concrete boat launch

Trailhead for 4-mile hiking trail to Black Creek Lake

VALLEY VIEW GROUP CAMP

15 camp units

double restroom

pavilion with charcoal grill

reservations by groups on first-come, first-served basis

fee required for group reservations

no potable water or sewage facilities

no fee except for group reservation

provides group access to the "blue" loop of the LBJ Multi-Use Trail System

LBJ Multi-Use Trail: the 75-mile-long LBJ Multi-Use Trail is open to horseback riding, mountain bikes and hiking. Access to the trail is provided by the TADRA Point Campsite, Valley View Group Campsite and numerous dispersed campsites. The trail system consists of five loops that begin and end at TADRA Point. Additionally, open areas of the Grasslands are popular for cross-country horseback riding. A vehicle/day fee is charged for parking.

TADRA (Texas Arabian Distance Riding Association) Trailhead is located south of Cottonwood Lake along FS Road 900. This site is used for various group events, including equestrian endurance rides.

The 75-mile long LBJ Multi-Use Trail consists of 5 loops that begin and end at TADRA Point.

LEWISVILLE LAKE

FOR INFORMATION

Lewisville Lake
1801 N. Mill Street
Lewisville, TX 75057-1821
972/434-1666

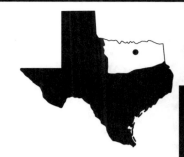

REGION 1

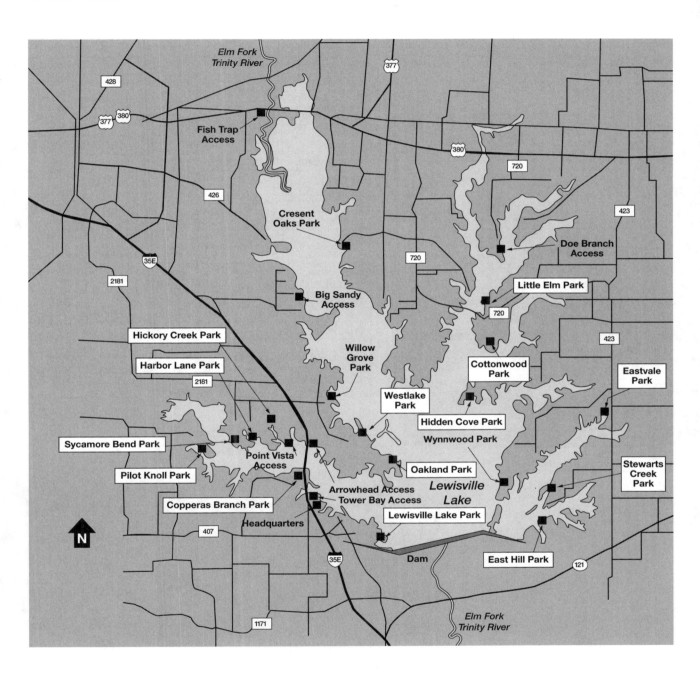

Elm Fork
Trinity River

377

428

377 380

Fish Trap
Access

426

Cresent
Oaks Park

35E

2181

Big Sandy
Access

380

720

423

Doe Branch
Access

Little Elm Park

720

Hickory Creek Park

Willow
Grove
Park

Cottonwood
Park

423

Harbor Lane Park

2181

Westlake
Park

Hidden Cove Park

Eastvale
Park

Sycamore Bend Park

Point Vista
Access

Wynnwood Park

Oakland Park

*Lewisville
Lake*

Stewarts
Creek
Park

Pilot Knoll Park

Copperas Branch Park

Arrowhead Access
Tower Bay Access

Headquarters

Lewisville Lake Park

N

407

35E

Dam

East Hill Park

121

1171

Elm Fork
Trinity River

LEWISVILLE LAKE
(CONTINUED)

LOCATION

Lewisville Lake is a 28,980-acre Corps of Engineers impoundment on the Elm Fork of the Trinity River with a 187-mile shoreline. The lake is about 27 miles north of downtown Dallas to the east of I-35E near Denton. Other nearby towns include Lewisville, Lake Dallas, The Colony, and Frisco.

Parks	Total Number of Campsites	Number of Campsites with Electrical Hookups	Camping Area for Groups	Toilets: F=Flush; V=Vault	Showers	Trailer Dump Station	Picnic Sites	Group Picnic Areas	Boat Launching Ramp	Swimming Area/Beach
Copperas Branch				V			•		•	
Cottonwood	7			V			•		•	
East Hill				V	•		•	•	•	•
Eastvale	4			V					•	
Harbor Lane						•				
Hickory Creek	134	124	•	F/V	•	•			•	•
Hidden Cove	74	50	•	F	•	•	•	•	•	
Lewisville Lake Park	113	91		F/V	•		•	•	•	
Little Elm Park	7			V			•	•	•	
Oakland	90	82		F	•	•			•	
Pilot Knoll	55	55		F/V	•	•	•	•	•	
Stewarts Creek	30			F		•	•		•	•
Sycamore Bend	15			V			•		•	
Westlake				F	•		•	•	•	•

Notes:
Hidden Cove has 38 screened shelters.
Pilot Knoll has hiking & equestrian trails; Hickory Creek has a hiking trail.
Lewisville Lake Park has an 18-hole golf course.

In the Dallas-Fort Worth metroplex, Lewisville Lake is immensely popular for water sports of every kind imaginable.

These sleek boats that display the seal of the U.S. Army Corps of Engineers appear to be motorized. Driving these has to be a new adventure for these youngsters.

MARTIN CREEK LAKE STATE PARK

FOR INFORMATION

Martin Creek Lake State Park
9515 CR 2181 D
Tatum, TX 75691-3425
903/836-4336

LOCATION

Martin Creek Lake State Park is located 20 miles southeast of Longview. The 287-acre park may be reached by driving 3 miles southwest of Tatum on TX 43, then turning south on County Road 2183. Due to the lake water being warmed by a nearby electric power plant, visitors enjoy excellent year-round fishing on this 5,020-acre lake.

A footbridge provides hikers and backpackers access to a small island.

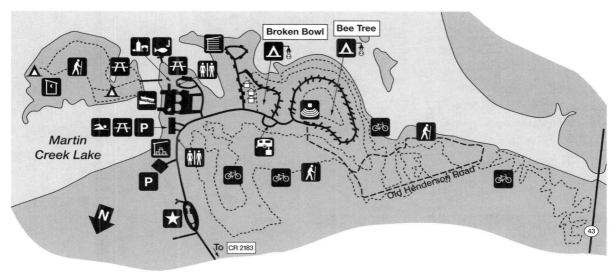

FACILITIES & ACTIVITIES

60 campsites with water/electricity	beach swimming area
12 primitive walk-in (¼-mile) or boat-in campsites	fishing/fish cleaning shelter
restrooms/showers	lighted fishing pier
trailer dump station	2 boat ramps
19 screened shelters	3 boat docks
2 cottages	boating/waterskiing
2 cabins	1½ miles of hiking trails
picnicking	6+ miles of mountain bike trails
group picnic pavilion	amphitheater
playground	park store at headquarters

MERIDIAN STATE PARK

FOR INFORMATION

Meridian State Park
173 Park Rd. 7
Meridian, TX 76665
254/435-2536

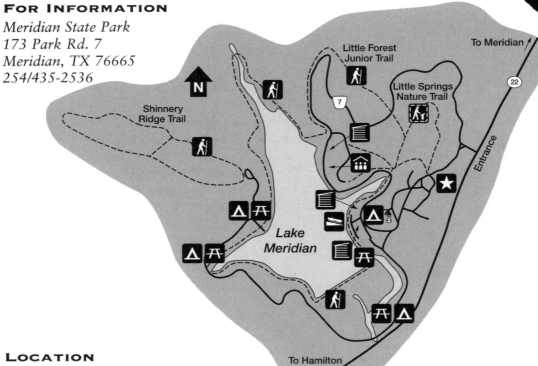

Little Forest
Junior Trail

Little Springs
Nature Trail

To Meridian

22

Entrance

Shinnery
Ridge Trail

N

Lake
Meridian

To Hamilton

LOCATION

Meridian State Park is located 3 miles southwest of Meridian off of TX 22. Park Road 7 provides access to the 505-acre park. A 73-acre lake, formed by a rock and earthen dam, was constructed by the Civilian Conservation Corps on Bee Creek. The endangered golden-cheeked warbler is a spring visitor.

The campsites that are adjacent to the water at Meridian State Park are considered primitive sites.

NAVARRO MILLS LAKE

FOR INFORMATION

Navarro Mills Lake
1175 FM 667
Purdon, TX 76679-3187
254/578-1431

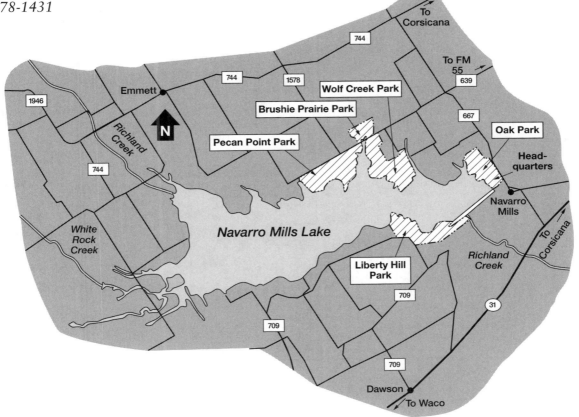

Parks	Total Number of Campsites	Number of Campsites with Electrical Hookups	Camping Area for Groups	Toilets: F=Flush; V=Vault	Showers	Trailer Dump Station	Picnic Sites	Group Picnic Areas	Boat Launching Ramp	Swimming Area/Beach
Brushie Prairie	10			V				•		
Liberty Hill	102	98	•	F/V	•	•			•	•
Oak	48	48	•	F/V	•	•	•		•	•
Pecan Point	35	5		V		•			•	
Wolf Creek	72	50	•	F/V	•	•		•	•	

Notes:
Oak Park has nature & hiking trails.

LOCATION

Navarro Mills Lake is a 5,070-acre Corps of Engineers impoundment of Richland Creek, a tributary of the Trinity River; it has 38 miles of shoreline. The lake is about 18 miles southwest of Corsicana, with access from Texas Highways 22, 31, and 171. Other nearby towns include Hillsboro, Hubbard, Dawson, and Purdon.

Pat Mayse Lake

For Information

Pat Mayse Lake
P.O. Box 129
Powderly, TX 75473-0129
903/732-3020

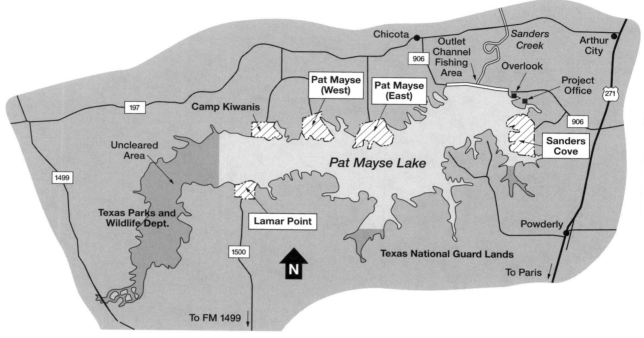

Parks	Total Number of Campsites	Number of Campsites with Electrical Hookups	Camping Area for Groups	Toilets: F=Flush; V=Vault	Showers	Trailer Dump Station	Picnic Sites	Group Picnic Areas	Boat Launching Ramp	Swimming Area/Beach
Lamar Point	26	26		V			•	•		•	•
Pat Mayse East	26	26		V			•	•		•	•
Pat Mayse West	88	83		F/V	•	•	•	•		•	
Sanders Cove	89	85	•	F/V	•	•	•	•		•	

Location

Pat Mayse Lake is a 5,993-acre Corps of Engineers impoundment of Sanders Creek, a tributary of the Red River, with a 67-mile shoreline. The lake is about 13 miles north of Paris off US 271. Other nearby towns include Chicota, Arthur City, and Powderly.

Cruising side by side on twin Jet Skis involves both concentration and adequate communication.

POSSUM KINGDOM STATE PARK

FOR INFORMATION

Possum Kingdom State Park
P.O. Box 70
Caddo, TX 76429
940/549-1803

LOCATION

To reach Possum Kingdom State Park, travel to Caddo on US 180, then go north for 17 miles on Park Road 33. The 1,529-acre park, located in the rugged canyon country of the Palo Pinto Mountains, is on the southwestern shoreline of Possum Kingdom Lake. Formed by impounding the Brazos River, the lake has 17,700 acres of the clearest, bluest water in the southwest.

FACILITIES & ACTIVITIES

61 campsites with water/electricity
   21 premium campsites
55 campsites with water only
10 primitive walk-in campsites
restrooms/showers
trailer dump station
7 cabins
picnicking
playground
lake swimming
fishing/lighted fishing pier
boat ramp
boating/waterskiing
marina/concessions
1-mile hiking trail

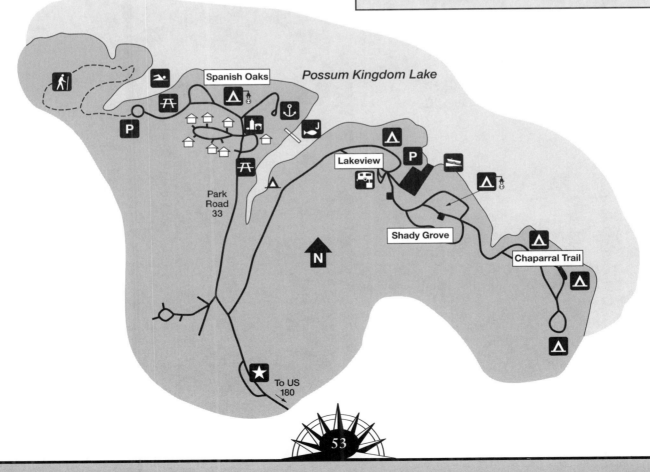

PROCTOR LAKE

FOR INFORMATION

Proctor Lake
Route 1, Box 71A
Comanche, TX 76442-9210
254/879-2424

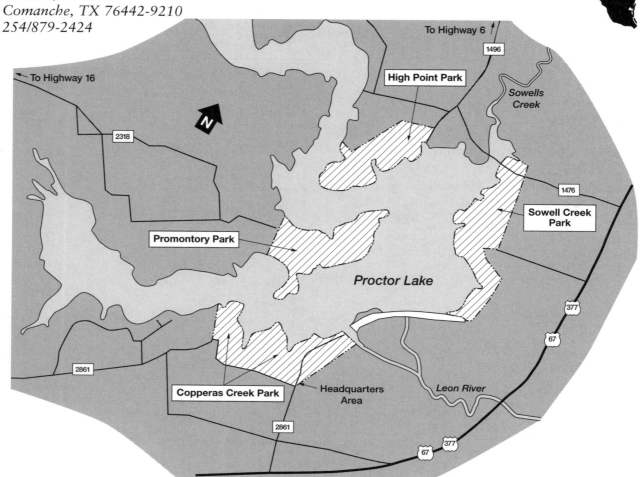

LOCATION

Proctor Lake is a 4,610-acre Corps of Engineers impoundment on the Leon River with a 38-mile shoreline. The lake is about 8 miles northeast of Comanche, off of US 67/377. Other nearby towns include Proctor, Dublin, and De Leon.

Parks	Total Number of Campsites	Number of Campsites with Electrical Hookups	Camping Area for Groups	Toilets: F=Flush; V=Vault	Showers	Trailer Dump Station	Picnic Sites	Boat Launching Ramp	Swimming Area
Copperas Creek	67	67	•	F/V	•	•	•	•	•
High Point							•		
Promontory	88	58	•	F/V	•	•		•	•
Sowell Creek	61	61	•	F/V	•	•	•	•	•

Notes:
Promontory Park has a nature trail.

PURTIS CREEK STATE PARK

FOR INFORMATION

Purtis Creek State Park
14225 FM 316
Eustace, TX 75124
903/425-2332

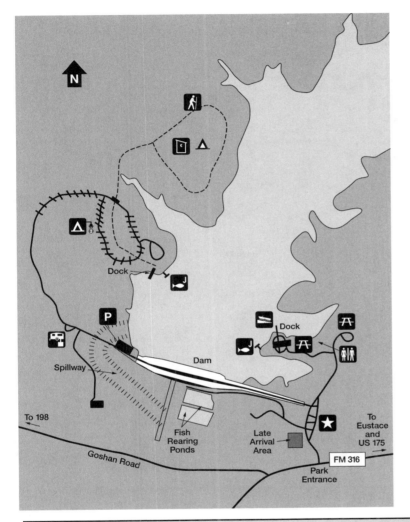

This lake was designed specifically for fishing.

LOCATION

Purtis Creek State Park is located about 65 miles southeast of Dallas and can be reached by traveling US 175 to Eustace, then left on FM 316 for about 3 miles to the park entrance. From Athens, travel 12 miles northwest on US 175 to Eustace, then right on FM 316. The 1,582-acre park includes a 355-acre lake. The lake is unique in that it was designed specifically for fishing where largemouth bass are plentiful and can be fished on a "catch and release" basis only.

FACILITIES & ACTIVITIES

59 campsites with water/electricity	2 lighted fishing piers
13 primitive walk-in campsites	boat ramp & 2 boat docks
restrooms/showers	boating (no wake, idle speed)
trailer dump station	lake use fee; 50-boat maximum
picnicking	reservations up to 90 days in advance available
playground	largemouth bass "catch-and-release" only
designated swimming area	1¼-mile loop hiking trail to walk-in campsites
fishing/2 fish cleaning shelters	park store
2 fish-rearing ponds	

RAY ROBERTS LAKE STATE PARK
ISLE DU BOIS UNIT

FOR INFORMATION

Ray Roberts Lake State Park
Isle du Bois Unit
100 PW 4137
Pilot Point, TX 76258-8944
940/686-2148

LOCATION

The Isle du Bois Unit of Ray Roberts Lake State Park is located off of FM 455 between Pilot Point on US 377 and Sanger on I-35. This park unit contains 2,263 acres on the south side of Ray Roberts Lake, a 29,350-acre impoundment of the Elm Fork of the Trinity River.

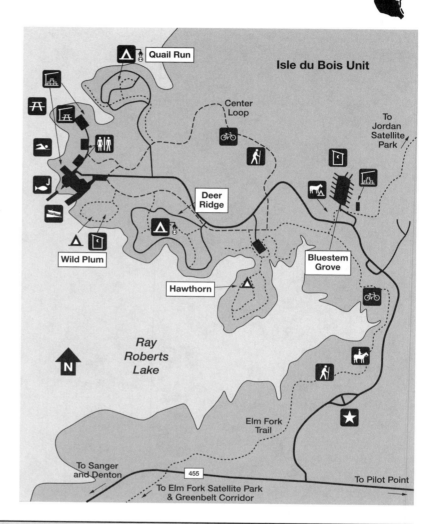

FACILITIES & ACTIVITIES

115 campsites with water/electricity
  17 premium campsites
53 hike-in campsites with water (¼ to ½ mile)
14 equestrian campsites with water
2 walk-in (¼ to ½ mile) group campsites
restrooms/showers
trailer dump station
overnight group pavilion at Bluestem Grove
  (in conjunction with 3 campsites)
picnicking
2 group picnic pavilions

playground
beach swimming area
fishing/fish cleaning shelter
lighted fishing pier
lighted boat ramp
boating/waterskiing
12 miles of dirt trails for hiking, bicycling,
  & equestrian
4½ miles of paved trails
12 miles of dirt trails to Jordan Satellite Park
park store

JOHNSON BRANCH UNIT

FOR INFORMATION

Ray Roberts Lake State Park
Johnson Branch Unit
100 PW 4153
Valley View, TX 76272-7411
940/637-2294

LOCATION

The Johnson Branch Unit of Ray Roberts Lake State Park is located off of FM 3002 east of I-35. From Sanger, travel north on I-35 to Lone Oak Road (exit 483), turn east on FM 3002, and travel 7 miles to the park entrance. This park unit contains 1,514 acres on the north side of Ray Roberts Lake, a 29,350-acre impoundment of the Elm Fork of the Trinity River.

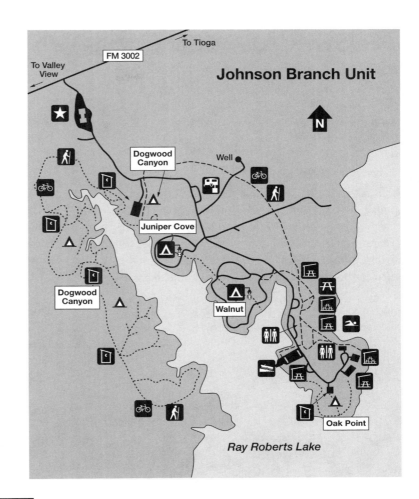

FACILITIES & ACTIVITIES

104 campsites with water/electricity
50 primitive walk-in campsites
   29 at Oak Point
   21 at Dogwood Canyon
1 primitive group camping area
showers/restrooms
trailer dump station
picnicking
2 group picnic pavilions
playgrounds
beach swimming area
fishing/fish cleaning facility
boat ramps
boating/waterskiing
4.8-mile paved hike/bike trail
10 miles of mountain bike trails
park store at headquarters

Fishing is so popular at Ray Roberts Lake that boaters often have to wait their turn at the boat launch.

RUSK-PALESTINE STATE PARK

FOR INFORMATION

Rusk-Palestine State Park
RR 4, Box 431
Rusk, TX 75785
903/683-5126

LOCATION

Rusk-Palestine State Park is adjacent to US 84 between Rusk and Palestine in the Piney Woods of East Texas. The park is located at each end of the Texas State Railroad State Historical Park, which offers 50-mile rides on antique coaches pulled by turn-of-the-century steam engines. The Palestine Unit of this 136-acre park is located 3 miles east of Palestine on US 84; the Rusk Unit is located 3 miles west of Rusk off US 84. The Rusk Unit has a 15-acre lake.

ABOUT THE TEXAS STATE RAILROAD

The railroad was built in 1896 to haul iron ore to a state-owned smelter. The round-trip, from either Rusk or Palestine, takes about 4 hours, including an hour-long stop for lunch. Separate trains are operated from each depot. Advance reservations are recommended. Contact: Texas State Railroad State Historical Park, P.O. Box 39, Rusk, TX 75785. Phone 1-800-442-8951 (in-Texas reservations) or 903/683-2561 (information and out-of-Texas calls).

Antique steam engines power vintage coaches 50 miles round-trip through dense East Texas forestlands between Rusk and Palestine in the nation's longest and narrowest state park.

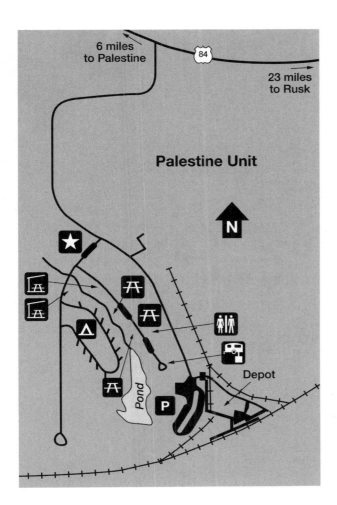

Palestine Unit

6 miles to Palestine

84

23 miles to Rusk

N

Pond

P

Depot

FACILITIES & ACTIVITIES

RUSK UNIT

32 campsites with water/electricity/sewage

23 group trailer campsites with water/electricity

16 tent sites with water/electricity

restrooms/showers

trailer dump station

15 picnic sites

open air gazebo-style pavilion with kitchen/dining area

playground

2 tennis courts

lake swimming

fishing/fishing pier

boating (no gasoline motors)

paddleboat rentals

¼-mile nature trail

park store

west terminus of the Texas State Railroad

PALESTINE UNIT

12 campsites with water

restrooms

trailer dump station

36 picnic sites

2 group picnic pavilions

playground

½-mile nature trail

park store

east terminus of the Texas State Railroad

REGION 1

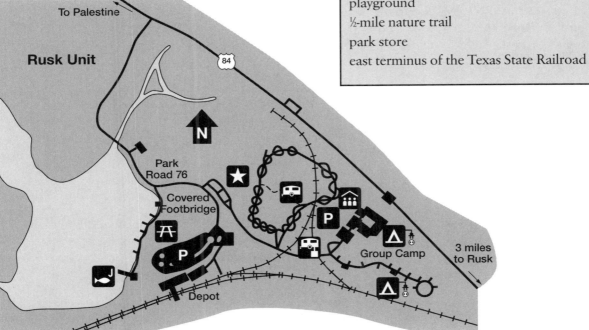

Rusk Unit

To Palestine

84

N

Park Road 76

Covered Footbridge

P

P

Depot

Group Camp

3 miles to Rusk

TYLER STATE PARK

FOR INFORMATION

Tyler State Park
789 Park Rd. 16
Tyler, TX 75706-9141
903/597-5338

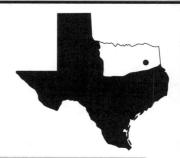

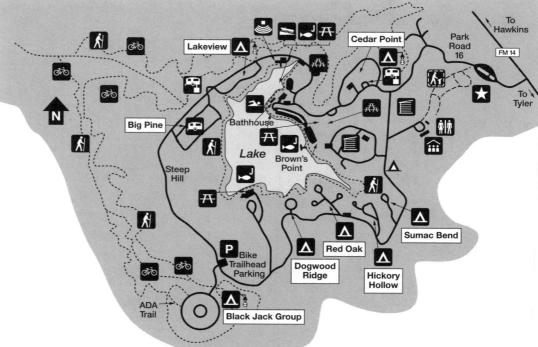

LOCATION

Tyler State Park is located off FM 14, about 8 miles north of Tyler from Loop 323; from I-20, the park is just 2 miles north off FM 14. From FM 14, turn left on Park Road 16. Surrounded by a mixed pine/hardwood forest, this 985-acre park has a spring-fed 64-acre lake.

FACILITIES & ACTIVITIES

77 campsites with water/electricity
  18 premium campsites
37 campsites with water only
restrooms/showers
trailer dump station
35 screened shelters
group trailer area with 30 sites with
  water/electricity
dining hall/kitchen for day use only
picnicking
2 group picnic areas

playground
lake swimming & bathhouse
fishing/3 fishing piers
boat ramp & dock
boating (no wake)
boat/canoe/paddleboat/kayak rentals
2½ miles of hiking trails
¾-mile nature trail
13 miles of pedestrian/bike trails
amphitheater

WACO LAKE

FOR INFORMATION

Waco Lake
3801 Zoo Park Drive
Waco, TX 76708-9602
254/756-5359

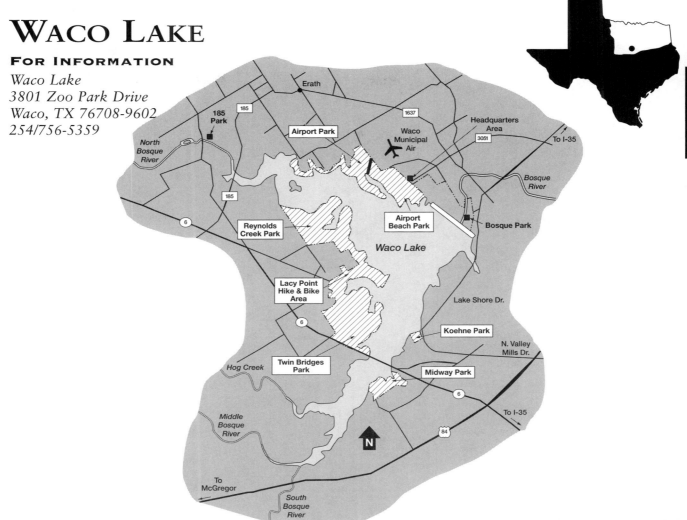

Since this lake is within the Waco city limits, residents can be boating on very short notice.

LOCATION

Waco Lake is a 7,270-acre Corps of Engineers impoundment of the Bosque River with a 60-mile shoreline. Located to the northwest of Waco, the lake is within the city limits of Waco. TX 6 crosses the southernmost arm of the lake.

Parks	Total Number of Campsites	Number of Campsites with Electrical Hookups	Camping Area for Groups	Toilets: F=Flush; V=Vault	Showers	Trailer Dump Station	Picnic Sites	Group Picnic Areas	Boat Launching Ramp	Swimming Area/Beach
Airport Park	53	20		F	•	•	•	•	•	•
Koehne Park				V			•		•	
Midway Park	38	33		F/V			•		•	
Airport Beach Park				V			•	•	•	•
Reynolds Creek Park	55	55	•	F/V	•	•		•		
Twin Bridges Park				F/V			•	•	•	•

Notes:
Airport and Twin Bridges have marinas.
Reynolds Creek Park has a hiking trail.

WHITNEY LAKE

FOR INFORMATION

Whitney Lake
285 CR 3602
Clifton, TX 76634
254/694-3189

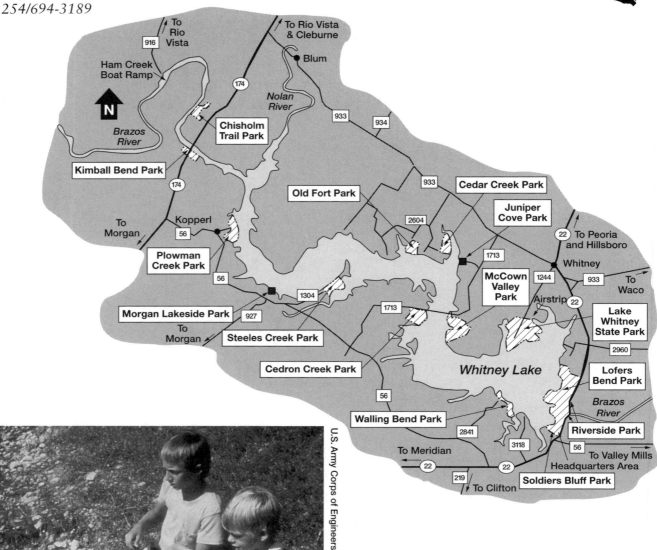

To Rio Vista
916

To Rio Vista & Cleburne

Blum

Ham Creek Boat Ramp

N

174

Nolan River

Brazos River

933

934

Chisholm Trail Park

Kimball Bend Park

174

Old Fort Park

933

Cedar Creek Park

2604

Juniper Cove Park

To Morgan

Kopperl

56

22 To Peoria and Hillsboro

1713

Whitney

Plowman Creek Park

56

McCown Valley Park

1244

933 To Waco

Airstrip

22

Morgan Lakeside Park

927

1304

1713

Lake Whitney State Park

To Morgan

Steeles Creek Park

2960

Cedron Creek Park

Whitney Lake

Lofers Bend Park

Brazos River

56

Walling Bend Park

2841

3118

Riverside Park

56 To Valley Mills

To Meridian

22

22

Headquarters Area

219

Soldiers Bluff Park

To Clifton

Whitney Lake stretches 45 miles up the Brazos River Valley. If you don't have a boat, fishing from the bank is the next best thing

LOCATION

Whitney Lake is a 23,560-acre Corps of Engineers impoundment of the Brazos River with a 190-mile shoreline. The lake is west of Hillsboro and east of Meridian; it is accessible via various FM roads off of TX 22, which connects these two towns. Other nearby towns include Laguna Park and Whitney.

Most campers prefer camping as near to the water as possible.

All water sports are popular at Whitney Lake, whether windsurfing, sailing, waterskiing, or scuba diving.

Parks	Total Number of Campsites	Number of Campsites with Electrical Hookups	Camping Area for Groups	Toilets: F=Flush; V=Vault	Showers	Trailer Dump Station	Picnic Sites	Group Picnic Areas	Boat Launching Ramp	Swimming Area
Cedar Creek	21			V				•	•	
Cedron Creek	57	57	•	F/V	•	•			•	•
Chisholm Trail	14			V					•	
Juniper Cove	100	100	•	F/V	•	•	•	•	•	
Kimball Bend	11			V					•	
Lake Whitney State Park	137	66	•	F	•	•	•	•	•	•
Lofers Bend	151	113	•	F	•	•	•	•	•	•
McCown Valley	61	32	•	F/V	•	•	•	•	•	•
Morgan Lakeside	15	15	•	F/V	•	•	•	•	•	•
Plowman Creek	34	20		F/V	•	•			•	
Riverside	5			V					•	
Soldiers Bluff	14		•	F				•		
Steeles Creek	21			V					•	
Walling Bend	10			V				•	•	

Notes:
Lake Whitney State Park also has 37 campsites with full hookups and 21 screened shelters.
Juniper Cove has 25 campsites with full hookups.
Juniper Cove & Morgan Lakeside are operated by concessionaires.
Marinas are located at Juniper Cove, Lofers Bend, & Morgan Lakeside.

U.S. Army Corps of Engineers

WRIGHT-PATMAN LAKE

FOR INFORMATION

Wright-Patman Lake
P.O. Box 1817
Texarkana, TX 75504-1817
903/838-8781

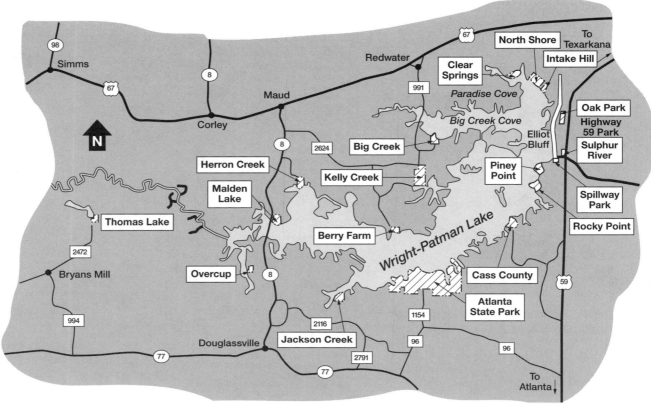

N

Simms

98

67

8

Maud

Corley

Redwater

67

991

North Shore

To Texarkana

Intake Hill

Clear Springs

Paradise Cove

Big Creek Cove

Oak Park

Highway 59 Park

Elliot Bluff

Sulphur River

8

2624

Big Creek

Herron Creek

Kelly Creek

Piney Point

Spillway Park

Rocky Point

Malden Lake

Thomas Lake

2472

Berry Farm

Wright-Patman Lake

Bryans Mill

Overcup

8

Cass County

59

994

Jackson Creek

2116

Atlanta State Park

1154

Douglassville

2791

77

96

96

To Atlanta

77

A screened shelter around the eating area can be a real asset when camping at an East Texas lake during the bug season.

LOCATION

Wright-Patman Lake is a 33,750-acre Corps of Engineers impoundment of the Sulphur River with a 203-mile shoreline. The lake is about 12 miles south of Texarkana with access off of US 67, US 59, and TX 77. Other nearby towns include Maud, Redwater, Queen City, Atlanta, and Douglassville.

This sturdily made climbing apparatus is typical of the playgrounds found at most Corps of Engineers parks.

Four parks at Wright-Patman Lake have designated swimming areas; usually, lifeguards are not on duty.

Parks	Total Number of Campsites	Number of Campsites with Electrical Hookups	Camping Area for Groups	Toilets: F=Flush; V=Vault	Showers	Trailer Dump Station	Picnic Sites	Group Picnic Areas	Boat Launching Ramp	Swimming Area/Beach
Atlanta State Park	59	59		F/V	•	•	•	•	•	•
Berry Farm	18			V					•	
Big Creek	29	29		V					•	
Cass County	45	45		F	•	•	•	•	•	
Clear Springs	101	88	•	F	•	•	•	•	•	
Herron Creek				V			•		•	
Intake Hill	27			V		•				
Jackson Creek	10			V			•		•	
Kelly Creek	77	77		F	•	•			•	
Malden Lake	39	39		F		•			•	
North Shore				F/V			•	•	•	•
Oak Park				F		•	•	•		
Overcup				V			•		•	
Piney Point	68	48		F/V	•	•	•	•	•	
Rocky Point	124	124		F	•	•		•	•	•
Spillway							•			
Sulphur River	12			V			•			
Thomas Lake	10								•	

Notes:
Big Creek, Kelly Creek, & Sulphur River are operated by a concessionaire.
Kelly Creek has a marina; Intake Hill is adjacent to a marina.
Full hookups available: Atlanta-8; Kelly Creek-30; Rocky Point-9.
Atlanta State Park, Clear Springs, North Shore, Rocky Point, and Piney Point have nature/hiking trails.

U.S. Army Corps of Engineers

REGION 2

1—ANGELINA NATIONAL FOREST, 67

2—BASTROP STATE PARK, 70

3—BELTON LAKE, 71

4—BIG THICKET NATIONAL PRESERVE, 73

5—BRAZOS BEND STATE PARK, 76

6—BUESCHER STATE PARK, 77

7—DAVY CROCKETT NATIONAL FOREST, 78

8—FORT PARKER STATE PARK, 80

9—GALVESTON ISLAND STATE PARK, 81

10—GRANGER LAKE, 82

11—HUNTSVILLE STATE PARK, 83

12—LAKE BASTROP, 84

13—LAKE FAYETTE, 85

14—LAKE GEORGETOWN, 86

15—LAKE HOUSTON STATE PARK, 87

16—LAKE LIVINGSTON STATE PARK, 88

17—LAKE SOMERVILLE STATE PARK AND TRAILWAY (BIRCH CREEK UNIT), 89

18—LAKE SOMERVILLE STATE PARK AND TRAILWAY (NAILS CREEK UNIT), 90

19—MARTIN DIES, JR. STATE PARK, 91

20—MISSION TEJAS STATE PARK, 92

21—MOTHER NEFF STATE PARK, 93

22—SABINE NATIONAL FOREST, 94

23—SABINE PASS BATTLEGROUND STATE PARK & HISTORIC SITE, 97

24—SAM HOUSTON NATIONAL FOREST, 98

25—SAM RAYBURN RESERVOIR, 100

26—SEA RIM STATE PARK, 102

27—SOMERVILLE LAKE, 103

28—STEPHEN F. AUSTIN STATE PARK, 105

29—STILLHOUSE HOLLOW LAKE, 106

30—TOLEDO BEND RESERVOIR, 107

31—TOWN BLUFF DAM/B. A. STEINHAGEN LAKE, 109

32—VILLAGE CREEK STATE PARK, 110

33—WOLF CREEK PARK, 111

ANGELINA NATIONAL FOREST

FOR INFORMATION

Angelina National Forest
701 N. First Street
Lufkin, TX 75901
936/639-8620

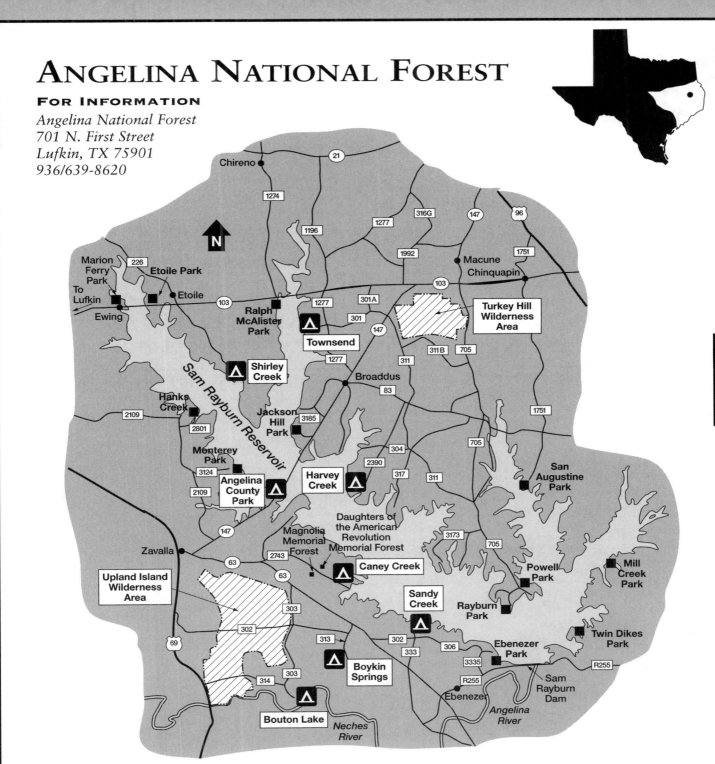

LOCATION

Angelina National Forest, located in Angelina, Jasper, San Augustine, and Nacogdoches counties, is the smallest of the 4 national forests in Texas and contains 153,179 acres. The forest surrounds much of Sam Rayburn Reservoir. Two of the state's 5 wilderness areas are on the Sabine National Forest: the 5,473-acre Turkey Hill Wilderness Area and the 13,331-acre Upland Island Wilderness Area.

Hiking and horseback riding are allowed in wilderness areas; bicycles and other wheeled vehicles are prohibited.

ANGELINA NATIONAL FOREST (CONTINUED)

DIRECTIONS TO RECREATION AREAS

▲ **Bouton Lake**—TX 63 southeast from Zavalla for 7 miles; turn right (south) on FSR 303 for 7 miles.

▲ **Boykin Springs**—TX 63 southeast from Zavalla for 10½ miles; turn right (south) on FSR 313 for 2½ miles.

▲ **Caney Creek**—TX 63 southeast from Zavalla for 6 miles; turn left on FM 2743 for 6 miles; then left (northeast) on FSR 336 for 1 mile.

▲ **Harvey Creek**—FM 83 east from Broaddus for 3½ miles; turn right (southwest) on FM 2390 for 6 miles.

▲ **Sandy Creek**—TX 63 southeast from Zavalla for 14½ miles; turn left (north) on FSR 333 for 2½ miles.

▲ **Townsend**—TX 103 east from Lufkin for 28 miles; turn right on FM 1277 and go 3½ miles; turn right at sign onto FM 2923 and go 1½ miles.

BOYKIN SPRINGS RECREATION AREA

FACILITIES & ACTIVITIES

37 campsites for tents/RVs

24-ft. max. trailer length

restrooms/showers

picnicking

picnic shelter (50)

swimming beach/bathhouse

fishing/boating (electric motors)

hiking trails

trailhead to the 5-mile Sawmill Hiking Trail to Bouton Lake

CANEY CREEK RECREATION AREA

FACILITIES & ACTIVITIES

61 campsites for tents/RVs

flush toilets/showers

trailer dump station

picnicking

fishing

boating/boat ramp

waterskiing

amphitheater (200)

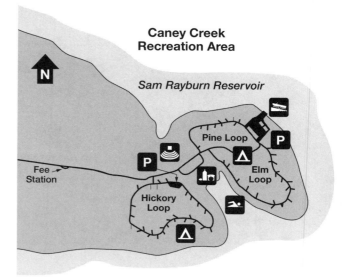

HARVEY CREEK RECREATION AREA

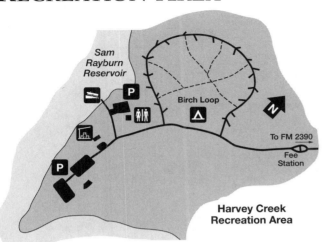

Sam Rayburn Reservoir

Birch Loop

To FM 2390

Fee Station

Harvey Creek Recreation Area

FACILITIES & ACTIVITIES

19 campsites for tents/RVs

24-ft. max. trailer length

vault toilets

no drinking water

picnicking

picnic shelter (50)

fishing

boating/boat ramp

waterskiing

Operated & maintained by San Augustine County (936/275-9472)

SANDY CREEK RECREATION AREA

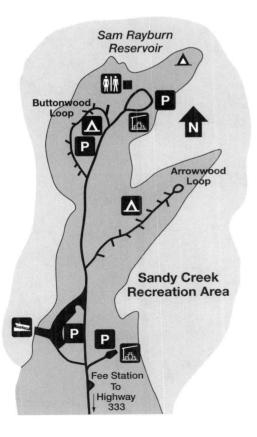

Sam Rayburn Reservoir

Buttonwood Loop

Arrowwood Loop

Sandy Creek Recreation Area

Fee Station To Highway 333

FACILITIES & ACTIVITIES

15 campsites for tents/RVs

24-ft. max. RV length

group covered campsites (25)

restrooms/showers

picnicking

1 picnic shelter (50)

fishing

boating/boat ramp

waterskiing

Other Recreation Areas*	Campsites	Drinking Water	Toilets	Swimming	Fishing	Boating/Boat Ramp	
Angelina County	27	•	P		•	•	Angelina County
Bouton Lake	7		P		•	E	U.S. Forest Service
Shirley Creek	103	•	F	•	•	•	Nacogdoches County
Townsend	19		P		•	•	San Augustine County

Notes:
*Campground maps not available.
Angelina County (409/384-5231) has 10 sites with electricity/water.
Bouton no boat ramp; use electric motors only.
Shirley Creek (936/854-2233) has 69 sites with full hookups, 34 with water/electricity, 13 cabins & marina.
Townsend (936/275-9472) has a group picnic shelter (50).

BASTROP STATE PARK

FOR INFORMATION

Bastrop State Park
P.O. Box 518
Bastrop, TX 78602-0518
512/321-2101

Park Road 1C
To Buescher State Park 10 miles
Shade-Shelter at Scenic Overlook
Lost Pines Hiking Trail
Pond
Old Road Bed
Park Road 1B
Copperas Creek
Park Road 1A
Creekside
Barracks
Pond
Golf Course
Piney Hill
Scout Camping Area
To Smithville
Deer Run
Park Road 1A
21
Park Road 1A
Golf Course
Dining Hall
150 Loop
To Bastrop
71
71
N

LOCATION

Bastrop State Park is located 1 mile east of Bastrop on TX 21; it is also accessible from the east on TX 71 or by way of Buescher State Park along Park Road 1C. This 5,926-acre park is situated among the famous Lost Pines of Texas; it includes a 10-acre lake.

FACILITIES & ACTIVITIES

35 campsites with water/electricity/sewer	picnicking
19 campsites with water/electricity	playground
11 campsites with water only	swimming pool (fee)
7 walk-in campsites with water near	fishing
backpacking campsites	hiking trail
restrooms/showers	8½ miles of hiking trails
trailer dump station	*13 miles of surfaced roads for bicycles on Park Road 1C to Buescher State Park
12 cabins	
Lost Pines Lodge	18-hole golf course/pro shop
group camp (4 dorms with bunk beds)	interpretive tour (fee)
group tent sites	park store
recreation hall/dining hall/kitchen	scenic drive to Buescher State Park
dining hall/kitchen (day use only)	

*Should be used only by experienced cyclists.

BELTON LAKE

FOR INFORMATION

Belton Lake
3740 FM 1670
Belton, TX 76513-9503
254/939-2461

LOCATION

Belton Lake is a 12,300-acre Corps of Engineers impoundment of the Leon River and several creeks with a 136-mile shoreline. The lake is northwest of Belton via FM 439 or TX 317 to Moody. SH 36 from Temple to Gatesville crosses the northernmost arm of the lake. Other nearby towns include Killeen, Nolanville, McGregor, and Morgan's Point Resort.

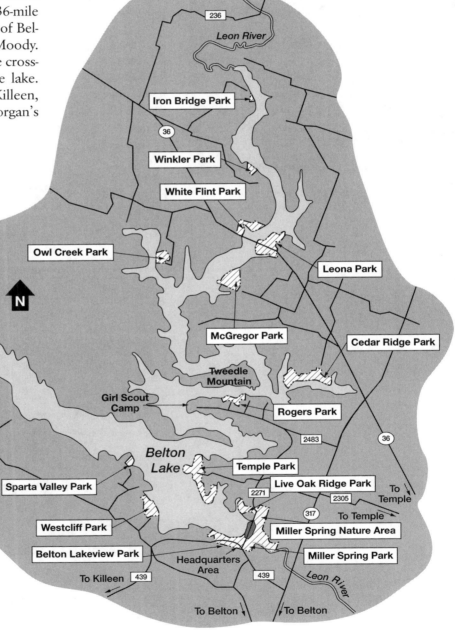

Leon River

236

Iron Bridge Park

36

Winkler Park

White Flint Park

Owl Creek Park

Leona Park

N

McGregor Park

Cedar Ridge Park

Tweedle Mountain

Girl Scout Camp

Rogers Park

Sparta Road

2483

36

Belton Lake

Temple Park

Sparta Valley Park

Live Oak Ridge Park

2271

2305

To Temple

317

To Temple

Westcliff Park

Miller Spring Nature Area

Belton Lakeview Park

Miller Spring Park

Headquarters Area

Leon River

To Killeen

439

439

To Belton

To Belton

REGION 2

BELTON LAKE (CONTINUED)

A neophyte gets her first lesson on how to jet ski.

Parks	Total Number of Campsites	Number of Campsites with Electrical Hookups	Camping Area for Groups	Toilets: F=Flush; V=Vault	Showers	Trailer Dump Station	Picnic Sites	Group Picnic Areas	Boat Launching Ramp	Swimming Area/Beach
Belton Lakeview				F			•	•	•	
Cedar Ridge	76	68	•	F	•	•	•	•	•	
Iron Bridge	5			V			•		•	
Leona				V					•	
Live Oak Ridge	48	48		F	•	•		•	•	
McGregor				V			•		•	
Miller Spring				V			•			
Owl Creek	7			V			•		•	
Rogers				V					•	
Sparta Valley	1			V					•	
Temple Park				F/V	•		•	•		•
Westcliff	31	27		F/V	•	•	•		•	•
White Flint	22	22		V					•	
Winkler	14			F	•					

Notes:
Cedar Ridge & Belton Lakeview have marinas.
6 parks do not have drinking water: Iron Bridge, Leona, McGregor, Miller Spring, Rogers, & Sparta Valley.
Temple Park has a 2-mile bike trail; Cedar Ridge has a 2-mile hiking trail; Belton Lakeview has a 2-mile fitness trail; and Miller Spring Nature Area has 10 miles of nature trails.

U.S. Army Corps of Engineers

Sunset over Belton Lake . . . a beautiful time of the day to relax around the campfire and relive the highlights of a great day at the lake.

BIG THICKET NATIONAL PRESERVE

FOR INFORMATION

Big Thicket National Preserve
3785 Milam
Beaumont, TX 77701
Headquarters 409/839-2689
Visitor Center 409/246-2337

*The Pitcher Plant Trail is located on the northeast
side of the Turkey Creek Unit.*

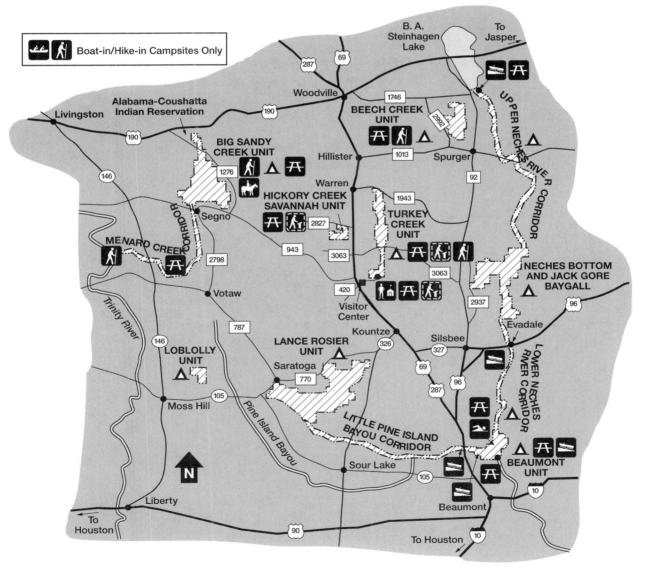

Boat-in/Hike-in Campsites Only

B. A. Steinhagen Lake

To Jasper

287
69
287

Woodville

1746

BEECH CREEK UNIT

2992

UPPER NECHES RIVER CORRIDOR

Livingston

Alabama-Coushatta Indian Reservation

190

Hillister

1013

Spurger

92

146

BIG SANDY CREEK UNIT

1276

Warren

1943

CORRIDOR

Segno

HICKORY CREEK SAVANNAH UNIT

2827

943

TURKEY CREEK UNIT

3063

MENARD CREEK

2798

3063

NECHES BOTTOM AND JACK GORE BAYGALL

Votaw

420

3063

2937

96

Visitor Center

Evadale

LOWER NECHES RIVER CORRIDOR

Trinity River

787

Kountze

Silsbee

LANCE ROSIER UNIT

326

327

LOBLOLLY UNIT

Saratoga

69

146

770

287

96

105

Moss Hill

LITTLE PINE ISLAND BAYOU CORRIDOR

Pine Island Bayou

Sour Lake

105

BEAUMONT UNIT

N

10

Liberty

Beaumont

To Houston

90

To Houston

10

BIG THICKET NATIONAL PRESERVE (CONTINUED)

LOCATION

The Big Thicket National Preserve, composed of 12 units of various sizes and spread over 50 square miles, contains more than 85,000 acres. The units range in size from 550 to over 25,000 acres. Scientists have termed the Big Thicket a "biological crossroads"; it is recognized internationally for its diversity. Factors contributing to this diversity are geology, geography, climate, and water. It is the first area to receive the preserve designation by the national park system, which means it will remain in its natural state. Located in southeast Texas, the 12 separate units are bounded by US 96 on the east, US 90 on the south, US 59 on the west and US 190 on the north.

POINTS OF INTEREST

▲ Five major North American biological influences meet in the Big Thicket, forming an area that combines the central plains, eastern forests, Appalachian mountains, southeastern swamps, and southwestern deserts in extremely close proximity.

▲ Canoe trips in the Big Thicket can range from traveling down the curving Neches River to quietly paddling into areas too shallow for boats. Using various canoe launch sites can create canoe trips lasting from a few hours to a few days.

▲ Hiking is one of the best ways to experience the Big Thicket. There are presently hiking or nature trails on 5 preserve units. Visitors may select from 9 trails ranging from ¼ mile to 18 miles in length.

▲ Backcountry camping for individuals or small groups is allowed in designated portions on 9 of the units.

▲ A variety of naturalist activities is offered by the preserve during the warmer months. Reservations are required for all programs, and can be made through the Visitor Center, 409/246-2337.

GENERAL INFORMATION

▲ An entry fee is not charged, nor is there a fee for backcountry camping.

▲ The Big Thicket Visitor Center is reached by traveling 7 miles north of Kountze on US 69. Turn east on FM 420, then left; it is open daily from 9 am to 5 pm. Information on the the preserve's resources, recreational opportunities, and facilities is available. A 20-minute video can be viewed. Phone: 409/246-2337.

▲ The Environmental Education Center is the former cabin of some early settlers of the Big Thicket. It is located 2½ miles beyond the Visitor Center on FM 420. The trailhead to the Kirby Nature Trail begins behind the Staley Cabin.

The Beech Woods Trail is a one-mile loop trail that meanders through a magnificent mature section of a beech-magnolia-loblolly forest.

▲ Park rangers conduct a large variety of programs throughout the year; ask for a schedule. Reservations are required, and some programs have a limit to group size. Make reservations at the Visitor Center, either by phone or in person.

▲ Several backcountry camping zones have been designated in isolated portions on 9 of the preserve units/corridors (see map). Backcountry users should pick up a copy of the special regulations that apply. Use is limited to a maximum of 5 days per trip and group size is limited to 8 persons.

▲ When camping in the backcountry, fires using camp stoves are allowed in wooded areas; open fires are allowed only on sandbars along the Neches River. Backcountry camping is suspended in all areas open to hunting (October 1 to January 15). A portion of the Turkey Creek Unit is open year-round.

▲ Before beginning an overnight canoe trip along the Neches River Corridor, check with a ranger for current and projected water conditions, weather forecasts, and road conditions to launch sites. Overnight camping on sandbars is permitted except in restricted areas.

▲ Backcountry permits are free and must be obtained prior to camping from any park ranger, or at 3 locations, either in person or by telephone:

—Visitor Center on FM 420 (409/246-2337).
—Preserve headquarters in Beaumont at 3785 Milam (409/839-2689).
—Woodville office on US 287, ½ mile northwest of the US 69/287 junction (409/283-5824).

▲ Five of the units have nature/hiking trails ranging in length from ¼ mile to 18 miles in length: Beech Creek, Big Sandy, Hickory Creek Savannah, Turkey Creek, and Menard Creek Corridor. Trail maps are available at the Visitor Center.

▲ Six of the units provide recreational opportunities for boating, fishing, and swimming: the Upper and Lower Neches River Corridor Units, Menard Creek Corridor Unit, Little Pine Island Bayou Corridor Unit, Beaumont Unit, and the Neches Bottom and Jack Gore Baygall Unit.

▲ Fishing is allowed in all preserve waters with a valid Texas license.

▲ Picnic areas are presently located at 10 of the units; they are open from 6 am to 11 pm. All the sites have outhouse facilities and most of them have ground level fire grates for charcoal fires. Water is not available at the sites. A drinking fountain is located at the Visitor Center and the Kirby Nature Trail trailhead. The picnic area at Hickory Creek Unit is sheltered and ideal for large groups.

FACILITIES & ACTIVITIES

backcountry camping on 9 units

14 picnic areas

swimming

canoeing/boating on 6 units

boat ramps

fishing/hunting

9 nature/hiking trails on 4 units

18-mile Big Sandy Creek Horse Trail (designed for horseback/hiking/mountain biking)

ranger-led talks/walks/canoe trips

exhibits

visitor center

This hiker is fascinated by the number of little cypress knees growing in the stream.

BRAZOS BEND STATE PARK

FOR INFORMATION

Brazos Bend State Park
21901 FM 762
Needville, TX 77461-9511
979/553-5101

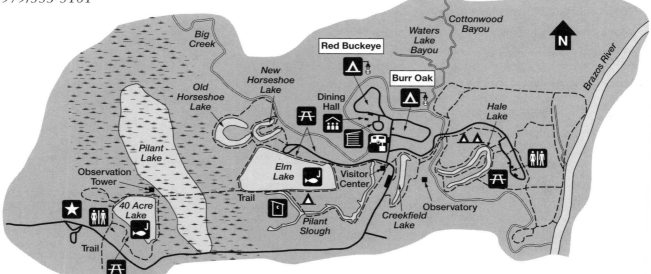

LOCATION

Brazos Bend State Park is on FM 762 about 20 miles southeast of the Rosenberg/Richmond area; access to FM 762 from this direction is via FM 2759 off of US 59. From Houston, travel south on TX 288, then 10 miles west through Rosharon on FM 1462, and north 1 mile on FM 762. The 4,897-acre park has sloughs, bayous, cutoff meanders called oxbow lakes, and several other small lakes created by levees.

Alligators do, indeed, inhabit the oxbow lakes at Brazos Bend. Park visitors are urged not to feed or annoy them.

FACILITIES & ACTIVITIES

77 campsites with water/electricity

3 primitive sponsored youth group camping areas (200–300-yard walk)

restrooms/showers

trailer dump station

14 screened shelters

dining hall/kitchen (day use only)

picnicking

2 group picnic pavilions

playground

observation tower & platforms

*½-mile accessible nature trail

21 miles of hiking/mountain bike trails (some surfaced)

nature center

park store

George Observatory—public stargazing programs each Saturday (limited passes available)

---

*Trail is accessible to those with vision, hearing, and mobility problems; it encircles Creekfield Lake.

BUESCHER STATE PARK

FOR INFORMATION

Buescher State Park
P.O. Box 75
Smithville, TX 78957-0075
512/237-2241

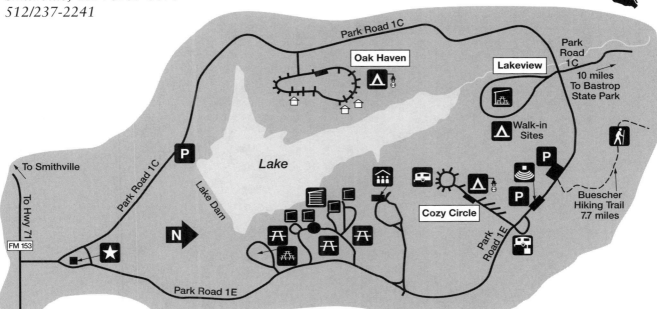

FACILITIES & ACTIVITIES

40 campsites with water/electricity

20 campsites with water only

10 walk-in sites

restrooms/showers

trailer dump station

4 screened shelters

3 mini-cabins

14-site group trailer area with water/electricity

group shelter (day use only)

recreation hall/kitchen (day or overnight use)

picnicking

group picnic area

playground

fishing

7.7 miles of hiking trails

*13 miles of surfaced road for bicycles on Park
   Road 1C to Bastrop State Park

park store

scenic drive to Bastrop State Park

---

*Should be used only by experienced cyclists.

LOCATION

Buescher State Park is located 2 miles north of Smithville. From TX 71, travel ½ mile north on FM 153 to Park Road 1; Loop 230 provides access to FM 153. The 1,017-acre park, located on the eastern edge of the famous Lost Pines of Texas, includes a 25-acre lake.

The campsites at the Oak Haven camping loop are very secluded.

DAVY CROCKETT NATIONAL FOREST

FOR INFORMATION

Davy Crockett National Forest
(in Ratcliff, east side of FM 227, just north of SH 7)
RR 1, Box 55-FS
Kennard, TX 75847
936/655-2299

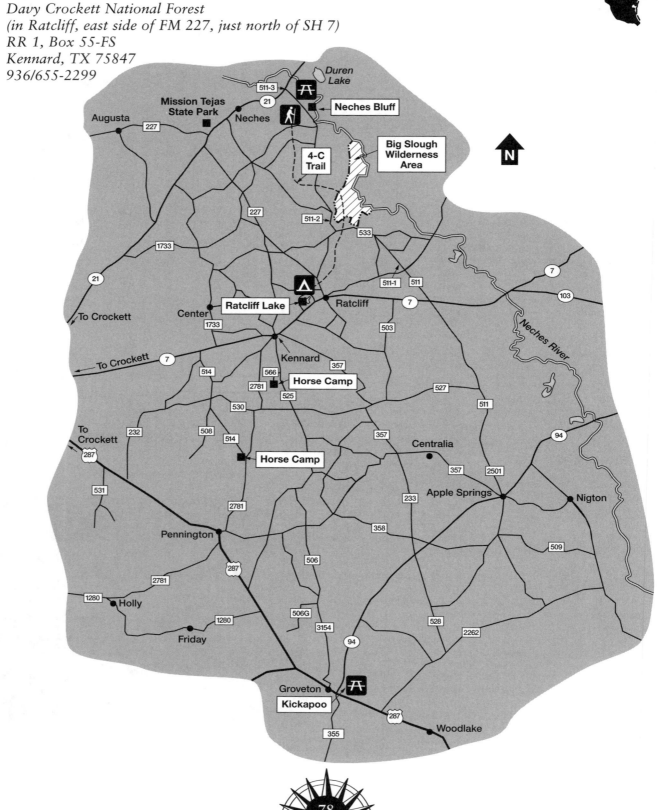

LOCATION

Davy Crockett National Forest, located in Houston and Trinity counties, contains 160,647 acres. The forest is west of Lufkin and east of Crockett. The 3,639-acre Big Slough Wilderness Area is located along the Neches River on the northeast portion of the forest.

DIRECTIONS TO RECREATION AREAS

▲ **Neches Bluff**—TX 21 northeast from Crockett for 25 miles; then turn right (east) on FSR 511-3 for 1 mile; then turn left (north) and follow entrance road for 1 mile. Picnicking and hiking trail available.

▲ **Ratcliff Lake**—On TX 7, 20 miles east of Crockett.

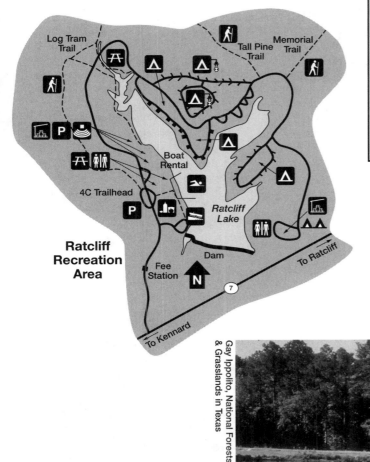

RATCLIFF LAKE RECREATION AREA

FACILITIES & ACTIVITIES

77 campsites
   27 with electricity
35-ft. max. RV length
trailer dump station
restrooms/cold showers
group camping area
picnicking
group picnic shelters (by reservation)
swimming beach/bathhouse
concessions
fishing at 45-acre lake
boating (electric motors only)
boat launch
canoe/paddleboat rentals
hiking trail
amphitheater
south trailhead to the 20-mile 4-C Hiking Trail

REGION 2

The lake at Ratcliff can best be described as tranquil, peaceful, quiet, and calm . . . a beautiful spot to pitch a tent!

Gay Ippolito, National Forests & Grasslands in Texas

FORT PARKER STATE PARK

FOR INFORMATION

Fort Parker State Park
194 Park Rd. 28
Mexia, TX 76667
254/562-5751

LOCATION

Fort Parker State Park is located 7 miles south of Mexia and 6 miles north of Groesbeck, off TX 14; the entrance is on Park Road 28. The park consists of the 724-acre Lake Fort Parker and 735 acres of gently rolling oak woodlands surrounding the lake.

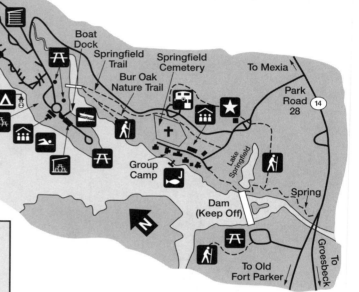

FACILITIES & ACTIVITIES

25 campsites with water/electricity

10 campsites with water only

sponsored youth group camping area

camping area for backpackers

restrooms/showers

trailer dump station

10 screened shelters

group camp: 4 dorms; staff bldg.; recreation hall; dining hall/kitchen; 2 modern restrooms

group recreation hall/kitchen (day-use only)

picnicking

group picnic pavilion

playground

lake swimming

fishing/fish cleaning shelter

fishing pier

boat ramp/boating

½-mile nature trail

2 miles of hiking/mountain bike trails

park store

Campers, don't leave your canoe at home! Small lakes are fun to canoe . . . just avoid the motorboats.

GALVESTON ISLAND STATE PARK

FOR INFORMATION

Galveston Island State Park
14901 FM 3005
Galveston, TX 77554
409/737-1222

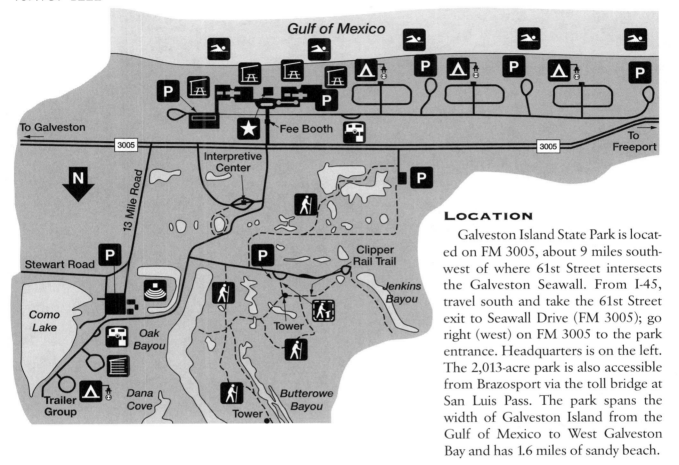

Gulf of Mexico

To Galveston

3005

Fee Booth

Interpretive
Center

N

13 Mile Road

Stewart Road

Como Lake

Oak Bayou

Trailer Group

Dana Cove

Tower

Butterowe Bayou

Tower

Clipper Rail Trail

Jenkins Bayou

To Freeport

3005

LOCATION

Galveston Island State Park is located on FM 3005, about 9 miles southwest of where 61st Street intersects the Galveston Seawall. From I-45, travel south and take the 61st Street exit to Seawall Drive (FM 3005); go right (west) on FM 3005 to the park entrance. Headquarters is on the left. The 2,013-acre park is also accessible from Brazosport via the toll bridge at San Luis Pass. The park spans the width of Galveston Island from the Gulf of Mexico to West Galveston Bay and has 1.6 miles of sandy beach.

FACILITIES & ACTIVITIES

150 campsites with water/electricity

campsites for cyclists who start or end trips in the park

restrooms/showers

trailer dump station

10 screened shelters

20-site group trailer area with water/electricity

picnicking

swimming in Gulf/bathhouses

surf fishing

ponds for freshwater fishing

fish cleaning shelter

boat ramp at Pirates Cove adjacent to park

kayaking

4 miles of nature trails with boardwalks & 1 observation platform

4 miles of mountain bike trails

interpretive exhibits

interpretive tour (fee)

park store

GRANGER LAKE

FOR INFORMATION

Granger Lake
3100 Granger Dam Road
Granger, TX 76530-5067
512/859-2668

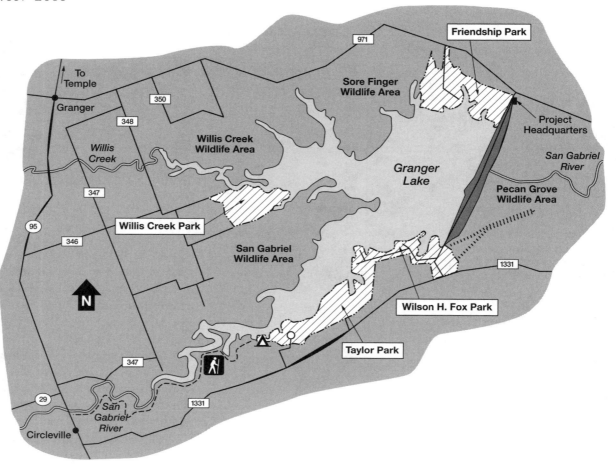

LOCATION

Granger Lake is a 4,400-acre Corps of Engineers impoundment of the San Gabriel River with a 34-mile shoreline. The lake is southeast of Granger; FM 971 and FM 1331 provide access from TX 95. Other nearby towns include Bartlett, Georgetown, and Taylor.

Parks	Total Number of Campsites	Number of Campsites with Electrical Hookups	Camping Area for Groups	Toilets: F=Flush; V=Vault	Showers	Trailer Dump Station	Picnic Sites	Group Picnic Areas	Boat Launching Ramp	Swimming Area/Beach
Friendship			•	F	•	•	•		•	•
Taylor	49	49		F/V	•	•	•		•	
Willis Creek	27	27		F/V	•	•	•	•	•	
Wilson H. Fox	58	58		F	•	•	•	•	•	•

Notes:
Taylor Park has a 6-mile hiking trail & a 4-mile bike trial.

HUNTSVILLE STATE PARK

FOR INFORMATION

Huntsville State Park
P.O. Box 508
Huntsville, TX 77342-0508
936/295-5644

LOCATION

Huntsville State Park is located 6 miles south of Huntsville off I-45; take exit 109 to Park Road 40. The 2,083-acre park includes 210-acre, man-made Lake Raven.

On weekends most of these canoes will be in use on Lake Raven.

FACILITIES & ACTIVITIES

64 campsites with water/electricity

127 campsites with water only

restrooms/showers

trailer dump station

30 screened shelters

group recreation hall "Raven Lodge"

picnicking

group picnic shelter

playgrounds

lake swimming/bathhouse

fishing/2 fish cleaning facilities

2 lighted fishing piers

boat ramp & dock/boating

canoe/kayak/rowboat rentals

¼-mile interpretive trail

11+ miles of hiking/bike trails (some surfaced)

*guided trail rides available through Lake Raven Stables

amphitheater

nature center

park store

*Lake Raven Stables: 936/295-1985.

LAKE BASTROP

FOR INFORMATION

LCRA South & North Shore Park
P.O. Box 761
Bastrop, TX 78602
512/303-7666

LOCATION

Lake Bastrop is located about 3 miles northeast of Bastrop. The lake was built by the LCRA as a cooling pond for the Sim Gideon Power Plant. The constant mix of warm and cool water at this 906-acre lake has created a fisherman's paradise. To reach the South Shore Park, take South Shore Road north from TX 21. To reach the North Shore Park take TX 95 north from TX 21, turn right on FM 1441, and drive 2½ miles to the park entrance. Both parks are operated by the Lower Colorado River Authority.

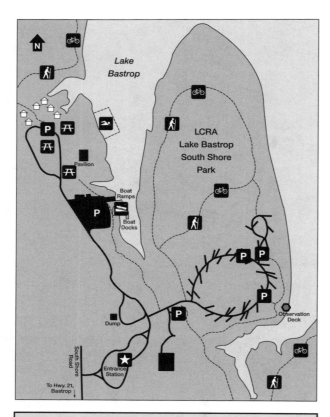

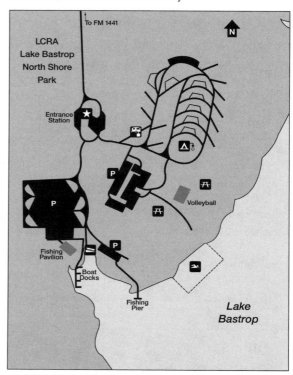

FACILITIES & ACTIVITIES
SOUTH SHORE PARK

38 campsites with water/electricity
6 mini-cabins
flush toilets/showers
sanitary dump
picnicking
group picnic pavilion
lake swimming
fishing
boating/boat ramp/boat dock
waterskiing/canoeing/sailing
canoe & paddleboat rentals
3½ miles of hiking/mountain bike trails

FACILITIES & ACTIVITIES
NORTH SHORE PARK

6 campsites with water/electricity/sewer
10 campsites with water/electricity
flush toilets/showers
sanitary dump
picnicking
lake swimming
fishing/fishing pier/fishing pavilion
boating/boat ramp/boat dock
waterskiing/canoeing/sailing

LAKE FAYETTE
OAK THICKET PARK AND
PARK PRAIRIE PARK

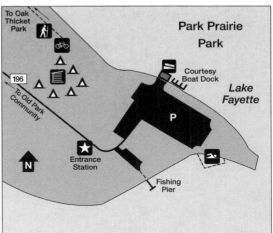

FOR INFORMATION

RPMF, Inc.
Lake Fayette Parks
P.O. Box 1248
La Grange, TX 78945

Oak Thicket Park: 979/249-3504
Park Prairie Park: 979/249-3344

LOCATION

Lake Fayette is located between La Grange and Fayetteville off of SH 159. Both parks are on the north shore of Lake Fayette. The lake was constructed as a 2,400-acre cooling pond for Fayette Power Project; it is owned jointly by the City of Austin and the Lower Colorado River Authority. Water discharged into the reservoir creates a warm-water lake that can be fished year-round. The parks are professionally managed by RPMF, Inc.

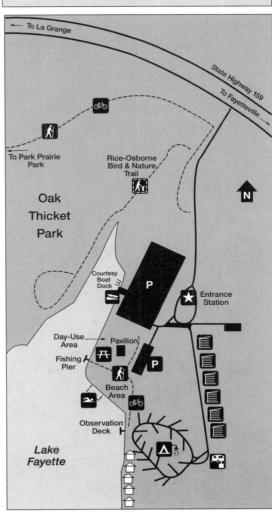

FACILITIES & ACTIVITIES
OAK THICKET PARK

20 campsites with water/electricity

8 cabins

6 screened shelters

restrooms/showers

dump station

picnicking

lighted pavilion

playground

sandy swim beach

fishing/fishing pier

boating/boat dock/boat ramp

nature trail

3-mile hike/bike trail to Park Prairie Park

PARK PRAIRIE PARK

12 primitive tent sites

large screened shelters with 3 campsites

restrooms

boating/boat dock/boat ramp

fishing/fishing pier

3-mile hike/bike trail to Oak Thicket Park

LAKE GEORGETOWN

FOR INFORMATION

Lake Georgetown
500 Cedar Breaks Rd.
Georgetown, TX 78626-4901
512/930-5253

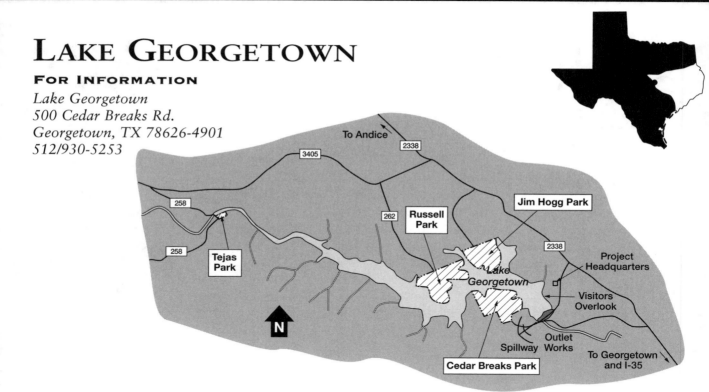

LOCATION

Lake Georgetown is a 1,310-acre Corps of Engineers impoundment on the North Fork of the San Gabriel River with a 25-mile shoreline. The lake is about 4 miles northwest of I-35 at Georgetown via FM 2388. Other nearby towns include Andice and Liberty Hill.

Parks	Total Number of Campsites	Number of Campsites with Electrical Hookups	Toilets: F=Flush; V=Vault	Showers	Trailer Dump Station	Picnic Sites	Group Picnic Areas	Boat Launching Ramp	Swimming Area/Beach
Cedar Breaks	64	64	F	•	•	•		•	
Jim Hogg	148	148	F	•	•			•	
Russell			F/V			•	•	•	•
Tejas	13		V			•			

Notes:
The 24-mile Good Water Trail connects Cedar Breaks Park to Russell Park, and passes through Tejas Park; a 5.6-mile portion of this trail is also designated as bicycle.

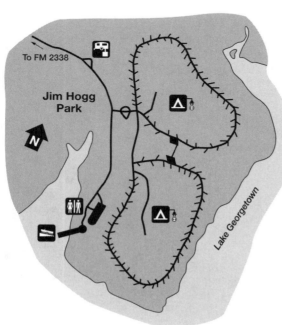

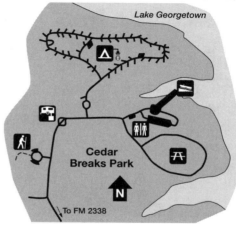

LAKE HOUSTON STATE PARK

FOR INFORMATION

Lake Houston State Park
22031 Baptist Encampment Road
New Caney, TX 77357-7731
281/354-6881

FACILITIES & ACTIVITIES

*24 walk-in campsites with water compost restrooms/showers available

*Lazy Creek Cottage (sleeps 26) with fireplace/kitchen/ceiling fans/flush toilets/showers/AC/heater

*Forest Cottage (sleeps 12) with kitchen/air-conditioned/flush toilets/showers/fireplace/heater

*Peach Creek Group Camp (50) with picnic pavilion/water/restrooms/showers

group dining hall/kitchen (day use)

group camp

primitive campsites

picnicking

group picnic pavilion

1-mile nature/interpretive trail

12 miles of hiking/mountain bike trails

8 miles of equestrian trails

*All have BBQ fire-ring

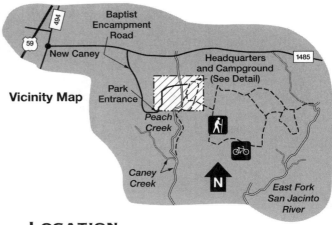

Vicinity Map

LOCATION

Lake Houston State Park is located 30 miles northeast of Houston off of US 59; at New Caney, exit to FM 1485. Travel east on FM 1485, then turn south on Baptist Encampment Road to the park entrance. The park has a total of 4,920 acres. Although there is no access to Lake Houston, there is walking access to Peach Creek and the East Fork of the San Jacinto River.

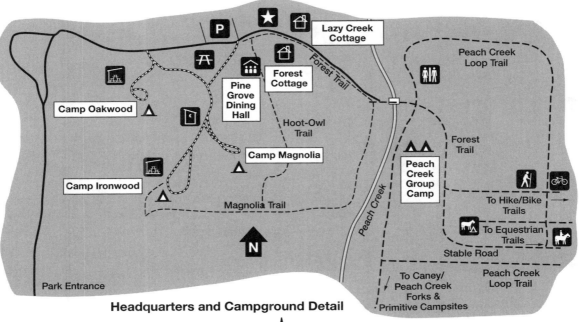

Headquarters and Campground Detail

LAKE LIVINGSTON STATE PARK

FOR INFORMATION

Lake Livingston State Park
RR 9, Box 1300
Livingston, TX 77351
936/365-2201

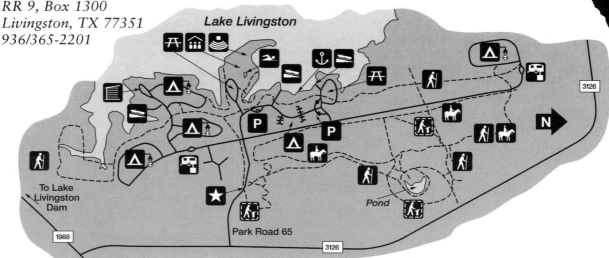

LOCATION

Lake Livingston State Park is located on the east shore of the 82,400-acre Lake Livingston. From Livingston, travel about 2 miles south on US 59, 4 miles west on FM 1988, and ½ mile north on FM 3126. The 635-acre park, dominated by loblolly pine and water oak, has about 2½ miles of shoreline

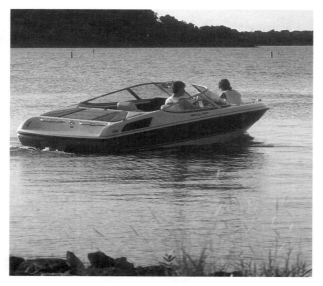

This park has three boat ramps to access Lake Livingston. Gas, bait, and dock facilities are available March through October.

FACILITIES & ACTIVITIES

56 campsites with water/electricity/sewer

21 premium campsites with water/electricity/sewer

70 campsites with water/electricity

32 campsites with water only

campsites for cyclists who start or end trips in the park

restrooms/showers

trailer dump station

10 screened shelters

picnicking

4 group picnic areas

playgrounds

swimming pool (fee)

bathhouse/recreation hall

fishing/fish cleaning shelters

lighted fishing pier

3 boat ramps/boating

waterskiing

park store

bait house/gas/dock facilities (March–October)

nature trails

5 miles of hiking/bike trails (some surfaced)

2½-mile guided trail rides available through Lake Livingston Stables (ph: 936/967-5032)

amphitheater

LAKE SOMERVILLE STATE PARK AND TRAILWAY
BIRCH CREEK UNIT

FOR INFORMATION

Lake Somerville State Park and Trailway
Birch Creek Unit
14222 Park Rd. 57
Somerville, TX 77879-9713
979/535-7763

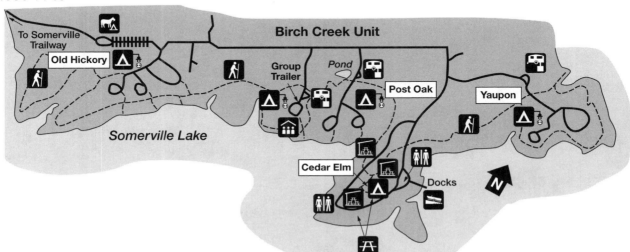

FACILITIES & ACTIVITIES

100 campsites with water/electricity

primitive campgrounds for backpackers and
    equestrians located along the 13-mile Trailway
    (10 sites at 3½ miles; 10 sites at 7 miles)

10 equestrian campsites with water

restrooms/showers

4 trailer dump stations

14-site group trailer area with water &
    electricity/dining hall

group dining hall/kitchen

picnicking

3 group picnic pavilions

lake swimming

fishing/fish cleaning shelter

boat ramps & docks

boating/waterskiing

19 miles of trails suitable for hikers, equestrians,
    & mountain bikers

park store

*These riders have gathered to ride the
Lake Somerville State Trailway.*

LOCATION

The Birch Creek Unit of Lake Somerville State
Park and Trailway is located on the north shore of
Somerville Lake and contains 2,365 acres. From TX
36, southeast of Caldwell at Lyons, travel 7.6 miles
west on FM 60 to Park Road 57, then south for 4.3
miles. From TX 21, southwest of Caldwell, travel FM
60 through Deanville to Park Road 57. The two units
of the park are connected by the 13-mile Somerville
Trailway.

Lake Somerville State Park and Trailway (Continued)

Nails Creek Unit

For Information

*Lake Somerville State Park
and Trailway
Nails Creek Unit
6280 FM 180
Ledbetter, TX 78946-7036
979/289-2392*

The Nails Creek Unit of Lake Somerville State Park and Trailway is located on the south shore of Somerville Lake; it has 3005 acres. From US 290 in Burton, take FM 1697 northwest for 11 miles, then FM 180 northeast for 4 miles. Or, from US 290, just east of Giddings, travel FM 180 northeast for about 15 miles. The main attraction for both units is the 11,400-acre Somerville Lake.

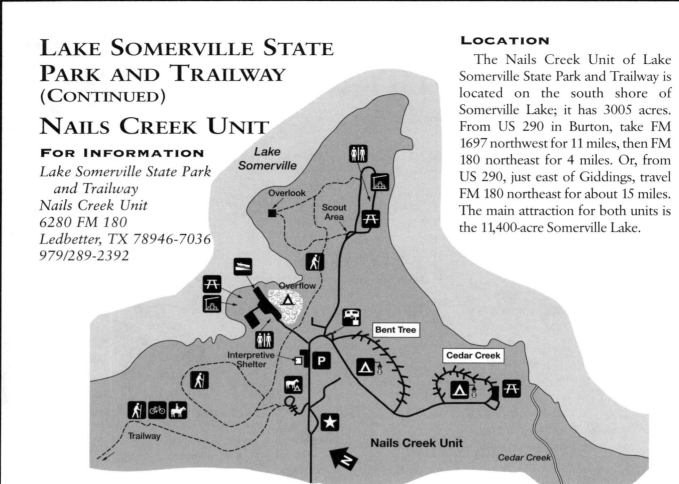

Facilities & Activities

40 campsites with water/electricity

10 campsites with water only (close to boat ramp)

6 primitive campgrounds for backpackers and equestrians located along the 13-mile Trailway (50 sites at 3½ miles)

10 equestrian campsites with water

restrooms/showers

trailer dump station

picnicking

2 group picnic pavilions

lake swimming

fishing/2 fish cleaning shelters

boat ramp

boating/waterskiing

3-mile nature trail

more than 20 miles of trails suitable for hikers, equestrians, & mountain bikers

interpretive shelter

park store

This family is enjoying fishing from the bank at Lake Somerville on a cold morning in March.

MARTIN DIES, JR. STATE PARK

FOR INFORMATION

Martin Dies, Jr. State Park
RR 4, Box 274
Jasper, TX 75951
409/384-5231

LOCATION

Martin Dies, Jr. State Park is located 17 miles east from Woodville, and 12 miles west from Jasper on US 190. Its 705 acres include 3 separate units on the shore of the 13,700-acre B.A. Steinhagen Lake. Camping facilities are located at Walnut Ridge and Hen House Ridge units, while Cherokee is a day-use area only.

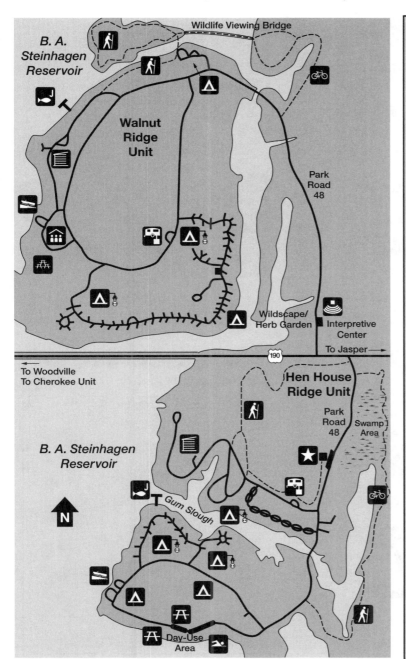

FACILITIES & ACTIVITIES

178 campsites
   56 at Hen House Ridge with
      water/electricity
   *68 at Walnut Ridge with water/
      electricity
   44 at Hen House Ridge with water only
   *10 at Walnut Ridge with water only
restrooms/showers
trailer dump station
44 screened shelters
   20 at Hen House Ridge
   24 at Walnut Ridge
2 limited use cabins
   1-Hen House Ridge
   1-Walnut Ridge
recreation hall with kitchen
picnicking
2 group picnic areas
3 playgrounds
lake swimming
fishing/2 fish cleaning shelters
2 lighted fishing piers
3 boat ramps
boating/waterskiing
canoe/boat rental
interpretive/nature trail
6 hiking/biking trails
4 miles of mountain bike trails
amphitheater
monthly interpretive canoe tour (fee)
park store at headquarters
nature center

*Walnut Ridge Unit is closed during the winter.

REGION 2

MISSION TEJAS STATE PARK

FOR INFORMATION

Mission Tejas State Park
RR 2, Box 108
Grapeland, TX 75844
936/687-2394

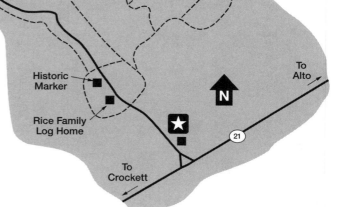

Pond

Mission
Commemorative

Dump

Historic
Marker

Rice Family
Log Home

N

To
Alto

To
Crockett

21

LOCATION

Mission Tejas State Park is located 21 miles northeast of Crockett and 12 miles southwest of Alto on TX 21; the entrance to the park is near Weches, where Park Road 44 intersects TX 21. Tall pine trees adorn the 669-acre park with its 2-acre pond; there are 2 historic structures.

J. Boutwell, U.S. Army Corps of Engineers

If you're really quiet while hiking the nature trail, you may be able to see a waterbird stalking its prey at the small pond.

FACILITIES & ACTIVITIES

5 campsites with water/electricity/sewage
7 campsites with water/electricity
3 tent campsites with water/electricity
2 tent campsites with water only
sponsored youth group camp
restrooms/showers
trailer dump station
picnicking
group picnic shelter
fishing
3½ miles of hiking trails
½-mile nature trail
2 historic structures
park store

MOTHER NEFF STATE PARK

FOR INFORMATION

Mother Neff State Park
1680 Texas 236 Hwy
Moody, TX 76557-3317
254/853-2389

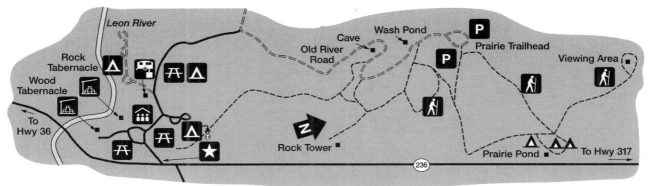

LOCATION

Mother Neff State Park is located 8 miles west of Moody. The park is about 16 miles from I-35 at Eddy; take FM 107 and travel west through Moody to TX 236, turn left and go 2 miles to the park. Or, from TX 36 between Temple and Gatesville, take TX 236 north for 5 miles. Mother Neff is the oldest state park in Texas; it has 259 acres and is adjacent to the Leon River.

FACILITIES & ACTIVITIES

6 campsites with water/electricity
15 campsites with water only
3 primitive walk-in campsites (¼-mile)
primitive walk-in group camping area
restrooms/showers
trailer dump station
picnicking
2 group shelters/one with kitchen (day-use)
playground
fishing (banks of Leon River)
2¾ miles of hiking trails
Tonkawa Indian Cave
observation tower

Tall trees provide lots of shade for campers in the beautiful Leon River bottom at Mother Neff State Park.

SABINE NATIONAL FOREST

FOR INFORMATION

Sabine National Forest
201 South Palm
P.O. Box 227
Hemphill, TX 75948
409/787-3870 or 2791
Toll Free: 866-235-1750

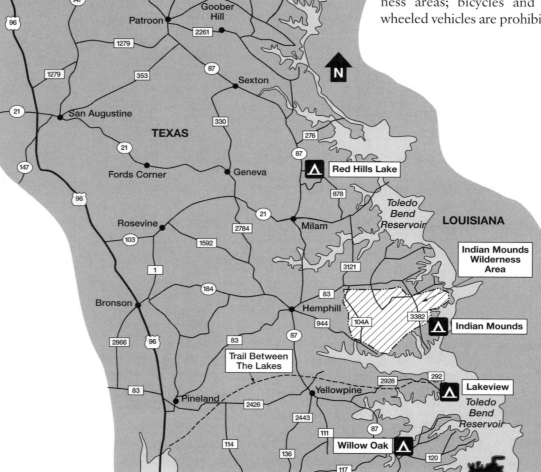

LOCATION

Sabine National Forest is located in Jasper, Sabine, San Augustine, Shelby, and Newton counties, and contains 160,680 acres. The forest is adjacent to Toledo Bend Reservoir its entire length along the west side. The 12,369-acre Indian Mounds Wilderness Area, the largest of the 5 wilderness areas in Texas, is on the Sabine National Forest. Hiking and horseback riding are allowed in wilderness areas; bicycles and other wheeled vehicles are prohibited.

DIRECTIONS TO RECREATION AREAS

▲ **Boles**—TX 87 south from Center for 4 miles; turn left (east) on FM 2694 for 8 miles to entrance.

▲ **Indian Mounds**—FM 83 east from Hemphill for 8 miles, turn right (south) on FM 3382 for 4 miles; then turn left (east) on FSR 130 for 1 mile.

▲ **Lakeview**—TX 87 south of Hemphill for 9 miles. Turn left on FM 2928 for 3 miles; follow signs and continue on gravel road for 4 miles.

▲ **Ragtown**—TX 87 southeast from Center for 11 miles; turn left (east) on FM 139 for 6 miles; bear left on FM 3184 and travel 5 miles to entrance.

▲ **Red Hills Lake**—TX 87 north from Milam for 2½ miles, then FSR 116 east for 1 mile.

▲ **Willow Oak**—TX 87 southeast from Hemphill for 11 miles, then FSR 120 east to entrance.

RAGTOWN RECREATION AREA

FACILITIES & ACTIVITIES

13 single-family campsites
12 double-family campsites
trailer/RV space
flush toilets/showers
trailer dump station
fishing (Toledo Bend Reservoir)
double boat ramp
1-mile nature trail

Operated and maintained by Sabine River Authority

REGION 2

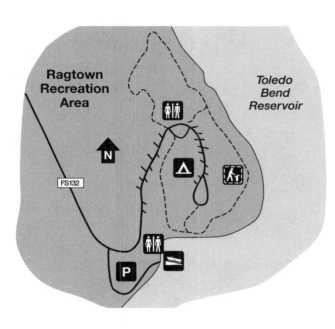

College students enjoy hiking the Trail Between the Lakes at spring break. The trail is a 28-mile hiking trail in the Sabine National Forest that extends from Lakeview Recreation Area on the Toledo Bend Reservoir to US 96 within sight of the easternmost point of Sam Rayburn Reservoir.

SABINE NATIONAL FOREST
(CONTINUED)

RED HILLS LAKE RECREATION AREA

FACILITIES & ACTIVITIES

28 campsites for tents/RVs
  9 sites with water/electricity
restrooms/cold showers
trailer dump station
picnicking
picnic shelter
swimming beach/bathhouse
fishing (19-acre lake)
boating (electric motors only)
launch for small boats
nature trail
hike/bike trail

Operated and maintained by the U.S. Forest Service

Other Recreation Areas*	Campsites	Trailer Space	Drinking Water	Toilets	Fishing	Boating/Boat Ramp
Boles Field	20	•	•	•			
Indian Mounds	36	•	•	•	•	•
Lakeview	10	•	•	•	•	
Willow Oak	10		•	•	•	•

*Campground maps not available.
Boles Field has electrical hookups, hot showers, covered shelter and amphitheater.
Note: Boles Field is operated and maintained by the U.S. Forest Service; all others are operated by the Sabine River Authority.

If you've never camped at one of the national forest campgrounds, you're missing a real treat. The setting is always peaceful and the scenery can be magnificent.

SABINE PASS BATTLEGROUND STATE PARK AND HISTORIC SITE

FOR INFORMATION

Sabine Pass Battleground State Park and Historic Site
P.O. Box 1066
Sabine Pass, TX 77655
409/971-2559 (Sea Rim State Park)

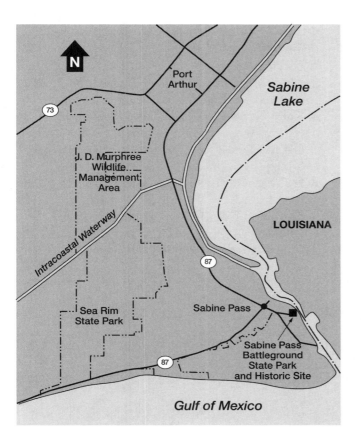

LOCATION

Sabine Pass Battleground State Park and Historic Site is located 1½ miles south of the city of Sabine Pass on Dick Dowling Road (FM 3322), and 15 miles south of Port Arthur via TX 87. (Note: TX 87 is closed between Sea Rim and High Island.) The 4-lane boat ramp at this 57-acre park provides access to Sabine Lake to the north and the Gulf of Mexico to the south.

FACILITIES & ACTIVITIES

7 campsites with water/electricity

primitive camping

restrooms (no showers)

trailer dump station

covered picnic tables

fishing along a ¼-mile waterfront

fish cleaning table

4-lane boat ramp with ADA-accessible dock that provides access to Sabine Lake to the north & the Gulf of Mexico to the south

historic site with monument, interpretive pavilion & walkway

REGION 2

This park is not located directly on the coast, but their 4-lane boat ramp provides access to Sabine Lake to the north and the Gulf of Mexico to the south.

Sam Houston National Forest

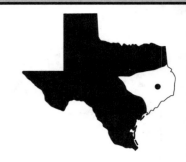

For Information

Sam Houston National Forest
394 FM 1375 West
New Waverly, TX 77358
936/344-6205
Toll Free: 888/361-6908

Location

Sam Houston National Forest, located in Montgomery, San Jacinto, and Walker counties, is the largest of the 4 national forests; it contains 163,037 acres. The forest extends northwest from Cleveland, is east and south of Huntsville, and encompasses about half of the northern portion of Lake Conroe. The 3,855-acre Little Lake Creek Wilderness Area is on the Sam Houston National Forest; the 129-mile Lone Star Hiking Trail passes through the area.

Directions to Recreation Areas

▲ **Double Lake**—From US 59 in Cleveland, take FM 2025 north for 17 miles; turn right on FSR 210 (entrance road) for 1½ miles.

▲ **Kelly Pond**—From I-45, take FM 1375 west from New Waverly for 10 miles; turn left (south) on FSR 204 for 1 mile; then turn right (west) on FSR 271 for 1 mile. (8 walk-in tent sites; picnic tables)

▲ **Stubblefield Lake**—From I-45, take FM 1375 west from New Waverly for 10 miles; turn right (north) on FSR 215 for 3 miles.

▲ **Cagle**—From I-45, take FM 1375 west from New Waverly for 8 miles; turn left at sign.

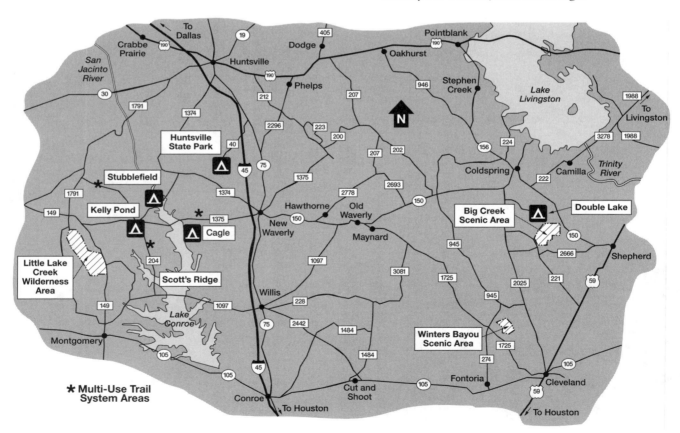

Double Lake Recreation Area

DOUBLE LAKE RECREATION AREA

FACILITIES & ACTIVITIES

65 campsites for tents/RVs
   20 with water/electricity/sewer
   21 with water/electricity

25-ft max. RV length

9 group campsites (25 max.); group shelter (100 max.)

restrooms/showers

dump station

picnicking

lodge for group meetings (50 max.)

swimming beach/bathhouse

concessions/amphitheater

fishing/3 piers (on 23-acre lake)

boating (electric motors only)

canoe/paddleboat rentals

nature trail/8-mile mountain bike trail

5-mile hiking trail to the Big Creek Scenic Area

access to the 129-mile Lone Star Hiking Trail

on NRRS reservation system (800-280-2267)

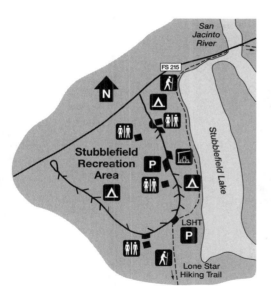

STUBBLEFIELD RECREATION AREA

FACILITIES & ACTIVITIES

30 campsites for tents/RVs

20-ft max. RV length

restrooms/cold showers

picnicking/picnic shelter

fishing

canoe/boat access to San Jacinto River

1.1-mile interpretive trail

access to the 129-mile Lone Star Trail

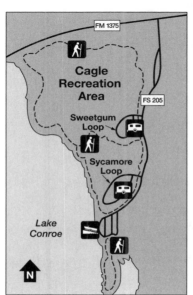

CAGLE RECREATION AREA

FACILITIES & ACTIVITIES

47 RV sites with water/electricity/sewer

45-ft max. RV length

each site has tent pad/lantern post/fire ring

restrooms/hot showers

boat ramp

boating/waterskiing

2-mile hiking trail

SAM RAYBURN RESERVOIR

FOR INFORMATION

Sam Rayburn Reservoir
Route 3, Box 486
Jasper, TX 75951-9598
409/384-5716

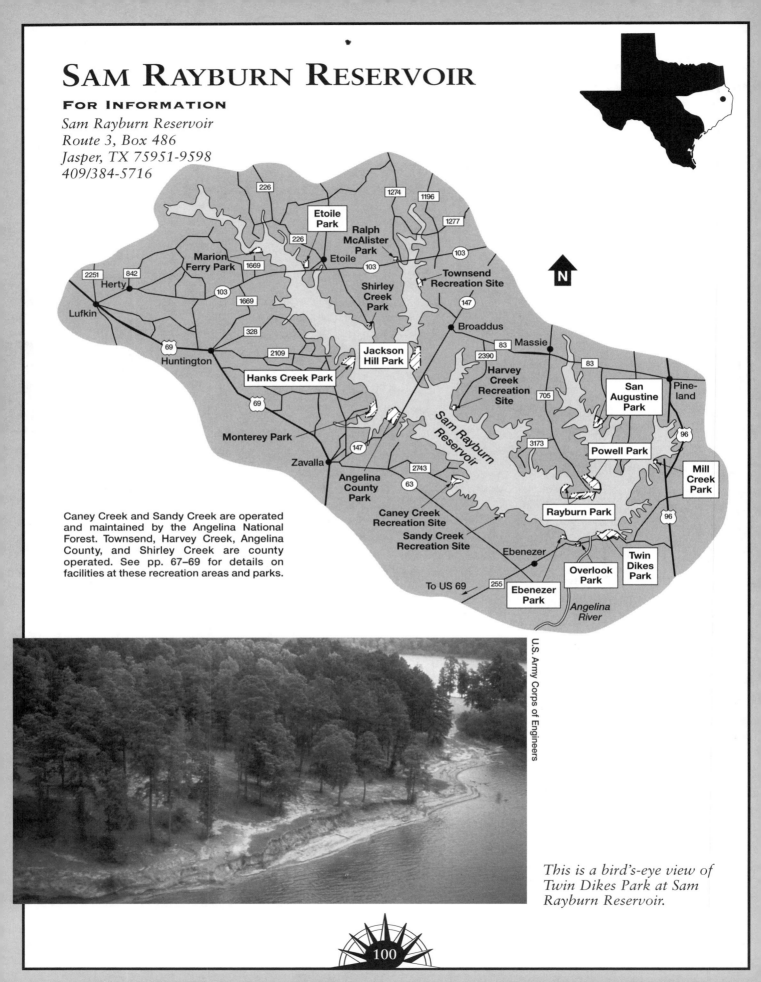

Etoile Park
Ralph McAlister Park
Marion Ferry Park
Townsend Recreation Site
Shirley Creek Park
Jackson Hill Park
Hanks Creek Park
Harvey Creek Recreation Site
San Augustine Park
Powell Park
Monterey Park
Mill Creek Park
Angelina County Park
Rayburn Park
Caney Creek Recreation Site
Sandy Creek Recreation Site
Twin Dikes Park
Overlook Park
Ebenezer Park

Herty · Lufkin · Huntington · Zavalla · Broaddus · Massie · Pineland · Ebenezer · Etoile

Sam Rayburn Reservoir

Angelina River

To US 69

Caney Creek and Sandy Creek are operated and maintained by the Angelina National Forest. Townsend, Harvey Creek, Angelina County, and Shirley Creek are county operated. See pp. 67–69 for details on facilities at these recreation areas and parks.

This is a bird's-eye view of Twin Dikes Park at Sam Rayburn Reservoir.

LOCATION

Sam Rayburn Reservoir, the largest body of water wholly within the state, is a 114,500-acre Corps of Engineers reservoir that impounds the Angelina River and several bayous; it has 560 miles of shoreline. The lake is surrounded by the Angelina National Forest; it is southeast of Lufkin with access via US 69 and TX 103, and northwest of Jasper with access via US 96. TX 147 from Zavalla to San Augustine crosses the lake near its midpoint. Other nearby towns include Broaddus, Pineland, Brookeland, Huntington, and Etoile.

Parks	Total Number of Campsites	Number of Campsites with Electrical Hookups	Toilets: F=Flush, V=Vault	Showers	Trailer Dump Station	Picnic Sites	Boat Launching Ramp	Swimming Area/Beach
Ebenezer	30	10	V		•			•
Etoile	9		V				•	
Hanks Creek	44	44	F	•	•		•	•
Jackson Hill	48		V		•	•	•	
Mill Creek	110	110	F	•	•		•	•
Overlook			F			•		
Powell**	68	19	F	•	•	•	•	•
Rayburn	77	24	V		•		•	•
San Augustine	100	100	F	•	•		•	
Twin Dikes	46	16	F	•	•		•	

Notes:
**Powell Park is operated by the Corps of Engineers. Powell Park Marina, located adjacent to it, is operated by a concessionaire. Facilities include 38 campsites with water/electricity, 14 cabins, and a lodge (409/584-2624).
San Augustine Park has a 2½-mile nature trail.
Ebenezer has a 1½-mile equestrian trail.

Sam Rayburn Reservoir is surrounded by the Angelina National Forest . . . and you know what that means . . . lots of beautiful flowering dogwood trees each spring!

The sun is setting . . . time to call it a day . . . it's been a great one!

SEA RIM STATE PARK

FOR INFORMATION

Sea Rim State Park
P.O. Box 1066
Sabine Pass, TX 77655
409/971-2559

LOCATION

Sea Rim State Park is located 10 miles west of Sabine Pass on TX 87; the highway between Sea Rim and High Island is closed, so the *only access* to the park is from the east. The park consists of 4,141 acres of gulf coast beach and marshland. TX 87 separates the park into 2 distinct areas: south of the highway lies the D. Roy Harrington Beach Unit and north of the highway is the Marshlands Unit, which comprises the greater portion.

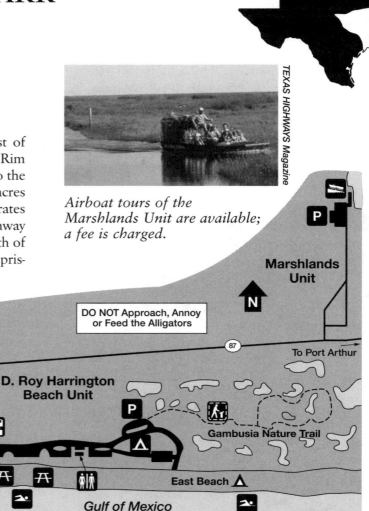

TEXAS HIGHWAYS Magazine

Airboat tours of the Marshlands Unit are available; a fee is charged.

DO NOT Approach, Annoy or Feed the Alligators

Marshlands Unit

To Port Arthur

Hwy 87 to Galveston is closed.

Willow Pond Birding Trail

West Beach

Fee Booth

D. Roy Harrington Beach Unit

Gambusia Nature Trail

Interpretive Center

East Beach

Gulf of Mexico

FACILITIES & ACTIVITIES

BEACH UNIT

20 campsites with water/electricity
10 campsites with water only
beach camping in designated areas
restrooms/showers
trailer dump station
picnicking
swimming beach
surf fishing
¼-mile birding trail
¾-mile boardwalk interpretive marsh trail
6 miles of mountain biking on beach

interpretive exhibits in visitor center/headquarters complex
observation deck at visitor center

MARSHLANDS UNIT

2 camping platforms with chemical toilets
fishing/crabbing in marshlands/lake system via boat
boat ramp
boat trails ideal for canoe/kayak/pirogue
canoe & paddleboat rentals
airboat tours of the marsh available (fee) (seasonal)

SOMERVILLE LAKE

FOR INFORMATION

Somerville Lake
P.O. Box 549
Somerville, TX 77879-0549
979/596-1622

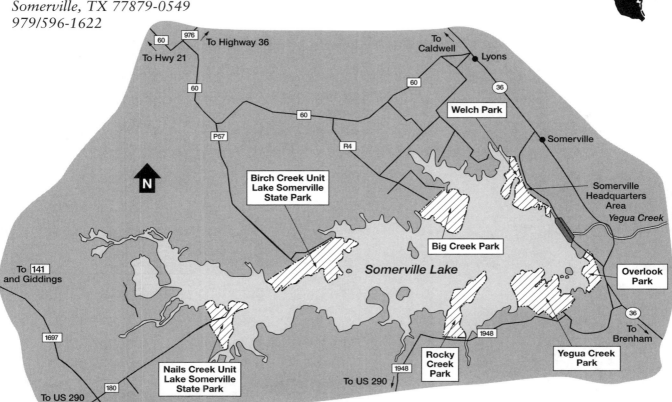

Map labels:
- To Highway 36
- 976
- 60
- To Hwy 21
- 60
- P57
- 60
- R4
- To Caldwell
- Lyons
- 60
- 36
- Welch Park
- Somerville
- N
- Birch Creek Unit Lake Somerville State Park
- Somerville Headquarters Area
- *Yegua Creek*
- Big Creek Park
- *Somerville Lake*
- To 141 and Giddings
- Overlook Park
- 36
- 1697
- Rocky Creek Park
- 1948
- Yegua Creek Park
- To Brenham
- Nails Creek Unit Lake Somerville State Park
- 180
- To US 290
- 1948
- To US 290
- To Burton

LOCATION

Somerville Lake is a 11,460-acre Corps of Engineers impoundment of Yegua Creek with an 85-mile shoreline. The lake is west of TX 36 at Somerville. Parks along the north shore are also accessible via TX 21 between Lincoln and Caldwell; parks along the south shore are also accessible via US 290 between Giddings and Brenham. Other nearby towns include Lyons, Gay Hill, and Burton.

At Somerville Lake, if you get tired of fishing from the boat, just pull in to the shore to try your luck.

SOMERVILLE LAKE
(CONTINUED)

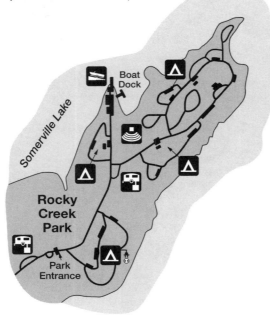

Somerville Lake

Boat Dock

Rocky Creek Park

Park Entrance

Parks	Total Number of Campsites	Number of Campsites with Electrical Hookups	Camping Area for Groups	Toilets: F=Flush; V=Vault	Showers	Trailer Dump Station	Picnic Sites	Group Picnic Areas	Boat Launching Ramp	Swimming Area
Big Creek	126	126	•	F/V	•	•	•	•	•	
Birch Creek State Park	124	114	•	F	•	•	•	•	•	•
Nails Creek State Park	60	40		F/V	•	•	•	•	•	•
Overlook	65	25		F/V	•	•	•		•	
Rocky Creek	203	82		F/V	•		•		•	
Welch	40			F/V			•	•	•	
Yegua Creek	82	47		F/V	•	•			•	

Notes:
Overlook Park has a marina.
The 13-mile Lake Somerville Trailway connects Birch Creek & Nails Creek; trail is designed for hikers, bikers, & horseback riders.
3 parks have interpretive trails: Big Creek (.1 mile), Rocky Creek (3 miles); Yegua Creek (1 mile).

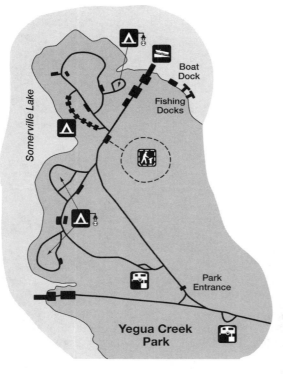

Somerville Lake

Boat Dock

Fishing Docks

Park Entrance

Yegua Creek Park

Fishing is popular at Somerville Lake; all 7 parks have boat launching ramps.

STEPHEN F. AUSTIN STATE PARK

FOR INFORMATION

Stephen F. Austin State Park
P.O. Box 125
San Felipe, TX 77473-0125
979/885-3613

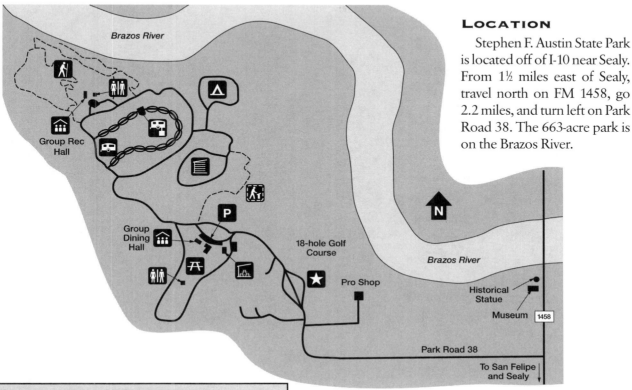

LOCATION

Stephen F. Austin State Park is located off of I-10 near Sealy. From 1½ miles east of Sealy, travel north on FM 1458, go 2.2 miles, and turn left on Park Road 38. The 663-acre park is on the Brazos River.

REGION 2

FACILITIES & ACTIVITIES

40 campsites with water/electricity/sewage

2 campsites with water/electricity

38 campsites with water only

restrooms/showers

trailer dump station

20 screened shelters

group dining hall (day use)

group recreation hall (overnight)

picnicking

2 playgrounds

fishing

5 hiking trails

nature trail

18-hole golf course/pro shop (979/885-2811)

museum—San Felipe State Historical Site

historic structure: log cabin

park store

Each spring the bluebonnets are quite beautiful in this area of Texas.

STILLHOUSE HOLLOW LAKE

FOR INFORMATION

Stillhouse Hollow Lake
3740 FM 1670
Belton, TX 76513-9503
254/939-2461

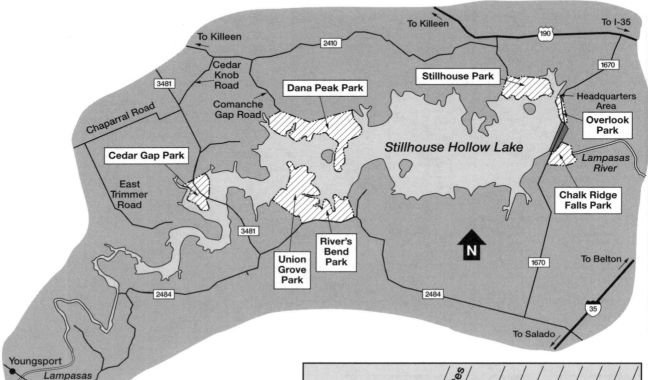

LOCATION

Stillhouse Hollow Lake is a 6,430-acre Corps of Engineers impoundment of the Lampasas River with a 58-mile shoreline. The lake is southwest of Belton with access off of US 190 west via FM 1670 or FM 2410. Or, from I-35 at Salado, travel west on FM 2484 and north on FM 1670. Other nearby towns include Killeen, Harker Heights, Nolanville, and Youngsport.

Parks	Total Number of Campsites	Number of Campsites with Electrical Hookups	Toilets: F=Flush; V=Vault	Showers	Trailer Dump Station	Picnic Sites	Group Picnic Areas	Boat Launching Ramp	Swimming Area/Beach
Cedar Gap			V					•	
Chalk Ridge Falls			V				•		
Dana Peak	25	25	F/V	•	•	•	•	•	•
Overlook			F			•			
River's Bend			V			•		•	
Stillhouse Park			F/V	•		•	•	•	•
Union Grove	37	37	F/V	•	•			•	•

Notes:
Union Grove has 3 screened shelters; Dana Peak has 2 minigroup shelters.
Stillhouse Marina is located at Stillhouse Park.
Dana Peak also has a 15-mile multi-use trail; Chalk Ridge has a 5-mile trail.

▲ *Lyndon B. Johnson State Park is famous for its spring wildflowers.*

◀ *Honey Creek is a special place; access to this protected natural area is through Guadalupe River State Park.*

▼ *The view from the end of the Lost Mine Trail in Big Bend National Park is spectacular.*

▲ *Fall colors brighten McKittrick Canyon in Guadalupe Mountains National Park.*

▼ *The strawberry pitaya cactus displays its beauty in Big Bend National Park.*

▼ *Canoeing these tranquil waters among the cypress is a paddler's paradise.*

▲ *A somewhat uncommon winter scene from the Texas Hill Country.*

◄ *Hikers at Lost Maples during the fall foliage changes.*

▼ *Riders of all ages enjoying an early morning trail ride.*

▲ *The cypress-lined banks of the clear-flowing Frio River at Garner State Park.*

▶ *Boating at sunset on an East Texas lake.*

▼ Amanita muscaria, *a poisonous mushroom, discovered by hikers on the 129-mile Lone Star Hiking Trail.*

▲ *On weekends, many of the Texas fishing spots buzz with activity; these fishermen have chosen a less crowded day.*

▼ *A typical field of Texas Bluebonnets found on many back roads in the Texas Hill Country.*

▼ *Yellow flowers adorn the rocky terrain at Enchanted Rock.*

Mickey Little

▲ *A typical scene at Guadalupe River State Park on a summer weekend.*

▼ *Camping at Ratcliff Recreation Area in the Davy Crockett National Forest.*

▼ *A hiking trail encircles this 23-acre lake at Double Lake Recreation Area in the Sam Houston National Forest.*

Texas Parks & Wildlife Dept. 2004

Mickey Little

▲ *Fall foliage is especially beautiful in the early morning sunlight.*

▼ *Flat-bottomed johnboats are ideal for the shallow waters of Steinhagen Lake near Magnolia Ridge Park.*

TEXAS HIGHWAYS Magazine

Mickey Little

Mickey Little

▲ *Prickly pear, yucca, and mesquite add pizzazz to this field of Texas Bluebonnets.*

◣ *A stately century plant graces this West Texas mountain scene.*

▶ *As the morning clouds ascend, the snow-dusted peaks of Guadalupe Mountains National Park are revealed.*

▼ *Sunrise at Rocky Creek Park at Somerville Lake.*

Jeanne Hardy

TOLEDO BEND RESERVOIR

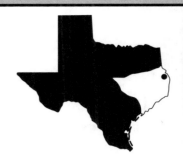

FOR INFORMATION

Sabine River Authority of Texas
Toledo Bend Division
Route 1, Box 270
Burkeville, TX 75932-9729
409/565-2273

LOCATION

Toledo Bend Reservoir, the largest man-made reservoir in the south, is a 186,000-acre impoundment on the Sabine River. A project of the Sabine River Authority, the reservoir has 1,200 miles of shoreline and extends up the river along the Texas-Louisiana border for 65 miles. The Sabine National Forest borders the lake on the Texas side. Numerous camping facilities are located on both the Texas and Louisiana sides of the lake; this guide includes only the agency parks on the Texas side. TX 87 parallels the reservoir on the west as it traverses the national forest north from Burkeville to Center. Access to the reservoir is via numerous FM roads from towns along TX 87—namely, Hemphill, Milam, Patroon, and Shelbyville.

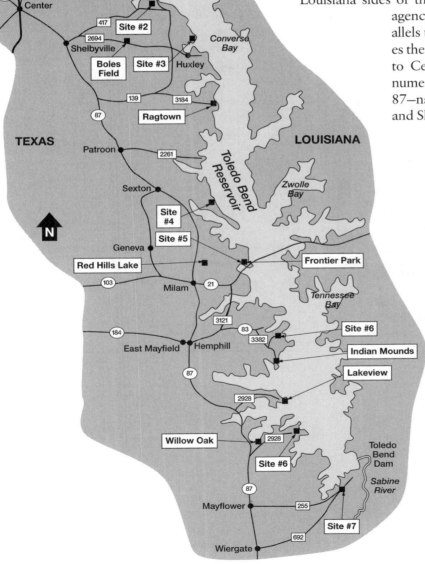

Toledo Bend Reservoir, as viewed from the observation point near the dam.

TOLEDO BEND RESERVOIR (CONTINUED)

There are several recreation sites at Toledo Bend Reservoir that have primitive facilities only. If you come prepared, the sites are quite comfortable, and usually quite private!

FACILITIES

The Toledo Bend Reservoir map distributed by the Sabine River Authority of Texas locates seven recreation areas by site numbers. Four of the recreation areas have primitive facilities only. Facilities at each site are listed below in the order that the sites appear on the map, reading from north to south.

In addition to these primitive sites, there are six developed recreation areas. Ragtown, Indian Mounds, Lakeview, and Willow Oak are operated by the Sabine River Authority. Boles Fields and Red Hills are operated by the U.S. Forest Service. See pp. 94–96 for campground maps and details on facilities.

Site 1 — Picnic tables, pavilion, playground, restrooms, & boat ramp
Site 2 — boat ramp
— **Boles Field** (U.S. Forest Service)
— **Ragtown**
Site 3 — Undeveloped & suitable for primitive camping
Site 4 — Undeveloped & suitable for primitive camping
— **Red Hills Lake** (U.S. Forest Service)
Site 5 — **Frontier Park** (commercial lease); full-service marina, tackle shop, swimming pool, restaurant, rental units, RV hookups, & campsites
— **Indian Mounds**
Site 6 — Undeveloped & suitable for primitive camping
Site 7 — Picnic tables, pavilion, playground, restrooms, and boat ramp
— **Lakeview**
— **Willow Oak**

TOWN BLUFF DAM/
B. A. STEINHAGEN LAKE

FOR INFORMATION

Town Bluff Dam/B. A. Steinhagen Lake
890 FM 92
Woodville, TX 75979-9509
409/429-3491

LOCATION

B. A. Steinhagen Lake, also known as Dam B and Town Bluff Reservoir, is a 13,700-acre Corps of Engineers impoundment of the Neches River and the Angelina River; it has 160 miles of shoreline. US 190 between Woodville and Jasper crosses the lake near its midpoint. FM 92 provides access to the lake along the west side.

Primitive camping by permit only is available at specific areas on the Angelina and Neches rivers. Details may be obtained by writing or calling the project office.

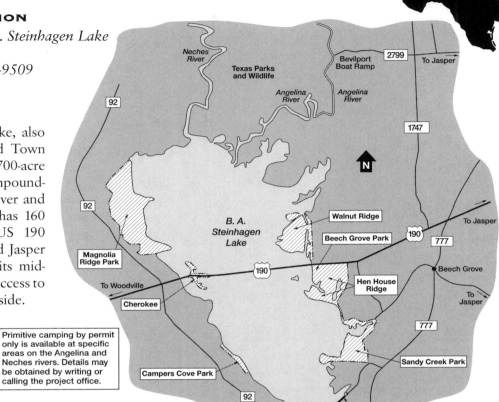

Neches River

Texas Parks and Wildlife

Bevilport Boat Ramp — 2799 — To Jasper

Angelina River

Angelina River

92

1747

92

N

B. A. Steinhagen Lake

Walnut Ridge

Beech Grove Park

190 — To Jasper

777

Beech Grove

Magnolia Ridge Park

To Woodville

190

Hen House Ridge

To Jasper

Cherokee

777

Campers Cove Park

Sandy Creek Park

92

East End Park

Headquarters Area and Bluff View Park

Neches River

To Woodville

Town Bluff

To Beaumont

Parks	Total Number of Campsites	Number of Campsites with Electrical Hookups	Toilets: F=Flush; V=Vault	Showers	Trailer Dump Station	Picnic Sites	Group Picnic Areas	Boat Launching Ramp	Swimming Area/Beach
Beech Grove	7	7	F					•	
Bluff View			F			•	•		
Campers Cove	25		V			•		•	
*Cherokee			F			•		•	
East End	6		V					•	
*Hen House Ridge	100	56	F	•	•	•		•	•
Magnolia Ridge	40	40	F/V	•	•		•	•	
Sandy Creek	78	78	F/V	•	•	•		•	•
*Walnut Ridge	78	68	F	•	•	•	•	•	

Notes:
*These 3 parks comprise Martin Dies, Jr. State Park.
Hen House, Magnolia Ridge, & Walnut Ridge have nature/hiking trails.
Beech Grove is operated by a concessionaire.

Magnolia Ridge Park provides access to the more shallow waters of Steinhagen Lake.

VILLAGE CREEK STATE PARK

FOR INFORMATION

Village Creek State Park
P.O. Box 8565
Lumberton, TX 77657
409/755-7322

FACILITIES & ACTIVITIES

25 campsites with water/electricity

16 walk-in campsites with water only

sponsored youth group camping area

restrooms/showers

trailer dump station

group recreation hall/kitchen
   (day or overnight use)

picnicking

group open-air picnic pavilion

playground

swimming

fishing

canoeing/canoe launch

8 miles of hiking trails

8 miles of mountain bike trails

nature/interpretive trail

park store

Note: canoe rental outfitters (in local area)

LOCATION

Village Creek State Park is located off US 69/96/287 in Lumberton on Alma Drive. From Beaumont, take US 69/96/287 to Mitchell Road, turn east on Mitchell Road, then immediately north on Village Creek Parkway for about 2 miles, then east on Alma Drive, cross the railroad tracks, veer to left, and park entrance will be on the left. The 1,050-acre park is located on Village Creek, a 63-mile long renowned float stream, that rises near the Alabama-Coushatta Indian Reservation and flows southeast to a junction with the Neches River.

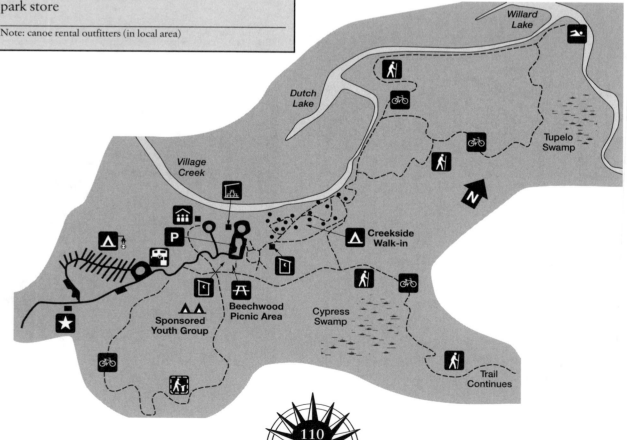

WOLF CREEK PARK

FOR INFORMATION

Wolf Creek Park
P.O. Box 309
Coldspring, TX 77331
936/653-4312

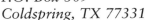

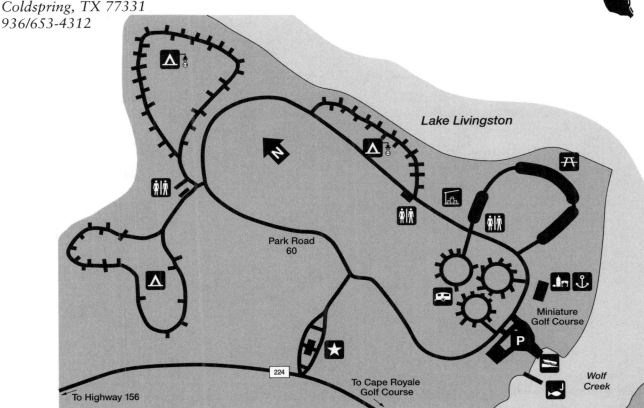

FACILITIES & ACTIVITIES

103 campsites
   30 campsites with water/electricity/sewage
   54 tent sites with water/electrity
   19 tent sites with water only
restrooms/showers
trailer dump station
picnicking
group shelter
playground/basketball/volleyball court
miniature golf course
lake swimming/bathhouse
fishing
fishing pier/fish cleaning facility
boat ramp/boat rentals
boating/sailing/waterskiing
marina & store

LOCATION

Wolf Creek Park is located off of US 190 east of Huntsville. At Pointblank, travel south on TX 156, then left on FM 224. The park is located on the west shore of Lake Livingston, an 82,600-acre Trinity River Authority impoundment on the Trinity River. Wolf Creek Park is owned and operated by the Trinity River Authority. The 18-hole Cape Royale Golf Course is 1 mile south of the park.

Note: The park closes for the winter each December 1 and reopens March 1.

REGION 3

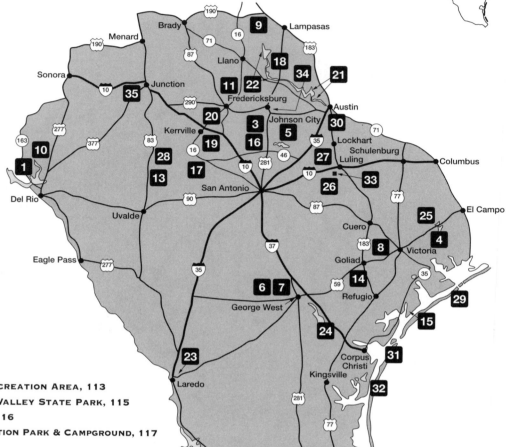

AMISTAD NATIONAL RECREATION AREA

FOR INFORMATION

Amistad National Recreation Area
HCR3, Box 5J
Del Rio, TX 78840
830/775-7491

LOCATION

Amistad National Recreation Area lies between Del Rio and Langtry; it is reached via US 90 from the east and west and US 277 from the north and south. The 6-mile-long Amistad Dam on the Rio Grande backs water up 3 major rivers: Rio Grande, 74 miles; Pecos, 14 miles; and Devils, 25 miles. The 67,000-acre reservoir boasts more than 850 miles of shoreline, 540 of which are in Texas. Steep-walled limestone canyons in biologically diverse near-desert settings typify the park. Amistad lies in a transition zone where 3 major biological regions meet: the Balconian, Chihuahuan, and Tamaulipan. The reservoir offers outstanding watersports.

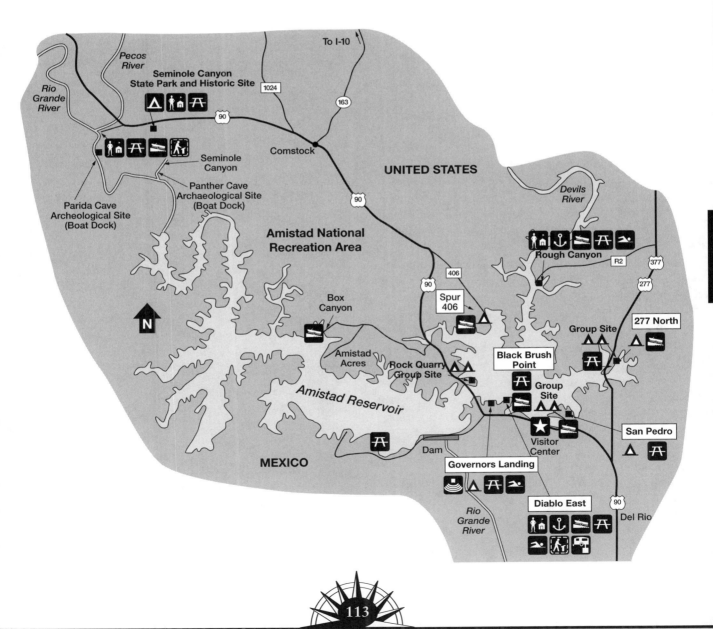

REGION 3

Amistad National Recreation Area
(Continued)

Points of Interest

▲ Amistad—the name means "friendship"—is an international recreation area on the United States-Mexico border; at the center of the dam stand two bronze eagles symbolizing the nations working together.

▲ The waters present an extraordinary blueness because of their great clarity and the area's limestone character and lack of loose soils.

▲ Black bass, stripers, channel and yellow catfish, crappie, and sunfish are the species that attract most anglers.

▲ Amistad lies in what archeologists call the Lower Pecos Region, which contains some of North America's largest and oldest rock art sites.

▲ Backcountry campers can stay at many remote spots along the 540 miles of US shoreline below the high-water mark.

General Information

▲ There is no entrance fee; camping fees are charged.

▲ For a schedule of programs, ask at the visitor center or at the ranger stations at Pecos, Rough Canyon, or Diablo East.

▲ Campgrounds are open all year on a first-come, first-served basis. All 4 campgrounds are primitive; chemical toilets are provided. Limit of stay is 14 days.

▲ Potable water is provided at Governors Landing only. Water is available at the dump station on the Diablo East entrance road.

▲ There are 3 campgrounds for organized groups. Reservations are required and are accepted up to 90 days in advance; contact the park. Groups must include at least 15 persons; one site can accommodate up to 200 persons.

▲ Lakeshore camping from boats is permitted all year along the US side of the lake below the high-water mark (contour 1,144.3 feet) except in restricted areas, such as near marinas, designated swimming beaches, and developed areas.

▲ Spectacular rock art panels up to 16 feet in height are found at Panther and Parida Caves, accessible only by boat. Please use the boat docks provided and stay on the trails.

▲ A protected swim beach is at the Governors Landing; the beach is not supervised.

▲ The Cliffs Area of Diablo East is a beautiful area, but do not dive or jump from the cliffs or rocks, because there are submerged rocks. The Cove, just east of the cliffs, is another excellent swimming spot.

▲ Winds can increase or change directions suddenly, causing high wave conditions. Don't try to cross the lake when winds and waves are high; find shelter and wait it out.

Facilities & Activities

80 RV & tent campsites at 4 campgrounds
    40 sites at San Pedro
    15 sites at Governors Landing
    17 sites at 227 North
    8 sites at Spur 406
3 group campgrounds
vault toilets/potable water at Governors Landing
dump station at Diablo East
boat-in camping along lakeshore
9 designated picnic areas
1 protected swimming beach area
waterskiing/sailing/sailboarding
scuba diving
boating/houseboating
2 marinas/boat & slip rentals/fuel
bait/ice/picnic supplies
8 boat launching sites
fishing/hunting
viewing archaeological sites
2 nature trails
amphitheater at Governors Landing
visitor center near lake

BENTSEN-RIO GRANDE VALLEY STATE PARK/WORLD BIRDING CENTER

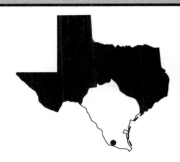

FOR INFORMATION

Bentsen-Rio Grande Valley State Park/
World Birding Center
2800 S. Bentsen Palm Drive
Mission, TX 78572
956/585-1107

LOCATION

The park is located about 6 miles southwest of Mission. Take West Expressway 83 to Bentsen Palm Drive (FM 2062). Travel south on Bentsen Palm Drive and enter the World Birding Center Headquarters on Park Road 43.

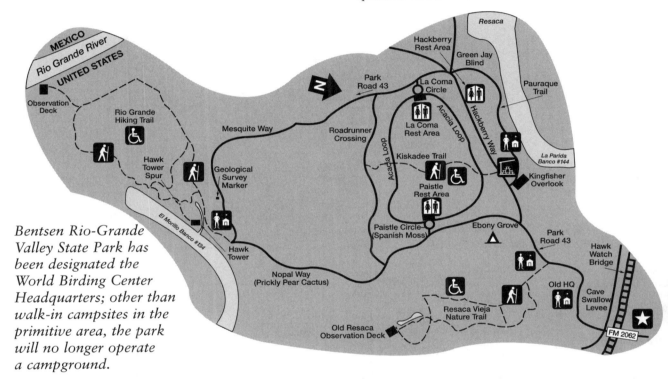

Bentsen Rio-Grande Valley State Park has been designated the World Birding Center Headquarters; other than walk-in campsites in the primitive area, the park will no longer operate a campground.

FACILITIES & ACTIVITIES

- primitive/walk-in campsites (reservations encouraged)
- restrooms/showers
- trailer dump station
- picnic tables
- covered group picnic area (capacity 100, reservations only)
- playground
- fishing on 60-acre resaca
- fish cleaning station
- boat ramp
- 2 bird blinds

- 24-foot high Hawk Tower
- 1.2-mile nature trail
- 1.8-mile hiking trail
- bike rentals
- World Birding Center Headquarters
  - conference center (multi-media room)
  - exhibit hall
  - gift store
  - café with outdoor patio
  - outdoor events courtyard
  - demonstration gardens

BLANCO STATE PARK

FOR INFORMATION

Blanco State Park
P.O. Box 493
Blanco, TX 78606
830/833-4333

LOCATION

Located on the banks of the Blanco River, just a block south of downtown Blanco, this 104-acre park is at the intersection of US 281 and FM 1623 on Park Road 23.

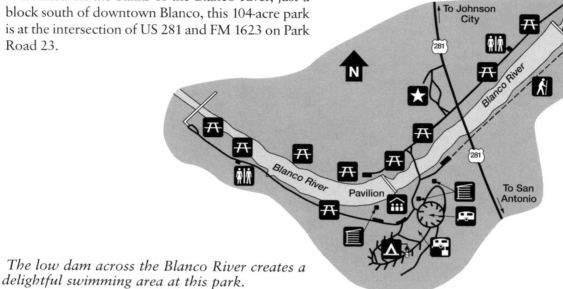

The low dam across the Blanco River creates a delightful swimming area at this park.

FACILITIES & ACTIVITIES

10 campsites with water/electricity/sewage
21 campsites with water/electricity
restrooms/showers
trailer dump station
7 screened shelters
picnicking
group pavilion with kitchen (day use)
group picnic area
3 playgrounds
river swimming
fishing
7/10-mile hiking trail
park store

BRACKENRIDGE PLANTATION PARK & CAMPGROUND

FOR INFORMATION

Brackenridge Plantation Park & Campground
891 Brackenridge Pkwy.
Edna, TX 77957
361/782-5456
www.brackenridgepark.com

LOCATION

Brackenridge Plantation Park & Campground is located east of Edna on the western shore of Lake Texana. Take TX 111 south from US 59 in Edna and travel about 7 miles; the campground is to the right before reaching the Lake Texana bridge. Lake Texana is a 11,000-acre reservoir that extends 18 miles up the Navidad River from Palmetto Bend Dam, and has 125 miles of shoreline. The campground and marina are owned by the Lavaca-Navidad River Authority.

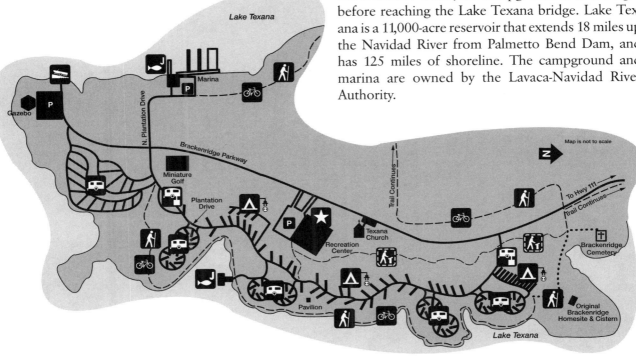

FACILITIES & ACTIVITIES

111 campsites with water/electricity/sewage	volleyball courts/
23 campsites with water/electricity	lake swimming
restrooms/showers (air conditioned)	fishing/lighted fishing pier
trailer dump station	boat ramp/boat dock
picnicking	marina with covered & open slips
bird watching gazebo	boating/sailing/waterskiing
covered pavilion	nature/historic trails
recreation center (auditorium/kitchen)	5-mile hike/bike trail
2 playgrounds	snack bar/groceries
9-hole minature golf	

CANYON LAKE

FOR INFORMATION

Canyon Lake
601 C.O.E. Road
Canyon Lake, TX 78133-4112
830/964-3341

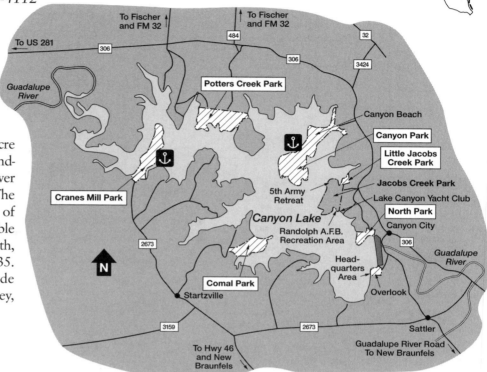

LOCATION

Canyon Lake is an 8,240-acre Corps of Engineers impoundment on the Guadalupe River with an 80-mile shoreline. The lake is about 20 miles north of New Braunfels and accessible via TX 46 and FM 2722 north, or via FM 306 north of I-35. Other nearby towns include Blanco, Fischer, Wimberley, San Marcos, and Sattler.

Canyon Lake is a popular lake for sailing; numerous regattas are held yearly.

Parks	Total Number of Campsites	Number of Campsites with Electrical Hookups	Camping Area for Groups	Toilets: F=Flush; V=Vault	Showers	Trailer Dump Station	Picnic Sites	Group Picnic Areas	Boat Launching Ramp	Swimming Area/Beach
Canyon	157		•	V			•	•	•	•
Comal				F/V			•		•	•
Cranes Mill	45								•	
Little Jacobs Creek				V			•		•	
North	19			V						
Potters Creek	97	97	•	F/V	•	•			•	•

Notes:
Canyon Park, Cranes Mill & Potters Creek are camping only; no day-use.
Canyon Beach is the day-use facility for Canyon Park.
Canyon Park has a hiking trail & a 3½-mile equestrian trail.
Jacobs Creek is controlled by Randolph A.F.B.

CHOKE CANYON STATE PARK
CALLIHAM UNIT

FOR INFORMATION

Choke Canyon State Park
Calliham Unit
P.O. Box 2
Calliham, TX 78007
361/786-3868

LOCATION

The Calliham Unit of Choke Canyon State Park is located 12 miles west of Three Rivers on TX 72. To reach the park, a 1,100-acre peninsula on Choke Canyon Reservoir, travel north on Park Road 8. The 26,000-acre reservoir is on the Frio River. Choke Canyon was most likely named for steep banks of resistant rocks near the dam site that "choked" the Frio River during floods.

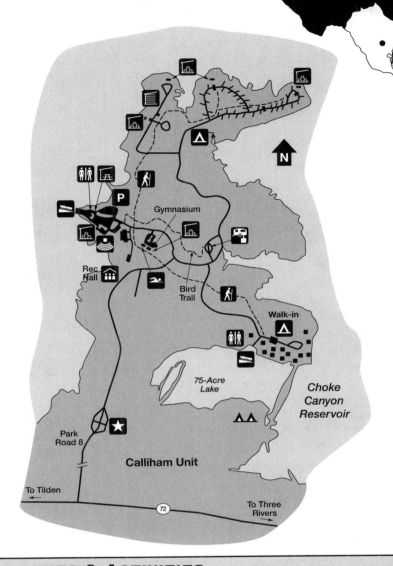

FACILITIES & ACTIVITIES

40 campsites with water/electricity

19 walk-in campsites with water only

3 primitive areas at boat ramps

sponsored youth group camping area

restrooms/showers

trailer dump station

20 winterized screened shelters

gymnasium with group dining hall

group recreation hall with kitchen (day use)

picnicking

group picnic pavilion

4 group picnic pavilions by reservation with 3 campsites

playgrounds

swimming pool & bathhouse (fee)

lake swimming

sports complex

fishing/fish cleaning shelter

fishing at a stocked 75-acre lake

boat ramp

boating/waterskiing

nature/interpretive trail

amphitheater

CHOKE CANYON STATE PARK
(CONTINUED)

SOUTH SHORE UNIT

FOR INFORMATION

Choke Canyon State Park
South Shore Unit
P.O. Box 1548
Three Rivers, TX 78071
361/786-3538

LOCATION

The South Shore Unit of Choke Canyon State Park is located 3½ miles west of Three Rivers off of TX 72 on Choke Canyon Reservoir. The 385-acre park provides access to the reservoir, as well as the Frio River below the dam. Two recreational areas are available—the main campground is below the dam, but near the headquarters is a large area used predominantly for day-use that also offers walk-in tent sites.

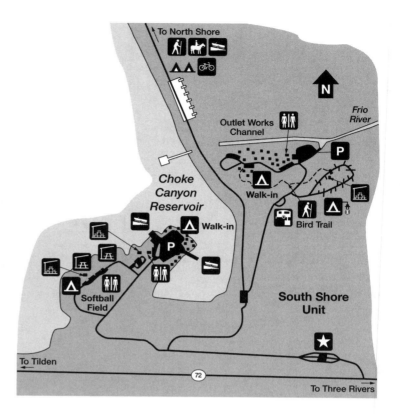

FACILITIES & ACTIVITIES

20 campsites with water/electricity

21 walk-in campsites with water only (below dam)

22 walk-in campsites with water only (above dam)

restrooms/showers

trailer dump station

picnicking

2 group picnic pavilions

1 group picnic pavilion in campground

2 playgrounds

lake swimming

fishing/3 fish cleaning shelters

2 boat ramps to lake

canoe/small boat launch to river

boating/waterskiing

access to 18 miles of hiking/mountain bike/equestrian trails (depending on lake level)

park store

NORTH SHORE EQUESTRIAN AND CAMPING AREA

The North Shore equestrian and camping area encompasses 1,700 acres of uncrowded South Texas Brush Country scenery; the terrain ranges from grassy shrubland to rugged and rocky and semi-rocky soil. Access to the North Shore area is through the South Shore Unit of Choke Canyon State Park. A paved access road across the dam leads to the facilities, which include 4 primitive group camping areas, 18 miles of designated trails for hiking, biking, and horseback riding, and a 6-lane boat ramp.

Trail users need to bring adequate water for human consumption; lake water may be used for horses. Sanitary facilities are not available at the North Shore area. The North Shore area has a 40–45 horse limit; neither corrals or horse rentals are available. Because of the remoteness of the group camping areas, there is an 8-person minimum requirement. Fees include a per-person entrance fee, a per-horse daily fee, and a fee for primitive overnight camping.

COLETO CREEK PARK

FOR INFORMATION

Coleto Creek Reservoir & Park
365 Coleto Park Rd.
Victoria, TX 77905
361/575-6366
www.coletocreekpark.com

LOCATION

Coleto Creek Reservoir is a 3,100-acre impoundment located at the confluence of Coleto and Perdido creeks; it serves as an electric generating plant and is operated by the Guadalupe-Blanco River Authority. The reservoir is midway between Victoria and Goliad on US 59. Access to the reservoir is through Coleto Creek Park, a 190-acre park, located on the southwest shore.

Campers appreciate fishermen who use a trolling motor when fishing along the bank.

FACILITIES & ACTIVITIES

58 campsites with water/electricity
flush toilets/showers/laundry
trailer dump station
4 cabins
picnicking
2 covered group pavilion
playgrounds
volleyball courts
lake swimming
fishing/200-ft lighted pier
boat ramp/boating
waterskiing
nature/hiking trails

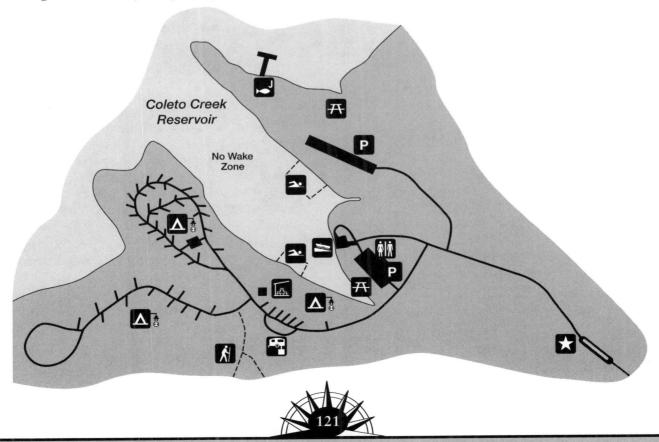

COLORADO BEND STATE PARK

FOR INFORMATION

Colorado Bend State Park
P.O. Box 118
Bend, TX 76824
325/628-3240

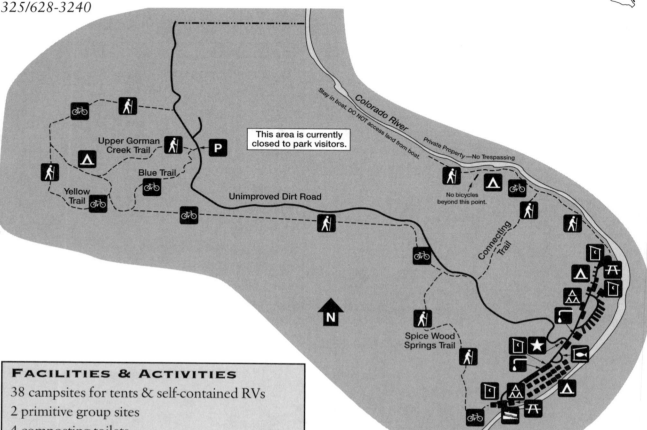

This area is currently closed to park visitors.

Colorado River

Stay in boat. DO NOT access land from boat.

Private Property —No Trespassing

Upper Gorman Creek Trail

Blue Trail

Yellow Trail

Unimproved Dirt Road

No bicycles beyond this point.

Connecting Trail

N

Spice Wood Springs Trail

FACILITIES & ACTIVITIES

38 campsites for tents & self-contained RVs

2 primitive group sites

4 composting toilets

drinking water at 2 locations

2 primitive campsites for backpackers
  (2-mile hike-in)

1 primitive campsite along river

picnicking

swimming in natural spring

river fishing

fish cleaning table

boat ramp/boating (access to Lake Buchanan)

16 miles of trails for hiking only

14 miles of hiking/mountain bike trails

*interpretive tours to Gorman Falls (fee)

*wild caves tours (both walking & crawling) (fee)

park store

*Tours are on weekends; phone park for reservations.

LOCATION

This state park is on the Colorado River about 10 miles above Lake Buchanan, west of Lampasas and southeast of San Saba. From the intersection of US 281 and US 183 in Lampasas, take FM 580 west for 24 miles to Bend. From San Saba, take US 190 about 4 miles to FM 580 and travel southeast for 13 miles to Bend. From Bend, follow the signs 4 miles to the park entrance. The headquarters and main camping area for this 5,328-acre park are 6 miles past the entrance on the gravel road.

Gorman Falls and several wild caves are accessible only through guided tours. The park is closed for wildlife management hunts—usually December through January.

DEVILS RIVER STATE NATURAL AREA

FOR INFORMATION

Devils River State Natural Area
HCR 1, Box 513
Del Rio, TX 78840
830/395-2133

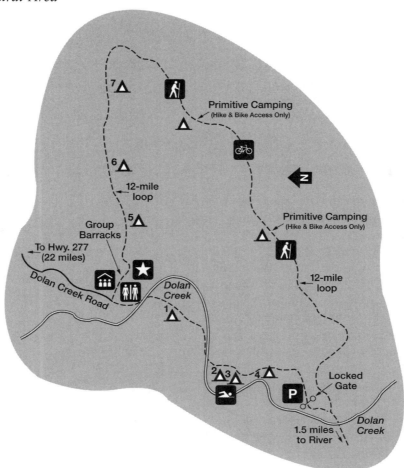

LOCATION

Devils River State Natural Area is located west of US 277 between Sonora and Del Rio. If you are coming from Del Rio, the turn off is 43 miles north, or from Sonora it is 47 miles south. To reach the park headquarters, turn off on a county maintained dirt road named Dolan Creek Road and drive west for 22 miles. This natural area encompasses 19,988 acres. Access to Dolan Falls is only through the Nature Conservancy of Texas; there is no access through the park.

Reservations Are Required—The park is open 7 days a week and is currently accessible by reservation only; make camping and lodging facility reservations through the Central Reservation Center. Park tours include visitation of archaeological pictograph sites and a canyon tour of Devils River area and springs. Contact the park for times and prices. Tours are scheduled at 9:00 am and 1:00 pm when staff is available to guide them; thus, all tours are on a pre-approved basis only. All persons entering the natural area for the day or overnight must have a permit. Visitors can buy permits at the headquarters office between 8 am and 5 pm, or self-register at the same location after 5 pm.

Devils River State Natural Area (Continued)

Additional Information:

▲ Primitive campsites 1–4 are located just off the main road leading to the river.

▲ Primitive campsites 5–7 are located just off the East Canyon jeep road; campers using these sites are not allowed to drive past their designated campsite as this road becomes a dedicated hike and bike trail beyond campsite #7.

▲ Parking for river access is at the locked river gate on the main road; access to the river from this point is 1½ miles and can be reached by foot, bicycle or park tour.

▲ No camping is permitted along the river except for canoeists arriving from Baker's Crossing for a one-night stay.

▲ Park is a put-in point only for canoes; canoe shuttle available (fee). Call ahead; 9 a.m. put-in only.

▲ Open fires of any kind, including charcoal and wood, are prohibited in the natural area.

▲ Provide your own water and containerized fuel at primitive campsites.

▲ All trash generated by visitor use must be carried out of the park.

▲ Hiking and biking are allowed *only* along the East Canyon road and along the main river road from designated camping areas. Hikers and bikers *must* remain on designated trail; cross-country travel is not allowed.

▲ Staying out of the streambeds, banks, and visible water in the canyons is also vital to the preservation of the fragile aquatic ecosystem.

▲ All creek crossings are subject to flash flooding.

▲ Swimming in the river is permitted but is "at your own risk."

▲ Pets are *not* allowed.

This scene is typical of the Devils River area north of Del Rio and the Amistad Reservoir.

Facilities & Activities

drinking water available

*7 backcountry primitive campsites (4 persons per site)

2 backcountry primitive campsites for hike & bike only

*primitive tent camping area on a 2-acre tract at headquarters

no primitive camping area along river except for canoeists arriving from Baker's Crossing for a one-night stay

5-room bunkhouse (10 max.)

group dining hall (20 max.)/kitchen/ conference room

restrooms/cold showers

fishing (catch & release with artificial lures only)

hiking

12-mile hike/mountain bike loop trail

park tours available (fee)

*Completely self-contained pop-ups and small RVs OK.

ENCHANTED ROCK STATE NATURAL AREA

FOR INFORMATION

Enchanted Rock State Natural Area
16710 Ranch Road 965
Fredericksburg, TX 78624
325/247-3903

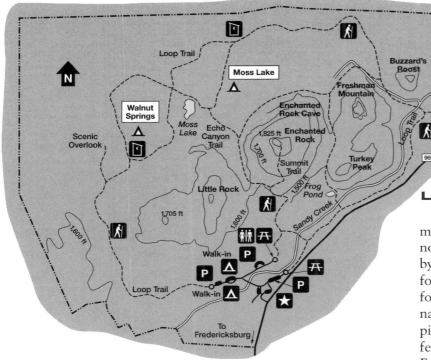

LOCATION

Enchanted Rock State Natural Area may be reached by traveling 18 miles north of Fredericksburg on RR 965 or by traveling south from Llano on TX 16 for 14 miles and then west on RR 965 for 8 miles. The 1,643 acres are dominated by massive dome-shaped hills of pinkish granite that rise more than 400 feet above the surrounding terrain. Enchanted Rock was designated as a National Natural Landmark in 1971.

FACILITIES & ACTIVITIES

*46 walk-in tent campsites with water near restrooms/showers
60 tent sites at 3 primitive camping areas for backpackers
composting toilets
picnicking
group picnic area with pavilion
playgrounds
*7 miles of hiking/backpacking trails
rock climbing (use of bolts or pitons prohibited)
exhibits/interpretive center
park store

---

*No vehicle or RV camping allowed.
No bicycles permitted on trails.

Enchanted Rock is one of the few state parks that allows walk-in tent camping only.

FALCON STATE PARK

FOR INFORMATION

Falcon State Park
P.O. Box 2
Falcon Heights, TX 78545
956/848-5327

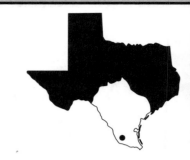

LOCATION

Located on the Texas-Mexico border, Falcon State Park may be reached by traveling 15 miles northwest of Roma on US 83, FM 2098 and Park Road 46. The 572-acre park is on the eastern shore of the 87,210-acre Falcon Reservoir on the Rio Grande River.

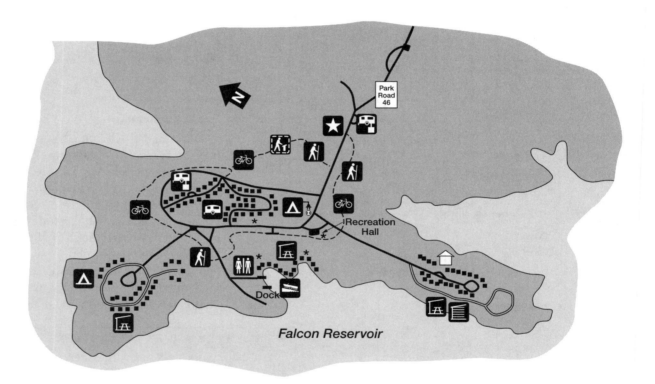

Falcon Reservoir

FACILITIES & ACTIVITIES

31 campsites with water/electricity/sewage

31 campsites with water/electricity

54 shade structure sites with water nearby
   are campsites in winter and picnic sites
   in summer

group trailer area

restrooms/showers

trailer dump station

12 enclosed shelters with AC

12 screened shelters

recreation hall

picnicking

*bird viewing area

lake swimming

fishing/fish cleaning facility

boat ramp & dock

boating/waterskiing

nature trail

3 miles of hiking/mountain bike trails

GARNER STATE PARK

FOR INFORMATION

Garner State Park
HCR #70, Box 599
Concan, TX 78838
830/232-6132

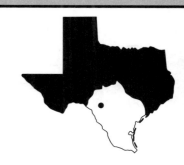

FACILITIES & ACTIVITIES

141 campsites with water/electricity
   41 premium campsites
203 campsites with water only
   55 premium campsites
restrooms/showers
2 trailer dump stations
37 screened shelters
   21 premium shelters
17 cabins
Cypress Springs Group Camp with 5 enclosed
   stone shelters and dining hall
picnicking
Old Group Shelter with kitchen (day use)
river swimming
tubing/canoeing
tube & paddleboat rentals (seasonal)
fishing
¼-mile nature trail
9 miles of hiking trails
.6 miles of surfaced hike/bike trail
18-hole miniature golf course (seasonal)
grocery store/laundry
concession pavilion with nightly dance
   during summer

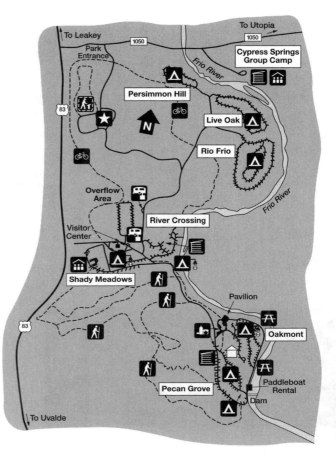

LOCATION

   This renowned state park is located north of Uvalde on US 83. From US 83, travel east on FM 1050 to the park entrance. FM 1050 is 9 miles south of Leakey and 8 miles north of Concan. The Frio River borders the east boundary of the 1,420-acre park for 1½ miles.

Successfully walking across the low dam that spans the Frio River at Garner State Park is a challenge that few youngsters pass up.

REGION 3

GOLIAD STATE PARK

FOR INFORMATION

Goliad State Park
108 Park Road 6
Goliad, TX 77963-3206
361/645-3405

LOCATION

Located about ¼-mile south of Goliad on US 183, this 188-acre park borders the San Antonio River.

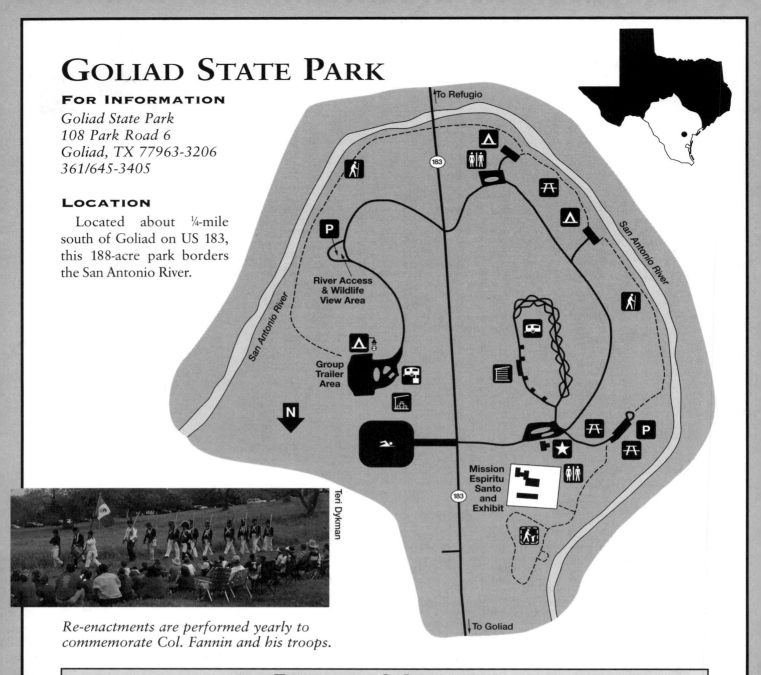

Re-enactments are performed yearly to commemorate Col. Fannin and his troops.

FACILITIES & ACTIVITIES

20 campsites with water/electricity/sewage
24 campsites with water/electricity
12 campsites with water only
restrooms/showers
trailer dump station
5 screened shelters
group dining hall
picnicking
group picnic area

playground
swimming pool complex (fee)
fishing/boating in San Antonio River
1-mile hiking trail
⅓-mile nature trail
historic site (Mission Espiritu Santo)
museum/exhibits/interpretive center
park store

GOOSE ISLAND STATE PARK

FOR INFORMATION

Goose Island State Park
202 S. Palmetto St. (Lamar)
Rockport, TX 78382
361/729-2858

FACILITIES & ACTIVITIES

102 campsites with water/electricity
    45 along bay front
    57 in wooded area
25 tent campsites with water only
youth group camping area
restrooms/showers
trailer dump station
picnicking
recreation hall (day use)
2 playgrounds
1,620-ft lighted fishing pier
fishing/boat ramp & loading dock
boating
1 mile of hiking trails
park store
"Big Tree," crowned State Champion Coastal
    Live Oak in 1967 by Texas Forest Service

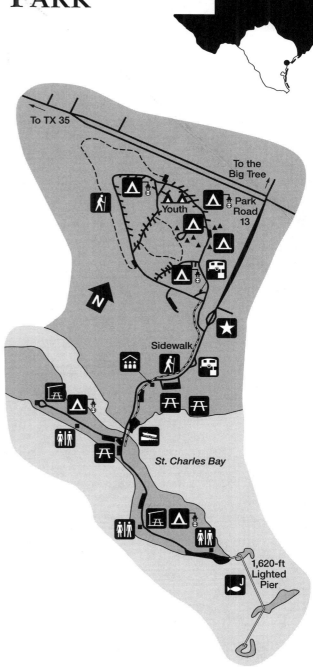

From the looks of the fishing gear, this family plans to spend the day. This 1,620-foot fishing pier is a real drawing card to Goose Island State Park.

LOCATION

This 321-acre park is on Aransas Bay between Copano Bay and St. Charles Bay. It can be reached by traveling 10 miles north of Rockport on TX 35 to Park Road 13, then 2 miles east to the park entrance.

GUADALUPE RIVER STATE PARK

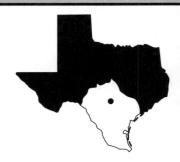

FOR INFORMATION

Guadalupe River State Park
3350 Park Rd. 31
Spring Branch, TX 78070
830/438-2656

FACILITIES & ACTIVITIES

48 campsites with water/electricity

37 campsites with water only

restrooms/showers

trailer dump station

9 primitive walk-in campsites with water

composting toilets

picnicking

playground

horseback riding

river swimming

fishing

river suitable for canoeing/kayaking/rafts/small johnboats

3 miles of hiking trails

5+ miles of bicycle/hiking/equestrian trails

Rust House Interpretive Center

amphitheater

park store

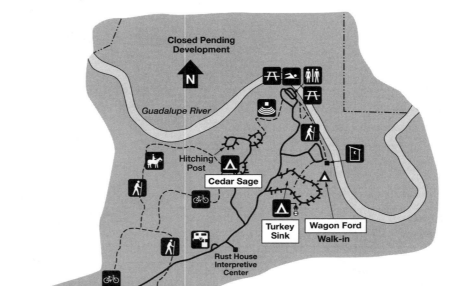

LOCATION

Bisected by the clear, flowing waters of the Guadalupe River, this state park comprises a 1,938-acre segment of the Texas Hill Country noted for its ruggedness and scenic beauty. The 3-mile road to the park (Park Road 31) can be reached by traveling 13 miles east of Boerne on TX 46, or 8 miles west of the US 281 intersection with TX 46.

HONEY CREEK STATE NATURAL AREA

Entrance to the 2,293-acre Honey Creek State Natural Area is through Guadalupe River State Park. The diverse geology, flora, and fauna make Honey Creek a special place for all visitors. Guided nature walks are scheduled almost every Saturday morning at 9:00 am. The tour lasts about 2 hours; reservations are not required. Tours are conducted by volunteer members of The Friends of Guadalupe; there is no fee but donations are encouraged. Please confirm the tour schedule with Guadalupe River State Park. In addition, a variety of guided tours are offered on Saturdays that are specific to birds, wildflowers, geology, photography, etc. Some of these tours may require a reservation.

HILL COUNTRY STATE NATURAL AREA

FOR INFORMATION

Hill Country State Natural Area
10600 Bandera Creek Rd.
Bandera, TX 78003
830/796-4413

LOCATION

Hill Country State Natural Area is located southwest of Bandera on FM 1077. From Bandera, travel south on TX 173, go across the Medina River and continue for about ¼ mile to FM 1077; turn right and go 10 miles to the end of the blacktop road. Continue on the caliche road. This 5,370-acre natural area is a scenic mosaic of rocky hills, flowing springs, oak groves, grasslands, and canyons. Park is open year round. Closed only for public hunts in December and January. Phone park office for specific dates.

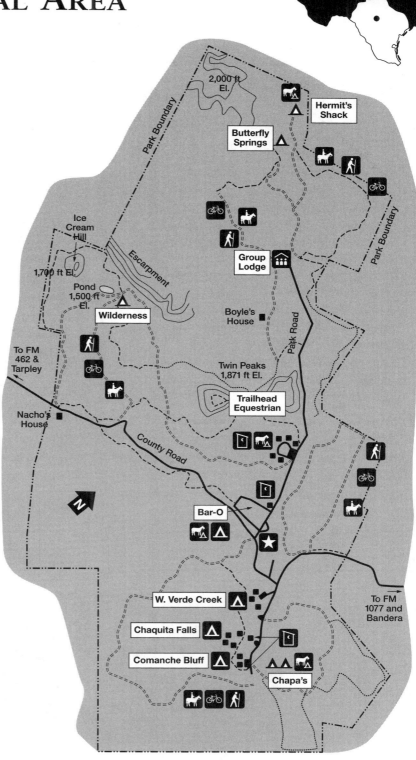

This park is already well known for its equestrian trails, but recently it has become the mecca for mountain biking.

HILL COUNTRY STATE NATURAL AREA
(CONTINUED)

FACILITIES & ACTIVITIES

CAMPGROUNDS WITH NEARBY PARKING:

*10 developed campsites at 3 walk-in tent-camping areas (no horses)
- West Verde Creek (3 sites)
- Chaquita Falls (4 sites)
- Comanche Bluff (3 sites)

*6 developed equestrian campsites at Trailhead Camp

*Chapa's Group Camp for equestrians (reservation required)—capacity for large groups on 10 acres, has large barn with concrete floor & electricity, 12 horse stalls, picnic tables, picket line, fire rings, and a nearby chemical toilet.

Bar-O day use area—for visitors with horse trailers or RVs. Used primarily by equestrians; can be used as an overflow camping area.

*group lodge—available to equestrian or non-equestrian use; can sleep 12. Pens, stables and an arena are available for horses.

CAMPGROUNDS ACCESSIBLE VIA TRAIL:

potable water is not available; all water must be treated. Bring drinking water.

springwater is available for horses

3 primitive camping areas for backpack, equestrian, & bikers

Hermit's Shack: 3½ miles from trailhead (horses allowed)

Wilderness Camp: 2½ miles from trailhead (no horses)

Butterfly Springs: 3½ miles from trailhead (no horses)

chemical or composting toilets are near most camping areas

fires are permitted in fire rings only; wood is scarce, so bring your own

all trash must be packed out, including hay and animal by-products

designated swimming areas on West Verde Creek

fishing along West Verde Creek

40 miles of designated multi-use trails open for backpacking, day hiking & horseback riding

travel only on designated trails; do not ride or hike cross-country

trails may be subject to closure during wet conditions

dogs and horses must be on a leash or lead rope, or tied at all times

bicyclists must yield to hikers & horses; hikers also yield to horses

park store

horse rentals are available from nearby ranches. Call Bandera County Convention and Visitors Bureau for information (830/796-3045)

---

*Reservations required through Central Reservation Systems.

Texas Parks & Wildlife Dept. 2004

Over 40 miles of trails at Hill Country are designated for multi-use; hikers and bicyclists yield to horseback riders.

INKS LAKE STATE PARK

FOR INFORMATION

Inks Lake State Park
3630 Park Road 4 West
Burnet, TX 78611
512/793-2223

LOCATION

Located along the southeastern shore of 803-acre Inks Lake, this 1,201-acre park is on Park Road 4. From Burnet, go 9 miles west on TX 29, turn left on Park Road 4 and go 3 miles to the park. Or, from Marble Falls, go north on US 281 to Park Road 4, turn left and go 12 miles to the park.

Deck boats offer a relaxing way to enjoy the scenery at Inks Lake.

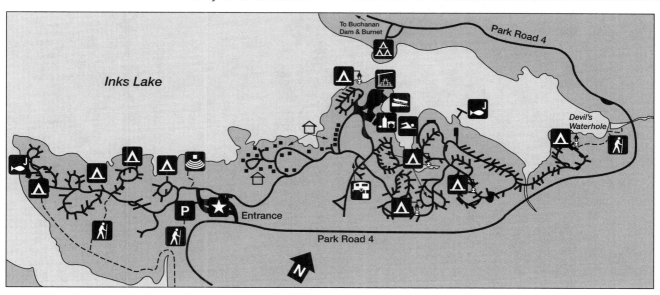

FACILITIES & ACTIVITIES

137 campsites with water/electricity	lake swimming
50 campsites with water only	fishing/2 fish cleaning shelters
10 walk-in campsites with electricity	2 lighted fishing piers
restrooms/showers	boat ramp
trailer dump station	canoe/paddleboat/surf bike rentals (year-round)
9 primitive backpack campsites	boating/waterskiing
youth sponsored camping area	7½ miles of hiking trails
22 mini-cabins	9-hole golf course/equipment rental
picnicking	amphitheater
covered group picnic area	park store
8 playgrounds	

KERRVILLE-SCHREINER PARK

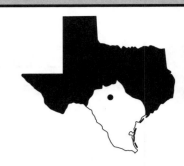

FOR INFORMATION

Kerrville-Schreiner Park
2385 Bandera Highway
Kerrville, TX 78028
830/257-5392
kerrpark@kerrville.org

LOCATION

Kerrville-Schreiner Park is located 3 miles southeast of Kerrville on both sides of SH 173. When approaching the park from the I-10 intersection with SH 16, continue toward Kerrville on TX 16, and turn left on Loop 534; after crossing the Guadalupe River, turn left on SH 173 and continue to the park entrance, located on the left. The park encompasses 517 acres, and is adjacent to the shores of the Guadalupe River, and is managed by the city of Kerrville.

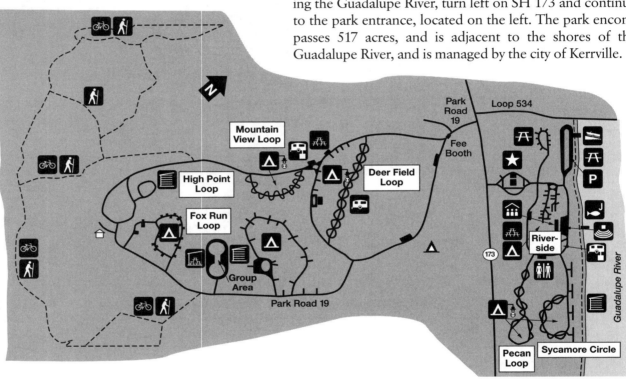

FACILITIES & ACTIVITIES

20 campsites with water/electricity/sewage	picnicking
42 campsites with water/electricity	group picnic areas (reservable)
10 premium campsites	playground
58 campsites with water only (no RVs or trailers)	river swimming
4 restrooms/showers	fishing
2 trailer dump station	lighted fishing pier
23 screened shelters	boat ramp/boating
group shelter area with 7 screened shelters	7.7 miles of hiking/mountain bike trails
screened shelter dining hall/kitchen (day use)	amphitheater
recreation hall/kitchen (day or overnight use)	

LADY BIRD JOHNSON MUNICIPAL PARK

FOR INFORMATION

Lady Bird Johnson Municipal Park
432 Lady Bird Johnson Drive
Fredericksburg, TX 78624-0111
830/997-4202

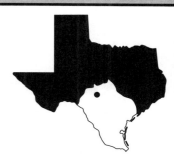

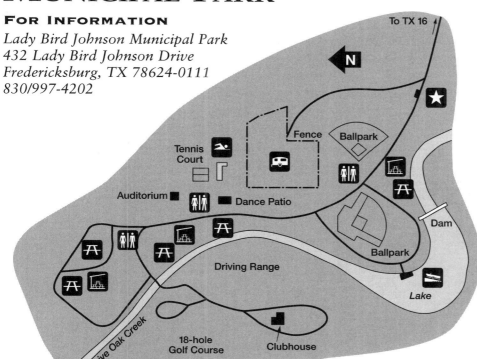

To TX 16

N

Fence
Ballpark
Tennis Court
Auditorium
Dance Patio
Driving Range
Dam
Ballpark
Lake
Live Oak Creek
18-hole Golf Course
Clubhouse

LOCATION

This municipal park is located on Live Oak Creek 3 miles southwest of Fredericksburg on TX 16. The 190-acre park has a 20-acre lake and is run by the city of Fredericksburg.

This area of the state is noted for its colorful fields of wildflowers each spring. Since this is a black-and-white photograph you'll just have to imagine the intensity of this yellow field against the backdrop of green trees and a blue sky.

FACILITIES & ACTIVITIES

113 campsites with water/electricity/
   sewage/TV cable
undeveloped tent sites
restrooms/showers
trailer dump station
picnicking
5 group pavilions
playground
swimming pool & bathhouse (seasonal)
fishing
boating (no motors)/boat dock
18-hole golf course
2 putting greens/driving range
baseball diamonds
volleyball & tennis courts
enclosed rental pavilion
1-mile nature trail
restaurant at pro shop

LAKE AUSTIN AND LAKE TRAVIS

FOR INFORMATION

Lower Colorado River Authority
P.O. Box 220
Austin, TX 78767-0220
512/473-4083 or
1-800-776-5272, ext. 3366

LOCATION

Lake Austin is a 1,830-acre Lower Colorado River Authority impoundment that begins within the western edge of Austin and winds up the Colorado River for 20¼ miles to the Mansfield Dam. The maximum width of Lake Austin is 1,300 feet.

The second lake of the famous Highland Lakes, which stairstep up the Colorado from Austin, is the 18,929-acre **Lake Travis.** It is 63¾ miles long with 270 miles of shoreline, and has a maximum width of 4½ miles.

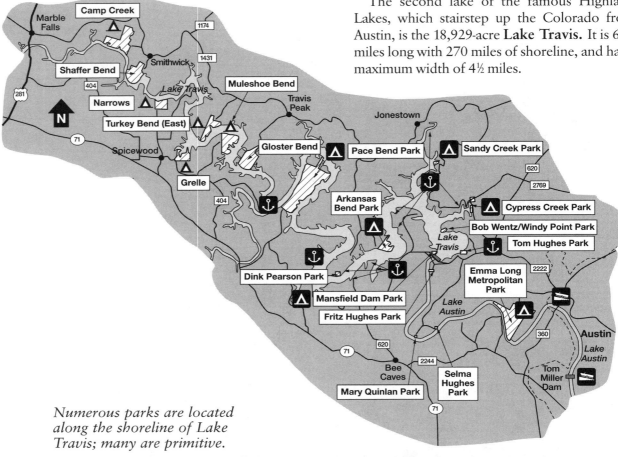

Numerous parks are located along the shoreline of Lake Travis; many are primitive.

Camping Parks

LCRA Parks	Daily Entrance Fee	Overnight Camping	Restrooms: F=Flush; V=Vault; P=Pit; C=Chemical	Picnicking	Trails	Boat Ramp	Lake Access	Equestrian
Camp Creek		Prim		•		•	•	
Grelle	•	Prim	C	•	•		•	•
Muleshoe Bend	•	Prim	C	•	•		•	•
Shaffer Bend		Prim		•	•		•	•
Turkey Bend (East)	•	Prim	P	•	•		•	
City of Austin								
Emma Long Metropolitan Park	•	46 Water 20 w/e	F	•	•	•	•	
Operated by Travis County (512/854-9437)								
Arkansas Bend	•	200 Tent	R	•	•	•	•	
Cypress Creek	•	5 Tent	P	•	•	•	•	
Mansfield Dam	•	6 Tent	F	•		•	•	
Pace Bend	•	400 Tent 20 w/e	F/V	•	•	•	•	
Sandy Creek	•	30 Tent	F	•	•	•	•	

Source: LCRA *Highland Lakes Camping and Boating Guide*, June 2003.
2 parks have RV sites & dump stations: Emma Long & Pace Bend.
3 parks have showers: Emma Long, Mansfield Dam & Pace Bend.
See next page for additional facilities at Pace Bend.

Day Use Parks

LCRA Parks	Daily Entrance Fee	Restrooms	Picnicking	Boat Ramp	Lake Access
Gloster Bend	•	C	•	•	•
Narrows		C	•	•	•
Operated by Travis County (512/854-9437)					
Bob Wentz at Windy Point	•	•	•		•
Dink Pearson		•	•	•	•
Fritz Hughes		•	•		•
Mary Quinlin		•	•	•	•
Selma Hughes		•	•		
Tom Hughes	•	•	•		•

Source: LCRA *Highland Lakes Camping and Boating Guide*, June 2003.
Bob Wentz has showers & trails.
Gloster Bend allows equestrian users.
Gloster Bend & Narrows have chemical toilets.

U.S. Army Corps of Engineers

Although jet skiing has become more popular in recent years, wind surfing remains a fun sport on all of the Highland Lakes.

REGION 3

LAKE AUSTIN AND LAKE TRAVIS
(CONTINUED)

PACE BEND PARK—ON LAKE TRAVIS

FOR INFORMATION

Pace Bend Park
2011 N. Pace Bend Rd.
Austin, TX 78669
512/264-1482

LOCATION

Pace Bend is located approximately 30 miles west of Austin on Lake Travis. From the intersection of RR 620 and SH 71, take SH 71 west 11 miles to RR 2322 (Pace Bend Park Road). Turn right on RR 2322 and travel 4.6 miles to the park entrance. This 1,368-acre park has more than 9 miles of shoreline along scenic Lake Travis. A 7-mile paved roadway loops the park; the interior of the loop can be reached only by foot, bicycle, or horseback. Pace Bend is an LCRA park operated by Travis County.

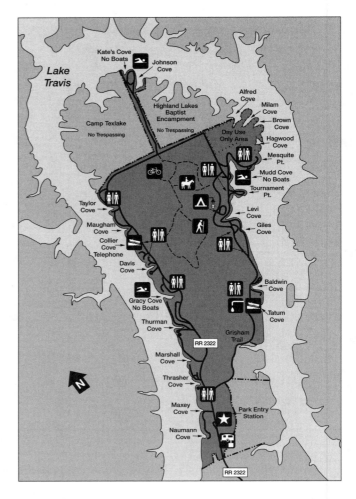

FACILITIES & ACTIVITIES

*20 back-in campsites with
water/electricity/restrooms/showers

**400+ primitive campsites

vault toilets

bulk potable water station opposite
Tatum Cove boat ramp

dump station

3 designated swim coves

picnic tables/grills/fire rings

hiking/bicycle/horseback trails (no vehicles)

fishing/boating/sailing/waterskiing

2 boat ramps: Collier Cove on west side and
Tatum Cove east side

---

*improved camping on the east side just above Levi Cove
  (reservations recommended)

**primitive campsites adjacent to the 7-mile loop road in the
designated coves; scattered along the cliffs on the west side and
along the gentle, sloping shorelines with sandy and gravel beaches
on the north and east side (first-come, first-served basis)

Note: Pace Bend charges by vehicle, not by site. A maximum of 2
vehicles may occupy a site; overflow parking is available.

*There are 2 boat ramps at Pace Bend
Park; Collier Cover on the west side,
and Tatum Cove on the east side.*

Lake Buchanan, Inks Lake, Lake LBJ, & Lake Marble Falls

For Information

Lower Colorado River Authority
P.O. Box 220
Austin, TX 78767-0220
512/473-4083 or
1-800-776-5272, ext. 3366

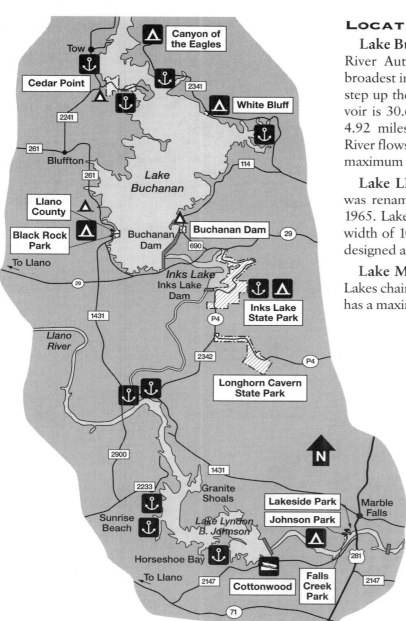

Location

Lake Buchanan is a 23,060-acre Lower Colorado River Authority impoundment, the highest and broadest in the series of 6 Highland Lakes that stair-step up the Colorado River from Austin. The reservoir is 30.65 miles long and its maximum width is 4.92 miles. From Lake Buchanan, the Colorado River flows into **Inks Lake;** it is 4.2 miles long, has a maximum width of 3,000 feet and covers 802 acres.

Lake LBJ, originally called Granite Shoals Lake, was renamed for President Lyndon B. Johnson in 1965. Lake LBJ is 21.15 miles long, has a maximum width of 10,800 feet, and covers 6,375 acres; it was designed as a constant level lake.

Lake Marble Falls, the smallest in the Highland Lakes chain, covers 780 acres, is 5.75 miles long, and has a maximum width of 1,080 feet.

REGION 3

Camping Parks	Daily Entrance Fee	Overnight Camping	Restrooms	Picnicking	Boat Ramp	Lake Access
Black Rock (LCRA: 512/473-3366)	•	•	•	•		•
Buchanan Dam (Burnet County: 512/756-4297)		Prim	•	•	•	
Canyon of the Eagles (Presidian Parks: 1-800-977-0081)	•	•	•	•		•
Cedar Point (LCRA: 512/473-3366)		Prim	•	•	•	•
Llano County (Llano County)		Prim	•	•	•	
White Bluff (Burnet County: 512/756-4297)		•	•	•	•	•
Day Use Parks						
Falls Creek (City of Marble Falls: 830/693-3615)			•	•		
Johnson Park (City of Marble Falls: 830/693-3615)			•	•	•	•
Lakeside Park (City of Marble Falls: 830/693-3615)			•	•	•	•

Source: LCRA *Highland Lakes Camping and Boating Guide,* June 2003.

Black Rock has 15 sites with water/electricity (3 with sewer), 25 tent sites, dump station & showers.

Canyon of the Eagles has 25 sites with full hookups, 35 tent sites & showers.

Cedar Point and Canyon of the Eagles offer trails; Cedar Point has equestrian trails.

See next page for additional facilities at Canyon of the Eagles.

Boating access to Inks Lake is via a two-lane boat ramp at Inks Lake State Park. The park also has a marina.

Just north of Canyon of the Eagles, the Colorado River provides many scenic views like this.

Canyon of the Eagles— on Lake Buchanan

FOR INFORMATION

Canyon of the Eagles
16942 RR 2341
Burnet, TX 78611
512/334-2070
1-800-977-0081
www.canyonoftheeagles.com

FACILITIES & ACTIVITIES

25 campsites with water/electricity/sewer

35 improved and primitive campsites

flush toilets/showers

64-room lodge

conference center/restaurant

lake & pool swimming/bathhouse

picnic area

fishing/fishing pier

boating/boat dock

canoe launch

14 miles of hiking trails

wildlife observation platform

open-air amphitheater

natural science center (capacity 120)

astronomical observatory

embarkation point for the Vanishing Texas
    River Cruise on Lake Buchanan

guided canoe/kayak trips on Colorado River
    offered by Lake Buchanan Adventures

park store

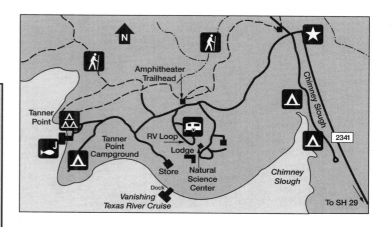

LOCATION

Canyon of the Eagles is a 940-acre nature park located northwest of Burnet on the shores of Lake Buchanan. From Burnet, travel west on SH 29, turn right on RR 2341 and travel 15 miles to the park entrance. The park is recognized internationally as a habitat for endangered wildlife, including the American bald eagle, black-capped vireo and golden-cheeked warbler. The LCRA owns the nature park and developed the camping areas and many of the recreation facilities. However, Presidian Destinations developed the lodge, conference center, and dining facilities and also operates the park and its facilities.

The embarkation point for the
Vanishing Texas River Cruise is Canyon
of the Eagles, a 940-acre nature park.

LAKE CASA BLANCA INTERNATIONAL STATE PARK

FOR INFORMATION

Lake Casa Blanca International State Park
P.O. Box 1844
5102 Bob Bullock Loop
Laredo, TX 78044
956/725-3826

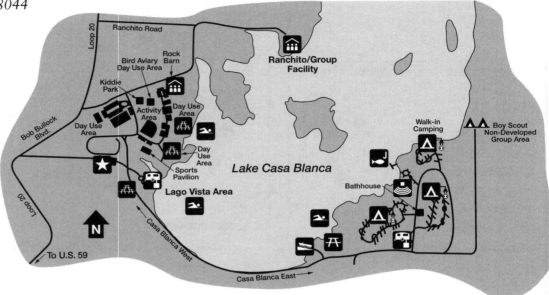

LOCATION

This state park is located east of the Laredo International Airport off of Bob Bullock Loop 20 on the shore of 1,100-acre Lake Casa Blanca. From I-35 north, the 371-acre park is accessible via Loop 20.

U.S. Army Corps of Engineers

This park has three beach swimming areas. Considering the warm temperature along the Texas-Mexico border, my guess is that the beaches are used at least nine months out of the year.

FACILITIES & ACTIVITIES

66 campsites with water/electricity
   36 multi-use
   18 trailer rally area
   12 walk-in
restrooms/showers
2 trailer dump stations
youth group camping area
group recreation hall (day use)
picnicking
5 group picnic pavilions
playground
3 beach swimming areas
fishing/fishing pier
boat ramp
boating/waterskiing
2 miles of mountain bike trails
sports area (tennis, basketball, volleyball, baseball)
amphitheater

Lake Corpus Christi State Park

For Information

Lake Corpus Christi State Park
P.O. Box 1167
Mathis, TX 78368
361/547-2635

Location

Lake Corpus Christi State Park is located 4 miles southwest of Mathis off of TX 359 via FM 1068 and Park Road 25. The 288-acre park is located on the 19,336-acre Lake Corpus Christi.

Facilities & Activities

25 campsites with water/electricity/sewage
23 campsites with water/electricity
60 campsites with water only
restrooms/showers
trailer dump station
25 screened shelters
picnicking
group covered pavilion (day use)
lake swimming
fishing/2 fish cleaning shelters
2 lighted fishing piers
2 boat ramps
boating/waterskiing

Lake Corpus Christi State Park has 2 boat ramps.

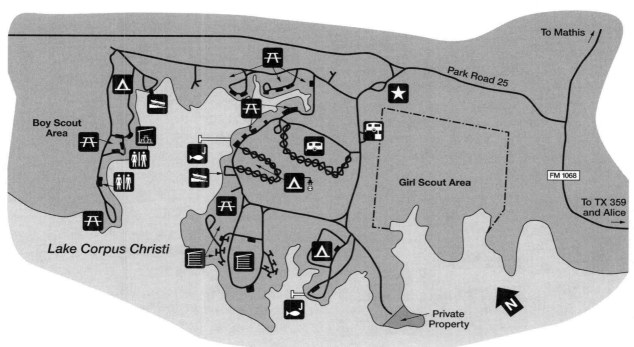

LAKE TEXANA STATE PARK

FOR INFORMATION

Lake Texana State Park
46 Park Rd. 1
Edna, TX 77957-0760
361/782-5718

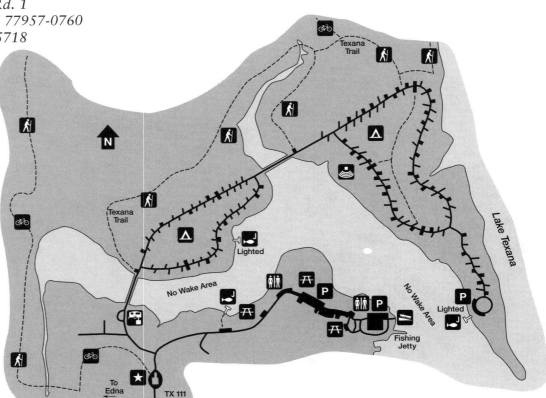

LOCATION

This state park is located on the west side of 11,000-acre Lake Texana; the lake backs up water from the Navidad River for 18 miles, and has 125 miles of shoreline. The park entrance is 6½ miles east of Edna off of TX 111. The park encompasses 575 acres of mixed oak/pecan woodlands associated with the Navidad River.

Mounting a jet ski is definitely not the same as mounting a horse.

FACILITIES & ACTIVITIES

86 campsites with water/electricity
55 campsites with water only
restrooms/showers
trailer dump station
picnicking
group picnic pavilion (day use)
3 playgrounds
lake swimming
fishing/4 fish cleaning facilities
2 lighted fishing piers/1 jetty
boat ramp/boating
waterskiing/jet skiing
canoe/kayak/hydrobike/rentals
6 miles of hiking/biking trails
park store

LAKE WOOD RECREATION AREA

FOR INFORMATION

Lake Wood Recreation Area
167 FM 2091 South
Gonzales, TX 78629
830/672-2779
www.gbra.org

LOCATION

Lake Wood Recreation Area is located west of US 183 at Gonzales; travel about 3 miles west on US 90A, then 3 miles south on FM 2091. Lake Wood is a 488-acre lake on the Guadalupe River; the 35-acre recreation area offers use of the lake and the river. The San Marcos River enters the Guadalupe River downriver from the park; the river is navigable the entire way to Gonzales. Lake Wood is operated by the Guadalupe-Blanco River Authority.

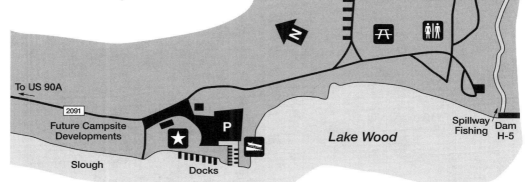

To US 90A

2091

Future Campsite Developments

Slough

Docks

P

Lake Wood

Spillway Fishing

Dam H-5

River Access

Guadalupe River

FACILITIES & ACTIVITIES

16 campsites with water/electricity/sewer
3 campsites with water/electricity
16 tent campsites
flush toilets/showers
trailer dump station
ice/groceries/laundry/live bait
picnicking
river swimming
fishing
lake boat ramp/boat docks
boating/waterskiing
boat access to river
canoeing

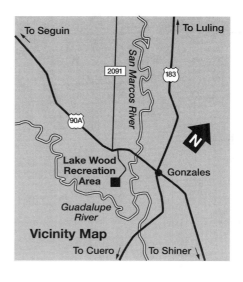

To Seguin

To Luling

2091

183

90A

San Marcos River

Lake Wood Recreation Area

Gonzales

Guadalupe River

Vicinity Map

To Cuero

To Shiner

LOCKHART STATE PARK

FOR INFORMATION

Lockhart State Park
4179 State Park Road
Lockhart, TX 78644-9716
512/398-3479

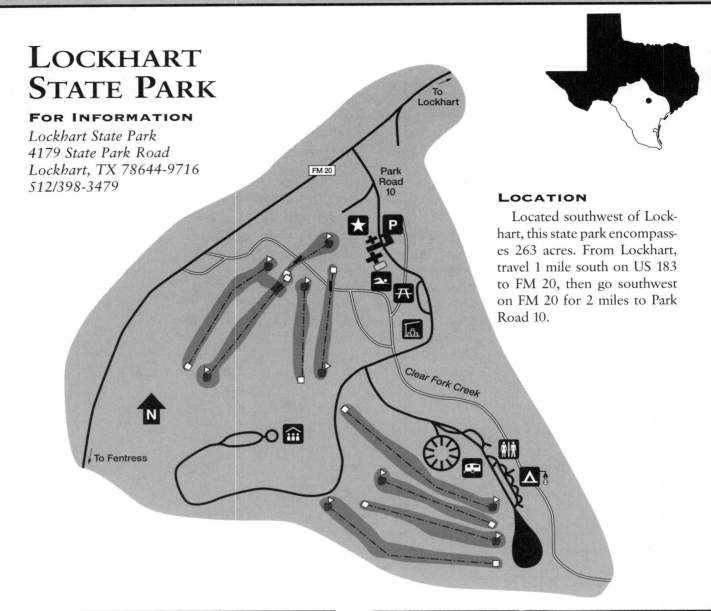

FM 20

To Lockhart

Park Road 10

Clear Fork Creek

N

To Fentress

LOCATION

Located southwest of Lockhart, this state park encompasses 263 acres. From Lockhart, travel 1 mile south on US 183 to FM 20, then go southwest on FM 20 for 2 miles to Park Road 10.

FACILITIES & ACTIVITIES

10 campsites with water/electricity/sewage
10 campsites with water/electricity
restrooms/showers
recreation hall/kitchen (day or overnight use)
picnicking
group picnic area
playground
swimming pool/bathhouse (fee)
fishing in Clear Fork Creek
short hiking trail (primitive)
9-hole golf course/golf cart rentals
pro shop/park headquarters
park store

Lockhart is one of four state parks that has a golf course.

LOST MAPLES STATE NATURAL AREA

FOR INFORMATION

Lost Maples State Natural Area
37221 FM 187
Vanderpool, TX 78885
830/966-3413

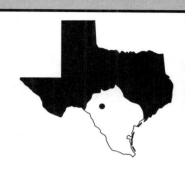

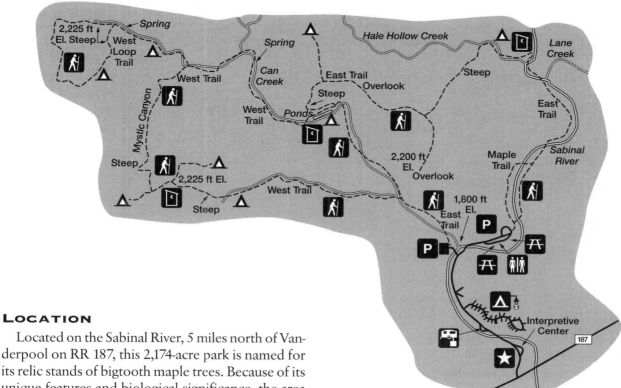

LOCATION

Located on the Sabinal River, 5 miles north of Vanderpool on RR 187, this 2,174-acre park is named for its relic stands of bigtooth maple trees. Because of its unique features and biological significance, the area was designated a National Natural Landmark in February, 1980.

ABOUT THE MAPLES

Fall displays of red, yellow, and orange foliage on the maple trees depend on the favorable combination of several factors, and these conditions do not occur every year. Generally, the foliage changes the last two weeks of October through the first two weeks of November. To obtain information on the condition of autumn coloration before planning a visit, call the toll-free number 1-800-792-1112 after the first of October.

FACILITIES & ACTIVITIES

30 campsites with water/electricity
8 primitive camping areas for backpackers
restrooms/showers
trailer dump station
picnicking
swimming
fishing
10½ miles of hiking/backpacking trails
⁹⁄₁₀-mile nature trail (Maple Trail)
scenic overlooks
interpretive center
park store

MATAGORDA ISLAND STATE PARK

FOR INFORMATION

Matagorda Island State Park
P.O. Box 117
Port O'Connor, TX 77982
361/983-2215

This fisherman is definitely serious about surf fishing.

TEXAS HIGHWAYS Magazine

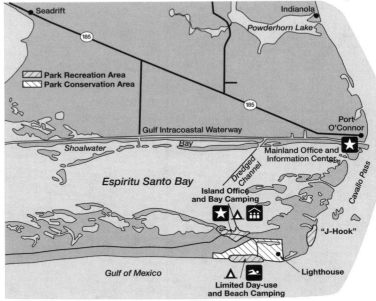

Park Recreation Area
Park Conservation Area

Seadrift • • Indianola
Powderhorn Lake
185
185
Port O'Connor
Gulf Intracoastal Waterway
Shoalwater Bay
Mainland Office and Information Center
Dredged Channel
Espiritu Santo Bay
Island Office and Bay Camping
Cavallo Pass
"J-Hook"
Lighthouse
Limited Day-use and Beach Camping
Gulf of Mexico

LOCATION

Matagorda Island is one of the barrier islands that borders the Gulf. Separated from the mainland by San Antonio and Espiritu Santo bays, the island is 38 miles long, ranges from ¾ to 4½ miles wide, and the highest elevation is 22 feet above mean high tide. The island is 56,668 acres in size and owned and managed by several state and federal agencies. A 7,325-acre tract at the northeastern end of the island is managed by the Texas Parks and Wildlife Department as a state park; it includes 2 miles of beach on the Gulf side.

Matagorda Island State Park is accessible only by boat. The headquarters is in Port O'Connor at the intersection of 16th Street and Intracoastal Canal. A passenger ferry now runs regularly between the state park docks in Port O'Connor and the island. A fee is charged. The ferry runs three times a day every Saturday, Sunday, and holidays. Surfboards and bicycles are allowed on the ferry. A shuttle vehicle is available to take visitors the 2½ miles across the island to the Gulf Beach.

FACILITIES & ACTIVITIES

There is no drinking water, concession, electricity, or telephone—there are 2 designated primitive camping areas

Army Hole Campground on the bay (located near boat dock) with shaded picnic tables, fire rings, new toilets, and outdoor cold water shower

Beach Campground on a 2-mile stretch of Gulf beach (2½ miles from boat dock; serviced by island shuttle) with covered picnic tables; no toilets

barracks (group or individuals)

picnicking

beach swimming area

fishing (surf/bayside lakes/tidal flats)

boating/limited docking space on bay side

beach walking

over 80 miles of beach, roadways and mowed pathways available for hiking and mountain biking

historic sites

exhibits/interpretive center

interpretive tours (fee)

park store

McKinney Falls
State Park

For Information

McKinney Falls State Park
5808 McKinney Falls Parkway
Austin, TX 78744
512/243-1643

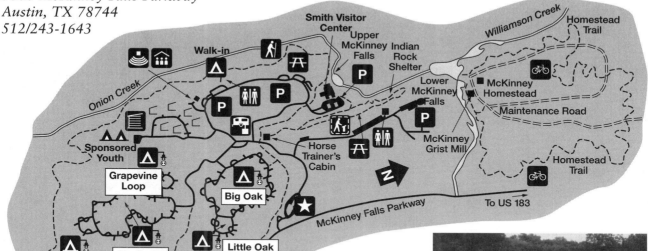

Location

This state park is located about 13 miles southeast of the State Capitol in Austin; it is east of I-35, south of Ben White Blvd. and west of US 183. The 744-acre park is named for the waterfall on Onion Creek. From the east, the park may be reached from US 183, either via traveling south on McKinney Falls Parkway, or via traveling west for 2 miles on Scenic Loop Road. From the west, the park may be reached off of I-35 by taking East William Cannon Drive (exit 228) to McKinney Falls Parkway.

Lower McKinney Falls is a great place to spend a hot afternoon.

FACILITIES & ACTIVITIES

81 campsites with water/electricity	fishing
8 walk-in campsites with water	short interpretive trails
restrooms/showers	3.2-mile paved hike & bike trail
trailer dump station	3 miles of unpaved trails for hiking & mountain biking
6 screened shelters with wooden bunks	
group dining hall with full kitchen	amphitheater
sponsored youth group camping area	historic sites
picnicking	interpretive center and tour (fee)
playground	park store
swimming	

MUSTANG ISLAND STATE PARK

FOR INFORMATION

Mustang Island State Park
P.O. Box 326
Port Aransas, TX 78373
361/749-5246

LOCATION

Mustang Island State Park is located on one of the coastal barrier islands that lie between the mainland and the open waters of the Gulf; it comprises 3,954 acres at the southern end of Mustang Island, including 5½ miles of beach. To reach the park, travel southeast from Corpus Christi to Padre Island on TX 358, cross the JFK Causeway, and continue one mile to a traffic light; turn left onto TX 361 and go 5 miles north to park headquarters. The park also can be reached by taking the toll-free ferry from Aransas Pass to Port Aransas and traveling south on TX 361.

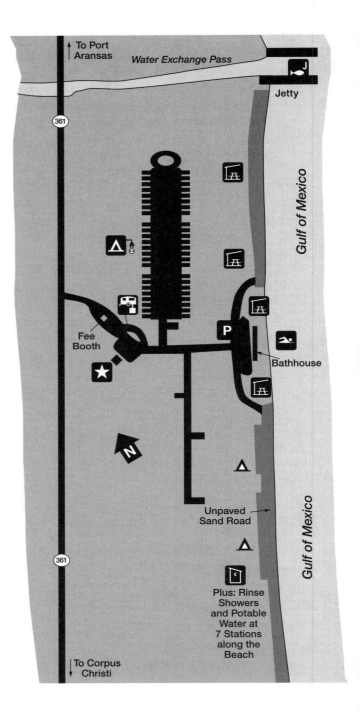

FACILITIES & ACTIVITIES

48 campsites with water/electricity/individual shade shelters/restroom with hot water showers nearby

300 open beach primitive campsites along a 7,000-foot stretch of coastline with 7 widely spaced convenience stations (each has chemical toilets, rinsing showers, and bulk-water supply)

trailer dump station

picnic tables with shade shelters

swimming beach

beach bathhouse with dressing rooms, restrooms, & outside rinsing showers

surf fishing

fishing off of 2 jettys

5 miles of biking—primarily beach riding

park store

PADRE ISLAND NATIONAL SEASHORE

FOR INFORMATION

Padre Island National Seashore
(20420 Park Rd. 22)
P.O. Box 1300
Corpus Christi, TX 78480-1300
361/949-8068 (Visitor Center)
361/949-8173 (Headquarters)
361/949-8175 (for recorded message
*   on tides, weather, beach conditions, etc.)*

LOCATION

Stretching for 113 miles along the Texas Gulf Coast from Corpus Christi on the north almost to Mexico on the south, this barrier island ranges in width from a few hundred yards to about 3 miles. The National Seashore encompasses the undeveloped central part of the island and is the longest stretch of primitive, undeveloped barrier island beach in the world. Access to the park is from the north end. There are two approaches: The first leads over a causeway from Corpus Christi (TX 358) to North Padre Island and then via Park Road 22; the other leads from Port Aransas down Mustang Island via TX 361. The visitor center is approximately 10 miles south of the junction of Park Road 22 and TX 361.

POINTS OF INTEREST

▲ This coastal wilderness embraces 65½ miles of white sand-and-shell beaches, picturesque windswept dunes, and wild landscapes of grasslands and tidal flats teeming with shore life.

▲ If you love the beach, you'll love Padre Island; the sun, sand, and surf are ideal for swimming and sunbathing almost all year.

▲ If you are a fisherman, you can choose between the Gulf of Mexico and the shallow, extremely salty waters of Laguna Madre—both are renowned for their bounty of game fish.

▲ If you delight in the discovery of a seashell of exquisite design, or a unique piece of driftwood, there are miles of shoreline for beachcombing.

▲ If it's adventure that you seek, you can hike or drive a 4-wheel-drive vehicle for 60 miles along the roadless Gulf beach.

Surf fishing is popular all along the Gulf coast.

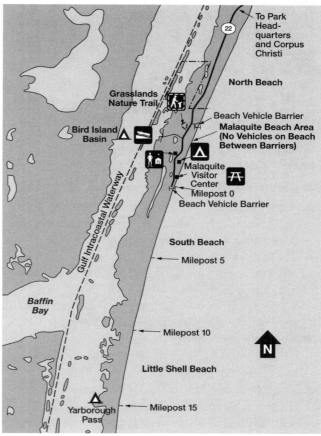

PADRE ISLAND NATIONAL SEASHORE (CONTINUED)

A day at the beach means doing whatever makes you happy!

GENERAL INFORMATION

▲ A park entrance fee is charged; a camping fee is charged at the Malaquite Beach Campground and Bird Island Basin but not at other locations.

▲ The visitor center is located in the Malaquite Pavilion overlooking the Gulf of Mexico; it is open daily and has books, brochures, maps, and exhibits. Schedules of special activities, such as beach walks and evening campfire programs, are posted.

▲ The complex includes an observation deck, snack bar and gift shop, restrooms, rinse-off showers, and changing rooms.

▲ The Malaquite Beach Campground, suitable for tents or RVs, is open all year on a first-come, first-served basis. The campground is paved, has picnic tables, restrooms, and cold showers. Fresh water and a dump station are located just outside the campground.

▲ All other camping areas are primitive; drinking water is not available but chemical or pit toilets may be available.

▲ Campers in primitive areas may use the showers and toilets at the Malaquite Visitor Center, which are free and open all night.

▲ Bird Island Basin permits primitive camping for tents and RVs.

▲ South Beach is open camping for self-contained RVs and tent campers. All campers must camp on the beach, not in the dunes. To access the beach, continue one mile past the Malaquite Visitor Center.

▲ When "traveling down island," whether by foot or 4-wheel-drive vehicle, plan your trip carefully; there are no services. Before you head out, stop at the visitor center or the ranger station to get up-to-date information on beach and weather conditions, tide time, etc.

▲ Fires are allowed only on the beaches between the water and the dunes. Fires are not permitted on Malaquite Beach.

▲ Gray water and sewage must be disposed of at a designated sewage dump station outside the Malaquite Campground.

▲ Items such as shells, driftwood, or other materials washed in with the tides may be collected as long as they are not used for commercial purposes.

▲ Only licensed vehicles may be driven on the beaches and established roadways. Driving in the dunes or grasslands is prohibited.

▲ Fishing in the park is permitted in accordance with state laws. A Texas fishing license and saltwater stamp are required.

FACILITIES & ACTIVITIES

50 RV & tent campsites at Malaquite Beach

sanitary dump

1 group campsite for tents only

primitive RV & tent camping at Bird Island Basin

primitive camping on South Beach between Milepost 0 and 5 (accessible by 2-wheel-drive vehicles)

primitive camping on beach beyond Milepost 5 (accessible only by 4-wheel drive vehicles)

primitive camping at Yarborough Pass (4-wheel-drive necessary)

picnicking

swimming/bathhouse

surfing

sailing/sail-boarding/boating/waterskiing in Laguna Madre

boat ramp at Bird Island Basin

fishing/surf fishing

¾-mile nature trail

beach hiking/backpacking

4-wheel-drive beach driving

concession store

interpretive activities/campfire programs

visitor center/exhibits

PALMETTO STATE PARK

FOR INFORMATION

Palmetto State Park
78 Park Road 11 South
Gonzales, TX 78629-5180
830/672-3266

Texas Parks & Wildlife Dept. 2004

Named for the Dwarf Palmetto, this park has 3 miles of nature and hiking trails. One trail passes this historic pump and water tower from the 1930's era.

LOCATION

Located in an area once known as the Ottine Swamp, Palmetto State Park closely resembles a tropical botanical garden. On the San Marcos River, the 270-acre park of swampy woodlands is located on Park Road 11 off of US 183, about 6 miles southeast of Luling and 12 miles northwest of Gonzales.

FACILITIES & ACTIVITIES

1 campsite with water/electricity/sewage
18 campsites with water/electricity
22 campsites with water only
  1 premium campsite
restrooms/showers
trailer dump station
picnicking
group picnic shelter with kitchen
2 playgrounds
swimming (lake & river)
fishing (lake & river)
fishing pier
3 miles of nature/hiking trails
bicycling allowed on paved roads only
historical structure
park store

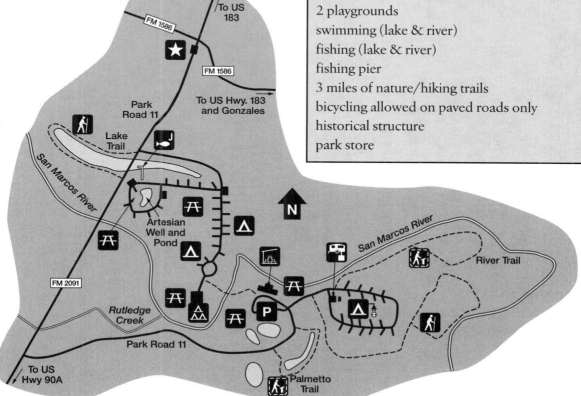

To US 183

FM 1586

FM 1586

To US Hwy. 183 and Gonzales

Park Road 11

Lake Trail

San Marcos River

Artesian Well and Pond

FM 2091

N

San Marcos River

River Trail

Rutledge Creek

P

Park Road 11

To US Hwy 90A

Palmetto Trail

PEDERNALES FALLS STATE PARK

FOR INFORMATION

Pedernales Falls State Park
2585 Park Road 6026
Johnson City, TX 78636
830/868-7304

LOCATION

Pedernales Falls State Park may be reached from US 281 at Johnson City, by traveling 9 miles east on FM 2766, or by traveling west of Austin for 32 miles on US 290, then north on FM 3232 for 6 miles. Located on one of the scenic stretches of the Pedernales River, the 5,212-acre park has more than 6 miles of river frontage and a rugged and picturesque gorge known as the Pedernales Falls.

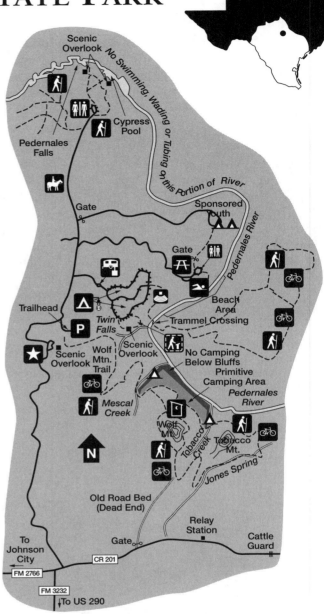

Pedernales Falls State Park has 21 miles of hiking trails.

FACILITIES & ACTIVITIES

69 campsites with water/electricity

21 backpacking campsites in a primitive camping area 2½ miles from trailhead

restrooms/showers

trailer dump station

youth group primitive camping area

picnicking

river swimming (begins 2½ miles below falls)

fishing

21 miles of hiking trails including the 7½-mile Wolf Mountain Trail

¼-mile nature trail

20 miles of mountain bike trails

10-mile equestrian trail

amphitheater

historical site

scenic views

park store

SOUTH LLANO RIVER STATE PARK

FOR INFORMATION

South Llano River State Park
1927 Park Rd. 73
Junction, TX 76849-9502
325/446-3994

LOCATION

South Llano River State Park and the adjoining Walter Buck State Wildlife Management Area are located 5 miles south of Junction off US 377 on Park Road 73. The winding South Llano River forms the northern park boundary with 1½ miles of river frontage. The park and wildlife management area encompass 2,657 acres.

The park is open year-round, except when wildlife management activities dictate closure of part of the park. The river frontage and bottomland is closed from October 1 to April 1 to protect the winter roosting areas for the Rio Grande turkey, while the closed dates of the Wildlife Management Area change from year to year. Check with the park ahead of time to be sure the area you plan to use is open.

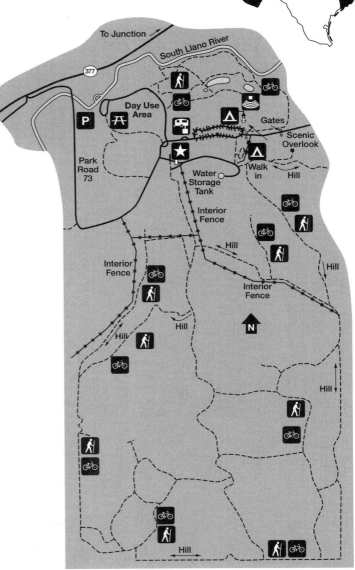

Birders agree that there is more to see than the Rio Grande Turkey at South Llano.

FACILITIES & ACTIVITIES

56 campsites with water/electricity

6 walk-in campsites with water

restrooms/showers

trailer dump station

picnicking

playground

swimming/canoeing/tubing in river

river & lake fishing

*2 miles of hiking/mountain bike trails in riverbottom section

*18 miles of hiking/mountain bike trails in Wildlife Management Area

historic site/museum

scenic views

park store

---

*Check with park in fall and winter for specific closure dates.

REGION 4

Dumas
Borger
Pampa
Amarillo
Canyon
Plainview
Vernon
Lubbock
Lamesa
Snyder
Abilene
Cisco
Big Spring
Colorado City
Midland
Brownwood
Odessa
Goldthwaite
San Angelo
Brady
El Paso
Menard
Van Horn
Balmorhea
Fort Stockton
Fort Davis
Alpine
Sonora
Marathon
Comstock

ABILENE STATE PARK

FOR INFORMATION

Abilene State Park
150 Park Road 32
Tuscola, TX 79562
325/572-3204

LOCATION

This state park is located 16 miles southwest of Abilene; from the US 83/84 bypass south off of I-20, take FM 89 through Buffalo Gap to the park entrance. The 529-acre park borders the 595-acre Lake Abilene on the east.

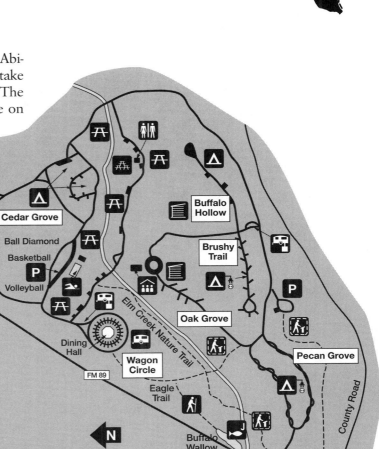

To Buffalo Gap and Abilene

Cedar Grove

Ball Diamond

Basketball

Volleyball

Buffalo Hollow

Brushy Trail

Oak Grove

Pecan Grove

Dining Hall

Wagon Circle

Elm Creek Nature Trail

Eagle Trail

Buffalo Wallow

FM 89

N

Spillway

Lake Abilene Dam

Lake Abilene

Elm Creek

County Road

To US 277

TEXAS HIGHWAYS Magazine

Abilene State Park also has a herd of Texas Longhorn.

FACILITIES & ACTIVITIES

3 campsites with water/electricity/sewer

37 campsites with water/electricity

12 campsites with water only

restrooms/showers

2 trailer dump stations

8 screened shelters

36-site group trailer area with water/electricity

2 recreation halls with kitchens (day use)

picnicking

2 group picnic areas

playground

game area (sand volleyball, basketball, baseball, horseshoes)

swimming pool/bathhouse

fishing

1½ miles of nature/hiking trail

park store at park headquarters

concessions (seasonal)

Texas Longhorn herd/buffalo

scenic views

REGION 4

BALMORHEA STATE PARK

FOR INFORMATION

Balmorhea State Park
P.O. Box 15
Toyahvale, TX 79786
432/375-2370

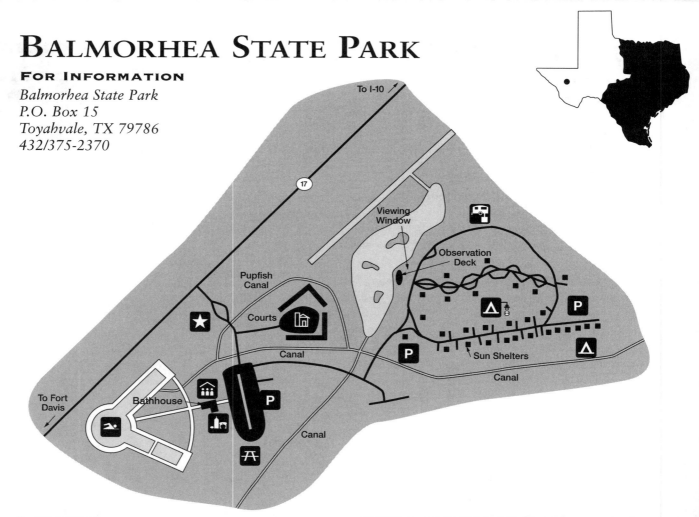

LOCATION

Balmorhea State Park is located 4 miles southwest of Balmorhea on TX 17, between Balmorhea and Toyahvale. From I-10, take the TX 17 exit to Balmorhea and travel southwest to the park entrance. Or, when traveling I-10 from the west, take the RR 3078 exit to Toyahvale, turn left on TX 17 at Toyahvale and continue to the park entrance. The waters of San Solomon Springs at this 46-acre park form the world's largest spring-fed swimming pool.

TEXAS HIGHWAYS Magazine

FACILITIES & ACTIVITIES

28 campsites with water/electricity

6 campsites with water only

restrooms/showers

trailer dump station

18-unit motel/some with kitchenettes (San Solomon Springs Court)

recreation hall/kitchen (day-use/fee)

picnicking

playground

spring-fed swimming pool/bathhouse/hot showers

concessions (seasonal)

exhibits/viewing area for pupfish canal

interpretive tour (fee)

park store at headquarters

The water of this world's largest spring-fed swimming pool stays at 76–78° year-round.

BIG BEND NATIONAL PARK

FOR INFORMATION

Big Bend National Park
P.O. Box 129
Big Bend National Park, TX 79834-0129
432/477-2251 Visitor Center/Headquarters

LOCATION

Big Bend National Park encompasses a vast area of 801,163 acres and is edged on three sides by the "big bend" of the Rio Grande, the international boundary between Mexico and the United States. US 385 leads from Marathon to the north entrance; TX 118 from Alpine leads to the west entrance; and RR 170, from Presidio, joins TX 118 at Study Butte before the west entrance.

The park can be thought of as having 3 natural divisions: the river, the desert, and the mountains. The Rio Grande, often referred to as a linear oasis, defines the park's southern boundary for 107 miles. The park is 97% Chihuahuan Desert; the Chisos Mountains interrupt it as a green island in a desert sea. At 4,500 feet the first trees begin to appear; higher up in the drainages you see masses of trees—junipers, small oak trees, and pinyon pines.

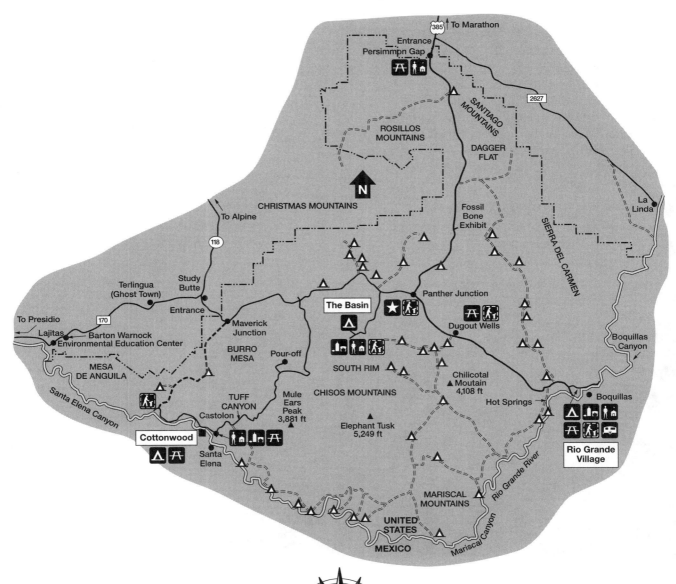

Big Bend National Park
(Continued)

POINTS OF INTEREST

▲ Paved roads and improved dirt roads enable park visitors to view many points of interest in the park. There are numerous places to stop along the way, such as overlooks, self-guided trails, exhibits, and historical sites. High-clearance vehicles and/or 4-wheel drive are necessary for travel on the back-country dirt roads.

▲ Big Bend is a birder's paradise; more than 400 species of birds have been seen. The larger migration through the park is in the spring. Ask a ranger about the best birding spots.

▲ The Rio Grande is a Wild and Scenic River for 234 miles along part of the park boundary and extending below. Easy floats include the Mariscal and Boquillas Canyons; Santa Elena and the Lower Canyons are more difficult.

▲ More than 200+ miles of trails offer opportunities for day-hikes or backpacking trips. Elevations range from 1,800 feet at the eastern end of Boquillas Canyon to 7,825 feet atop Emory Peak in the Chisos Mountains.

GENERAL INFORMATION

▲ A park entrance fee is charged; fees are good for 7 days. Campground fees are also charged.

▲ The visitor centers at the Basin and Panther Junction are open daily all year. The visitor center at Rio Grande Village is open mid-October through mid-May. A variety of maps and guides can be purchased. Information stations are at Persimmon Gap, the Basin, and Castolon.

▲ Campgrounds for RVs and tents are located in the Basin, Rio Grande Village, and Castolon. There is a concessionaire-operated trailer park with utility hookups at Rio Grande Village; full hookup capability is required; no reservations are taken.

▲ All campgrounds are on a first-come, first-served basis, with the following exception: From November 15 to April 15, reservations for 43 sites in Rio Grande Village Campground and 26 sites in the Chisos Basin Campground may be made. Contact www.reserveusa.com or call 1-817-444-6777.

▲ A parkwide limit of 14 days occupancy is in effect February 1 to April 15 for any developed campsite. During the rest of the year, occupancy beyond 14 days may be authorized on a day-to-day basis if sites are available for new arrivals.

▲ Campgrounds are available for organized groups at the Basin, Cottonwood, and Rio Grande Village. Various size groups can be accommodated. Advance reservations are required; they may be made 360 days in advance.

▲ Camping is also allowed in designated backcountry campsites. A permit is required for all overnight trips into the backcountry, and can be obtained up to 24 hours in advance of the trip in person only on a first-come, first-served basis.

The view of the Sierra del Carmen Mountain Range from the Dugout Wells area is quite breathtaking.

▲ Backcountry users should pick up a copy of the hiking/backpacking regulations in order to be well informed. Carry a topographic map and know how to use it. Detailed 7.5 minute topo maps can be purchased at the visitor center or ordered in advance. Building a ground fire is prohibited.

▲ Permits for the high Chisos designated campsites are available at the Basin Ranger Station. The maximum group size is 15.

▲ Carry a minimum of 1 gallon of water per person per day in the summer, slightly less in the winter. Springs are unreliable; springwater should be treated before use as it may be unsafe to drink. Don't drink the river water.

▲ A free river permit is required for floating the river and is available at park headquarters and ranger stations. A river guidebook is sold at park headquarters. There are no equipment rentals in the park. Call or write the park for a list of river outfitters in the area.

▲ Fishing is allowed in the Rio Grande. No license is required. Hunting is not allowed.

▲ Groceries are available near all campgrounds. Gas is available at Panther Junction and Rio Grande Village; there is no gas at Cottonwood/Castolon or in the Basin. Showers and laundry facilities are available only at the grocery store/service station at Rio Grande Village between 9:00 am and 5:00 pm.

▲ Prepared food and lodging are available only in the Chisos Basin. Call 432/477-2291 for room reservations. Advance reservations are recommended.

▲ Groceries, cold drinks, camping supplies, and film are sold at the Basin, Rio Grande Village, Castolon, and Panther Junction. The Chisos Mountains Lodge has a gift shop. Minor auto repairs can be obtained at Panther Junction.

▲ There are steep grades and sharp curves to the Basin and north out of Castolon. These roads are not advised for automobiles towing trailers over 20 feet in length or RVs over 24 feet in length.

▲ Typically, winter and spring are dry seasons; the rains usually begin in June and last into the fall. Summer brings hot days and warm nights. Winter is variable; cold spells are common and are interspersed with warm days; high winds are common and nights are almost always below freezing.

▲ Come well prepared because weather changes can be dramatic and unexpected. The weather in Big Bend National Park, hot or cold, causes more injuries and kills more hikers than any other factor.

▲ Weather Information Hotline: 432-477-1183.

FACILITIES & ACTIVITIES

200 RV & tent campsites at 3 campgrounds
concessionaire-operated trailer park
3 group campgrounds
designated backcountry campsites
lodge/restaurant in Basin
picnicking
canoeing/rafting on the Rio Grande River
fishing
hiking/backpacking
8 self-guided trails
bicycling
museum/exhibit
self-guided auto tours
snacks/groceries/ice
nature walks/workshops/evening slide
    programs
historic buildings/exhibits/amphitheater
visitor centers

Campgrounds	Elevation (Feet)	Number of Sites	Toilets: F=Flush P=Pit	Dump Station
Chisos Basin	5,400	63	F	•
Cottonwood	2,169	35	P	
Rio Grande Village	1,850	100	F	•
Rio Grande Village RV Park	1,850	25	Concessionaire-operated; full hookup capability required; NO reservations	

Note:
All campsites have drinking water, picnic tables, & grills.

REGION 4

BIG BEND RANCH STATE PARK

FOR INFORMATION

*Big Bend Ranch State Park Complex
(North of FM 170)
P.O. Box 2319
Presidio, TX 79845
915/229-3416*

*Big Bend Ranch State Park
Sauceda
432/385-4444*

*Big Bend Ranch State Park
(South of FM 170)
℅ Barton Warnock Environmental
  Education Center
HC 70, Box 375
Terlingua, TX 79852
915/424-3327*

*Fort Leaton State Historic Site
P.O. Box 2439
Presidio, TX 79845
915/229-3613*

LOCATION

Big Bend Ranch State Park is located just west of Big Bend National Park. The 299,623-acre park lies both south and north of FM 170, which parallels the Rio Grande River for 23 miles between Lajitas and Presidio. FM 170, called "El Camino del Rio," offers one of the most spectacular drives in Texas. Contact points for the Big Bend Ranch Complex include Fort Leaton State Historic Site, which is 4 miles southeast of Presidio on FM 170 (River Road), and Barton Warnock Environmental Education Center, located just east of Lajitas on FM 170.

Guided vehicle tours to Madrid Falls and several other sites are offered upon prior arrangement.

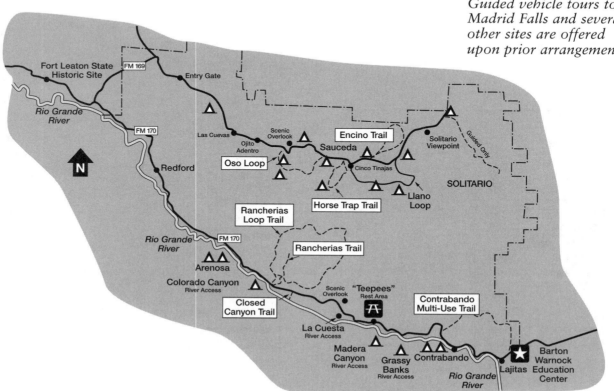

To enter the interior, visitors must contact either the complex office, Fort Leaton or the Warnock Center to obtain permits, pay fees, and *receive instructions for vehicular access into the interior of the park.* The interior is reached by traveling east on FM 170 from Fort Leaton for about 4 miles, and turning left onto a dirt road called Casa Piedra Road. When the road forks, turn right where the sign says Big Bend Ranch and follow the main road to the locked entrance gate. It is 28 miles from the turnoff on FM 170 to Sauceda, the old ranch headquarters. An additional 7 miles to the Solitario viewpoint are open to visitors; high-clearance vehicles are recommended.

FACILITIES & ACTIVITIES

ALONG FM 170 (RIVER ROAD):

camping: primitive areas at 4 river access points—Madera (Monilla) Canyon, Grassy Banks, La Cuesta and Colorado Canyon; they have self-composting toilets, but no other facilities

group camping: primitive areas at Contrabando and Arenosa; they have self-composting toilets

picnicking: at "the Tepees"—a rest area on FM 170 about 10 miles west of Lajitas

swimming: allowed only at designated locations at the campgrounds along the Rio Grande River; however, it is not recommended for health reasons

fishing: only at designated locations at the campgrounds along the Rio Grande River

backpacking: the 19-mile Rancherias Loop Trail, with trailheads located at both ends of the loop trail; access is from FM 170, near the Colorado Canyon River Access (25 max.), and the 11-mile Contrabando Multi-Use Trail with 1 primitive campsite. Trailheads are at both ends of the loop.

day-hiking: Rancherias Canyon Trail (9.6 miles round-trip) and Closed Canyon Trail (1.4 miles round-trip), with access off of FM 170

rafting/canoeing: a 9-mile section through Colorado Canyon, with 4 access points; bring own gear or hire a commercial outfitter in nearby Lajitas or Terlingua

park store at Warnock Environmental Education Center and Fort Leaton SHS

self-guided botanical garden at the Warnock Center

scenic drive along River Road FM 170

ALONG INTERIOR ROAD (SAUCEDA):

camping:
11 primitive drive-in/hike-in backcountry areas (20/site max.) along the 35-mile interior road to Sauceda (need a high-clearance vehicle)
2 backpacking campsites along the 7½-mile Encino Mountain Bike Trail

other accommodations:
*Sauceda Lodge, a group bunkhouse that accommodates 30 (15 male, 15 female); arrange in advance; meals available; showers/restrooms
*Big House, 3 bedrooms, accommodates 8; kitchen privileges available or arrange for meals in Lodge dining area

picnicking: at Sauceda

day-hiking: 3 short hiking trails off of gravel park road in the backcountry, leading to Ojito Adentro, Cinco Tinajas, and a short Sauceda Nature Trail

mountain biking: 17 miles on designated trails including 5 miles on Horsetrap Trail and 7½ miles on Encino Trail.

*horseback riding: daily/hourly rides at Sauceda Ranch Headquarters (Oso Loop, Llano Loop Trails)

mountain bike rentals at Visitor Center

seminars, workshops, & special events: a variety of educational seminars and workshops are held periodically (fee)
Phone the Park Complex for special activity information

park store

Texas Longhorn herd

---

*Phone the Big Bend Ranch State Park Complex for reservations.
**Reservations required through Central Reservation System.

BIG SPRING STATE PARK

FOR INFORMATION

Big Spring State Park
#1 Scenic Drive
Big Spring, TX 79720
432/263-4931

LOCATION

Located within the city limits of Big Spring, the entrance to Big Spring State Park is from FM 700. The 382-acre park covers what is locally known as "Scenic Mountain," a 200-foot-high, limestone-capped mesa overlooking the city. The park is easily accessed south from I-20, or west from US 87.

FACILITIES & ACTIVITIES

1 campsite with water/electricity
1 campsite with electricity
10 developed tent sites
restrooms
picnicking
group picnic pavilion (day or overnight)
open-air shelter/picnic tables at headquarters building
playground
⅓-mile nature trail
interpretive center
park store
prairie dog town
scenic drive

A large population of prairie dogs lives at this park.

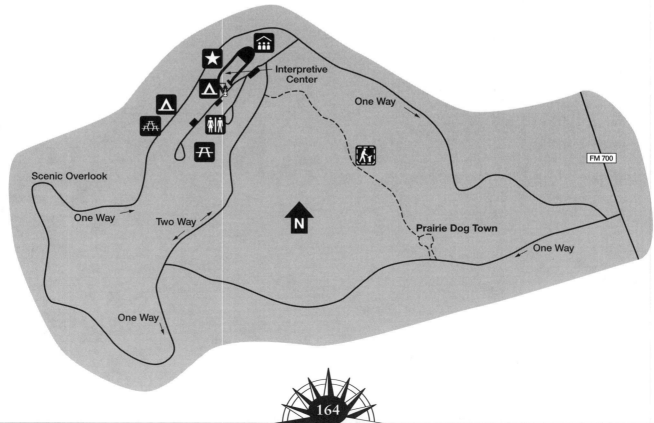

CAPROCK CANYONS
STATE PARK AND TRAILWAY

FOR INFORMATION

Caprock Canyons State Park and Trailway
P.O. Box 204
Quitaque, TX 79255
806/455-1492

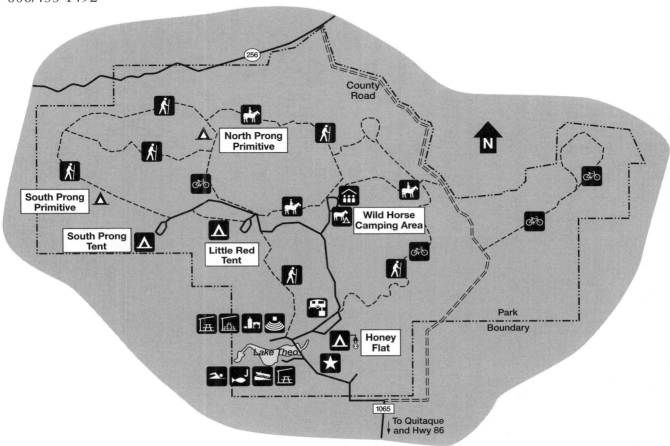

LOCATION

Caprock Canyons State Park and Trailway is located 3 miles north of Quitaque. Although bordered on the north by TX 256, the park entrance is on the south and most easily accessible by traveling north through Quitaque on RR 1065. Quitaque is on TX 86, which runs east from I-27/US 87 at Tulia and west from US 287 at Estelline. Lake Theo, a 120-acre lake, is a feature attraction of this 15,160-acre park.

The "Official Texas State Bison Herd"—descendents of the Charles Goodnight bison herd—are pastured and protected here.

Caprock Canyons State Park and Trailway (Continued)

Caprock Canyons Trailway

The Caprock Canyons Trailway is the longest rail-to-trail conversion in the state of Texas and the fourth longest in the United States. The 64.25-mile trail begins in South Plains, moves through Quitaque and Turkey near the state park and ends in Estelline. The first 22-mile segment of the trail opened on June 5, 1993; it runs from South Plains to Quitaque. This segment is in good shape for hiking, mountain biking, and horseback riding. The trailway is administered by Caprock Canyons State Park; all overnight trail campers must obtain permits from them and pay fees. Contact them for up-to-date information concerning camping areas, water availability, and trail maps. Horses are available for rent from Quitaque Riding Stables; phone 806/455-1208.

FACILITIES & ACTIVITIES

35 campsites with water/electricity

30 developed walk-in tent sites with no utilities

2 primitive backpack camping areas with 10 sites each (1 mile walk-in)

20 ride-in/hike-in primitive equestrian campsites (1 mile)

equestrian camping area with 12 campsites/water for horses

restrooms/showers

trailer dump station

picnicking

2 group picnic pavilions

playground

beach swimming area/outdoor shower

fishing/fishing pier

boat ramp/boating

nature trail

28 miles of hiking/equestrian/mountain bike trails

amphitheater

roadside exhibits/interpretive pavilion

scenic overlooks

park store

buffalo & pronghorn antelope

This state park is named for the scenic and rugged escarpment that separates the tablelands of the Southern High Plains from the Rolling Plains to the east.

COPPER BREAKS STATE PARK

FOR INFORMATION

Copper Breaks State Park
777 Park Rd. 62
Quanah, TX 79252-7679
940/839-4331

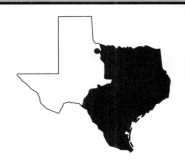

LOCATION

Copper Breaks State Park is located 13 miles south of Quanah or 11 miles north of Crowell on TX 6. The park contains 1,899 acres, primarily juniper breaks and grass-covered mesas, and a 60-acre lake formed by impoundment of Devil's Creek.

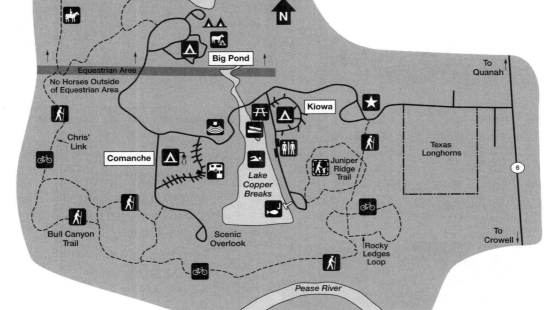

FACILITIES & ACTIVITIES

25 campsites with water/electricity
11 premium campsites with water only
10 equestrian campsites with water
restrooms/showers
trailer dump station
group camping area
picnicking
group picnic area
playgrounds
beach swimming area
fishing/fishing pier

boat ramp/boating (limit 5 mph)
10 miles of hiking trails
½- mile nature trail
9½ miles of equestrian trails
9½ miles of mountain bike trails
amphitheater
interpretive center/audio-visual programs periodically
park store
Texas Longhorn herd

DAVIS MOUNTAINS STATE PARK

FOR INFORMATION

Davis Mountains State Park
P.O. Box 1707
Fort Davis, TX 79734
432/426-3337

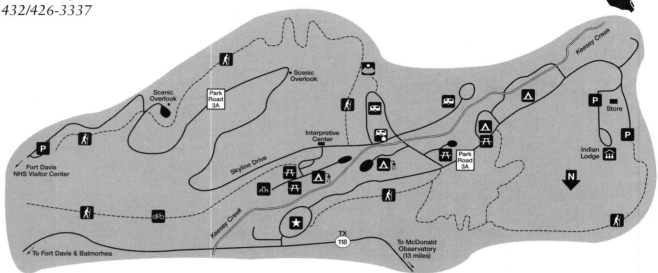

LOCATION

Davis Mountains State Park is located 4 miles northwest of Fort Davis; from just north of Fort Davis on TX 17, go west on TX 118 to Park Road 3. The park contains 2,709 acres and is adjacent to Fort Davis National Historic Site.

Skyline Drive is a scenic road that winds to the park's highest ridges. A hiking trail from the Stone Tower scenic overlook descends to Fort Davis National Historic Site, pictured here.

FACILITIES & ACTIVITIES

27 campsites with water/electricity/sewage

34 campsites with water/electricity

33 campsites with water only

*6 campsites for backpackers (4½ miles one way)

restrooms/showers

trailer dump station

**39-unit pueblo-style hotel (Indian Lodge)/restaurant

picnicking

group picnic area

playground

4½-mile hiking trail to Fort Davis National Historic Site

3½-mile mountain bike trail

3-mile scenic hiking trail

6½ miles of backcountry hiking/equestrian trails

amphitheater

interpretive center (open June through August)

interpretive tour (fee)

park store

Skyline Drive/scenic overlooks

---

*Trailhead north of park entrance across TX 118.
**For reservations, phone 432/426-3254.

E. V. SPENCE RESERVOIR

FOR INFORMATION

E. V. Spence Reservoir
Colorado River Municipal Water District
Box 869
Big Spring, TX 79721-0869
432/267-6341

Each of the 4 parks at this reservoir are relatively small, but each one has a boat launching ramp.

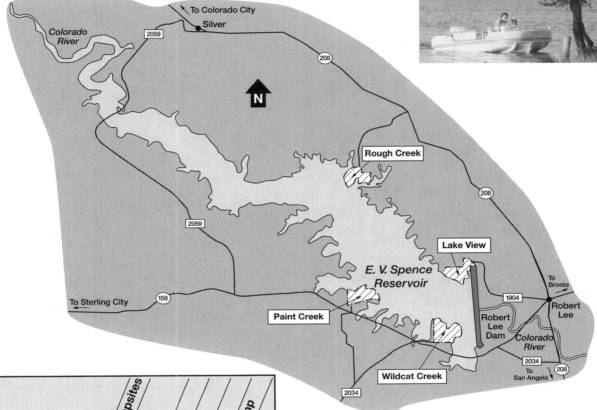

Parks	Total Number of Campsites	Toilets; F=flush; V=vault	Showers	Trailer Dump Station	Picnic Sites	Boat Launching Ramp
Lake View	7				•	•
Paint Creek	10	F		•	•	•
Rough Creek	7	V		•	•	•
Wildcat Creek	18	V	•	•	•	•

Notes:
Drinking water is not available, nor are there designated
   swimming areas at any of the parks.
Paint Creek & Wildcat Creek have marinas; they are
   operated by concessionaires; Wildcat has showers.
Full hookups: 10 at Paint Creek; 14 at Wildcat Creek.
Wildcat Creek has 4 screen shelters and 4 motel rooms.

LOCATION

E. V. Spence Reservoir, a 14,950-acre impoundment on the Colorado River, has a 137-mile shoreline; it was completed in 1969. Owned and operated by the Colorado River Municipal Water District, it was the second of three reservoirs constructed on the Colorado River to supply quality water to the citizens of West Texas. The lake is 2 miles west of Robert Lee; its 4 parks are accessible via TX 158 west and TX 208 north from Robert Lee. Other nearby towns include Bronte, Sterling City, and Silver.

FORT GRIFFIN STATE PARK & HISTORIC SITE

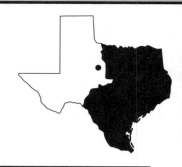

FOR INFORMATION

Fort Griffin State Park & Historic Site
1701 North U.S. 283
Albany, TX 76430
325/762-3592

LOCATION

This 506-acre state park is on the Clear Fork of the Brazos River, 15 miles north of Albany on US 283.

Fort Griffin is one of seven state parks that pasture Texas Longhorns.

FACILITIES & ACTIVITIES

2 campsites with water/electricity/sewer
20 campsites with water/electricity
5 walk-in campsites with water nearby
2 group equestrian primitive camping areas
restrooms/showers
trailer dump station
1 winterized shelter (day or overnight)
picnicking
group picnic pavilion
playground
sports area: baseball, basketball, volleyball, horseshoes, washers
fishing
hiking trail
1½ miles of hiking trails
2 miles of nature trails
area for equestrian use
amphitheater
historic site: Fort Griffin ruins
visitor center
park store
Texas Longhorn herd

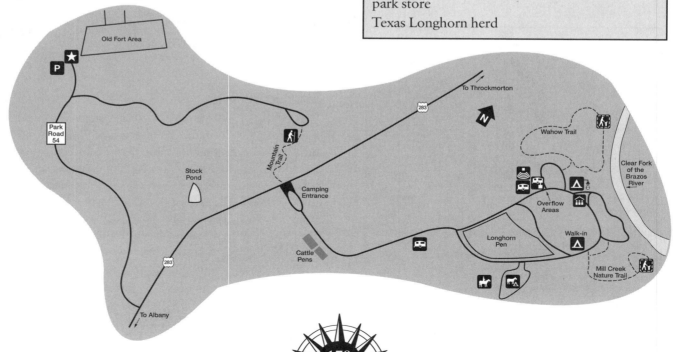

FRANKLIN MOUNTAINS STATE PARK

FOR INFORMATION

Franklin Mountains State Park
1331 McKelligon Canyon Road
El Paso, TX 77930
915/566-6441

To Aztec Caves

Primitive Camping Sites

Schaeffer Shuffle

RV Area

To W. Cottonwood Spring

Sneed's Cory

Rock Climing

To I-10 East

Upper Sunset

Nature Walk

Loop 2

Lower Sunset

Note: Stay on trails.

Loop 375—Trans-Mountain Road

N

To I-10 West

Tom Mays Unit

LOCATION

This state park is located completely within the city limits of El Paso; it is the largest urban wilderness park in the nation. The 24,050-acre park, with about 45 miles of boundary, includes an entire Chihuahuan Desert mountain range soaring to an elevation of 7,192 feet at the summit of North Franklin Peak, some 3,000 feet above the city of El Paso. State Loop 375 (Woodrow Bean Trans-Mountain Road) traverses the park. To reach the park entrance from the east, travel north on US 84 from I-10, then left on Loop 375. From the west, the park entrance is located 3.8 miles east of I-10. Take the Canutillo/Trans-Mountain exit and travel toward the mountains on Loop 375.

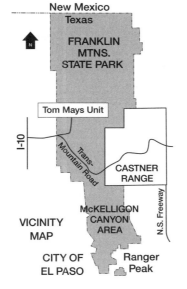

New Mexico
Texas

FRANKLIN MTNS. STATE PARK

Tom Mays Unit

I-10

Trans-Mountain Road

CASTNER RANGE

N.S. Freeway

McKELLIGON CANYON AREA

VICINITY MAP

CITY OF EL PASO

Ranger Peak

FACILITIES & ACTIVITIES

primitive camping (tents only) in Tom Mays section
    5 walk-in developed campsites (tables/grills)
    *5 RV sites (self-contained)
    self-composting toilets
    shaded picnic/barbecue sites
NO water/electricity in park
NO ground fires allowed
125 miles of multi-use trails
    22 miles of equestrian trails
    51 miles of mountain bike trails
    52 miles of nature/hiking trails
picknicking
day use group facility
rock climbing
*ranger-led tours (fee)
amphitheater
park store

*Reservations taken at the park for a limited number of RV sites.

GUADALUPE MOUNTAINS NATIONAL PARK

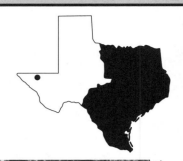

FOR INFORMATION

Guadalupe Mountains National Park
HC 60, Box 400
Salt Flat, TX 79847-9400
915/828-3251

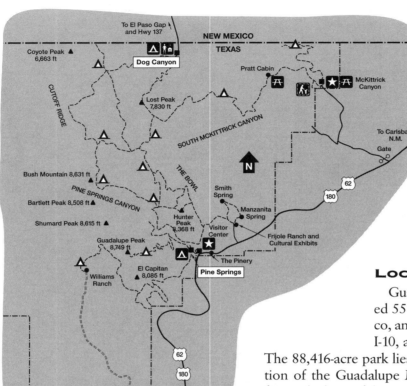

You've missed a real treat if you haven't backpacked in the Guadalupe Mountains.

LOCATION

Guadalupe Mountains National Park is located 55 miles southwest of Carlsbad, New Mexico, and 110 miles east of El Paso on US 62/180; I-10, at Van Horn, is 60 miles south via TX 54. The 88,416-acre park lies astride the most scenic and rugged portion of the Guadalupe Mountains. Elevations range from 3,650 feet at the base of the western escarpment to 8,749 feet on the summit of Guadalupe Peak, the highest point in Texas. The Capitan Reef is the most extensive fossil reef of Permian age on record. Geologists come here from around the world to marvel at this extraordinary natural phenomenon.

FACILITIES & ACTIVITIES

Pine Springs Campground
   19 RV sites (no hookups)
   20 tent sites (limited to 6 people or 2 tents)
   2 group sites
   flush toilets/drinking water
Dog Canyon Campground
   RV sites (no hookups)
   9 tent sites
   1 group site
   flush toilets/drinking water
10 backcountry campsites (no water)

3 picnic areas
interpretive trail
80 miles of hiking trails
backpacking
horseback riding
4-wheel-drive road to Williams Ranch
ranger-led talks/walks
evening ranger programs
historic buildings/exhibits/amphitheater
2 visitor centers

Points of Interest

▲ The hike to the summit of Guadalupe Peak is a popular all-day trip; the view is outstanding. The ascent is steady after leaving the floor of the canyon, and involves a climb of about 2,400 feet.

▲ The park's 80 miles of trails offer a wide range of opportunities for exploring the desert, canyons, and highlands of the Guadalupe Mountains. Trails vary greatly in length and difficulty.

▲ One of the park's most popular areas is McKittrick Canyon; you can hike a trail, enjoy a variety of plants and wildlife, and picnic beneath the canyon's high cliffs. In late October and early November, the trees' foliage turns brilliant reds, yellows, and oranges, creating a lushness that is rarely found in this part of Texas.

▲ At the foot of the Guadalupe Mountains lie the sparsely populated plains of the Chihuahuan Desert. Many of the desert's most common plants are abundant in the park: agaves, prickly pear cacti, walking-stick chollas, yuccas, and sotol.

▲ Among the trees found in the canyons is the rare and picturesque Texas madrone. It is easily identified by its smooth, reddish-colored bark and evergreen leaves.

Visitor Centers/Campgrounds

▲ **Headquarters Visitor Center**—On US 62/180, 55 miles southwest of Carlsbad, New Mexico, and 110 miles east of El Paso, Texas. Open daily 8:00 a.m. to 4:30 p.m. (MST) in winter, 8:00 a.m. to 6:00 p.m. in summer.

▲ **Pine Springs Campground**—¼ mile west of the Headquarters Visitor Center.

▲ **Dog Canyon Campground**—in the northern part of the park near the New Mexico border, 70 miles from Carlsbad, NM, via US 285 and NM 137.

▲ **McKittrick Canyon Visitor Center**—7 miles northeast of Headquarters Visitor Center on US 62/180 to McKittrick Canyon turnoff; another 5 miles northwest to the end of the road.

General Information

▲ A park entry fee is charged; it is good for 7 days. A camping fee is charged at Pine Springs and at Dog Canyon.

▲ There are 2 visitor centers: Pine Springs and McKittrick Canyon. They offer brochures, books, trail guides, maps, exhibits, a slide program, and a schedule of park activities. The visitor center near Pine Springs is open daily. Information is also available at the Dog Canyon Ranger Station.

▲ Rangers give evening programs at the Pine Springs Campground amphitheater daily in the summer and less frequently during the rest of the year.

▲ There are 2 RV & tent campgrounds: Pine Springs and Dog Canyon. Both are open all year on a first-come, first-served basis. Both have flush toilets and drinking water; both have several walk-in sites. Only campstoves are permitted in the park. No fires, including charcoal.

▲ Two group campgrounds at Pine Springs and one at Dog Canyon are available for reservation up to 60 days in advance. Each site can accommodate a minimum of 10 and a maximum of 20 persons; a fee is charged.

▲ Backcountry camping is allowed at designated sites only; pick up a required permit at a visitor center or ranger station. Campsites are first-come, first-served.

▲ There is no drinking water in the backcountry; carry at least 1 gallon per person per day. Only campstoves are allowed. A topographic map is essential for backcountry trips. Maps and trail guides are available.

▲ There are 80 miles of hiking trails; some are short nature hikes, while others may take a half day or a full day. Day-hikers do not need a permit but they should sign the register at the trailhead and carry an adequate water supply.

▲ McKittrick Canyon is a popular spot. Picnic areas have tables, but no water; fires are permitted only in campstoves. The canyon is open for day-use only; the access road is closed at the entrance from US 62/180 each night. Trails range up to 7 miles round-trip.

▲ The 7-mile road to historical Williams Ranch is open only to 4-wheel-drive vehicles. Persons wanting to travel this road must obtain a key to the entrance gate at the visitor center.

▲ Horseback riding is permitted on some of the trails; contact the park for specifics. Horses are not permitted in the backcountry overnight.

▲ Sudden changes in the weather are common in the park. High winds up to 60 to 80 miles per hour, or higher, can occur in the mountains and are particularly prevalent in the spring. Thunderstorms occur most often in late summer.

▲ The Salt Basin Dunes, on the park's west side, feature white gypsum and red quartzose dunes. Day use only. Obtain directions and a key at Pine Springs Visitor Center.

HORDS CREEK LAKE

FOR INFORMATION

Hords Creek Lake
HCR 75, Box 33
Coleman, TX 76834-9320
915/625-2322

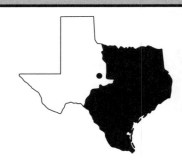

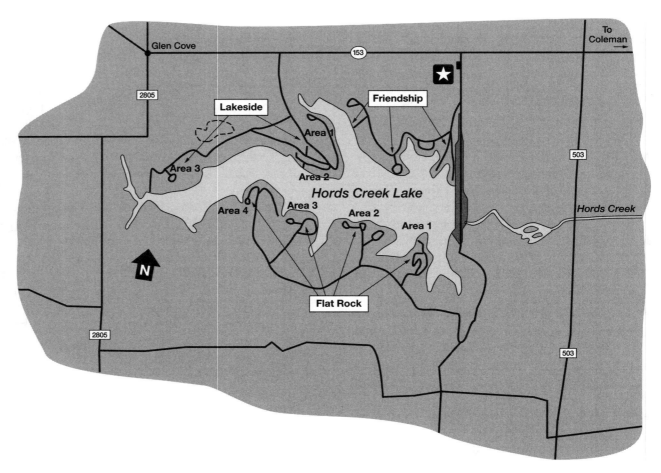

LOCATION

Hords Creek Lake is a 510-acre Corps of Engineers lake in the Colorado River Basin on Hords Creek with an 11-mile shoreline. The site is about 13.5 miles upstream from Coleman and may be reached by driving 8.7 miles west along TX 153 from Coleman. Other nearby towns include Ballinger, Winters, Crews, Glen Cove, and Valera.

Parks	Total Number of Campsites	Number of Campsites with Electrical Hookups	Camping Area for Groups	Toilets: F=flush; V=vault	Showers	Trailer Dump Station	Picnic Sites	Boat Launching Ramp	Swimming Area/Beach
Flat Rock	62	61	•	F/V	•	•		•	•
Friendship				F			•	•	•
Lakeside	74	72	•	F/V	•	•		•	•

Notes:
Lakeside has 6 screened shelters; Flatrock has 3 screened shelters.
¾-mile self-guided nature trail near Lakeside Park.

HUECO TANKS STATE HISTORIC SITE

FOR INFORMATION

Hueco Tanks State Historic Site
6900 Hueco Tanks Rd. #1
El Paso, TX 79938
915/857-1135
Reservation: 915/849-6684

LOCATION

Located about 32 miles east of El Paso just north of US 62/180 on RR 2775, this 860-acre park is named for the natural rock basins, or huecos, that trap and store water from infrequent rains in this arid region of West Texas.

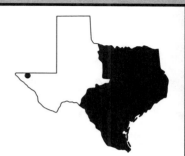

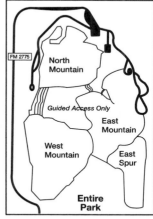

Note: Only the North Mountain section of the park is accessible without a guide. Reservations are recommended. For guided tours, contact the park.

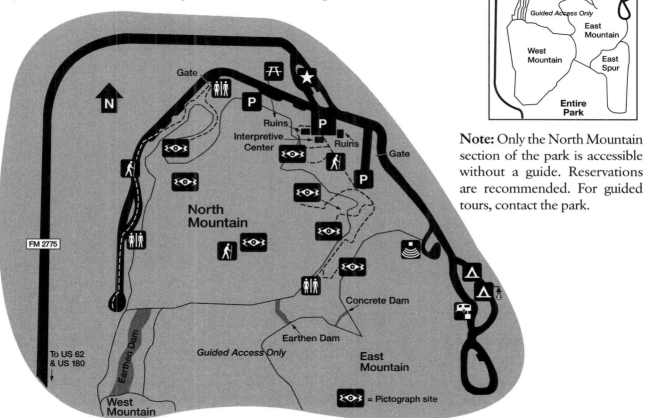

FACILITIES & ACTIVITIES

17 campsites with water/electricity	rock climbing
3 campsites with water only	amphitheater
restrooms/showers	historic structures
trailer dump station	pictographs (rock paintings)
picnicking	interpretive tour
nature trail	park store
hiking	

LAKE BROWNWOOD STATE PARK

FOR INFORMATION

Lake Brownwood State Park
200 State Park Rd. 15
Brownwood, TX 76801
325/784-5223

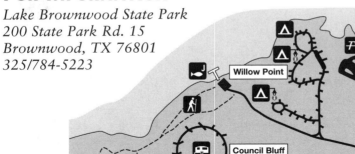

LOCATION

Lake Brownwood State Park is named for its primary attraction, a 7,300-acre reservoir created by damming Pecan Bayou, a tributary of the Colorado River. To reach this 537-acre park from Brownwood, take TX 279 north to Park Road 15, turn east and travel 5 miles to the park entrance, then 1 mile to headquarters. From US 183, take FM 2273 west to the FM 2559, then south on FM 2559 to Park Road 15.

FACILITIES & ACTIVITIES

20 campsites with water/electricity/sewage
55 campsites with water/electricity
12 campsites with water only
restrooms/showers
trailer dump station
10 screened shelters (tents only; no RVs)
16 cabins
Loma Vista Lodge/kitchen
Beach Lodge/kitchen
Fisherman Lodge/kitchen
Oak Lodge/kitchen
group camp: 4 bunkhouses and *group dining hall/kitchen

group recreation hall: dining hall/kitchen & meeting rooms (day-use)
picnicking
playgrounds
beach swimming area/bathhouse
fishing/fish cleaning facility
lighted fishing pier
boat ramp & dock
boating/waterskiing
1.8 miles of nature & hiking trails
park store
concessions (seasonal)

*Group hall may be rented with bunkhouses or separately for day-use.

LAKE COLORADO CITY STATE PARK

FOR INFORMATION

Lake Colorado City State Park
4582 FM 2836
Colorado City, TX 79512
325/728-3931

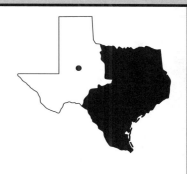

LOCATION

This state park is located about 11 miles southwest of Colorado City. Travel 5 miles west of Colorado City on I-20, exit south on FM 2836 and go 6 miles to the park entrance. Or, from downtown Colorado City, travel south on TX 163 for 7 miles, turn right on FM 2836, then ½ mile to the park entrance. This 500-acre park is on the southwest shore of Lake Colorado City—a 1,612-acre lake, created by damming Morgan Creek, a tributary of the Colorado River.

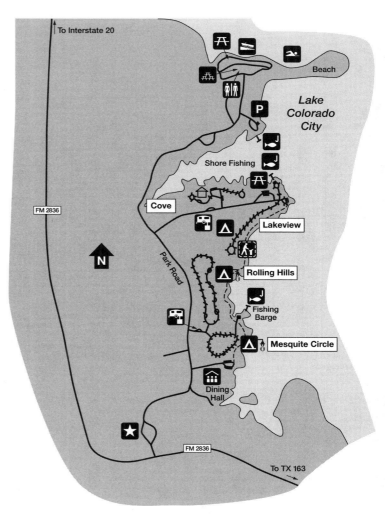

FACILITIES & ACTIVITIES

78 campsites with water/electricity
34 campsites with water only
restrooms/showers
2 trailer dump stations
11 cabins
group dining hall (overnight)
picnicking
group picnic area
playground
beach swimming area
nature trail
fishing/fish cleaning facility
2 fishing piers (1 lighted)/
   covered fishing barge
boat ramp
boating/waterskiing
kayak/hydrobike rentals
park store

Life is good when you take time to "wet a line."

LAKE J. B. THOMAS

FOR INFORMATION

Lake J. B. Thomas
Colorado River Municipal Water District
Box 869
Big Spring, TX 79721-0869
432/267-6341

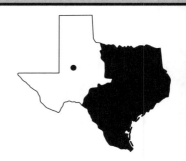

LOCATION

Lake J. B. Thomas, an 8,000-acre impoundment on the Colorado River has a shoreline of 75 miles; it was completed in 1952. Owned and operated by the Colorado River Municipal Water District, it was the first of three lakes constructed on the Colorado River to supply quality water to the citizens of West Texas. Visit the lake by going about 18 miles southwest of Snyder via TX 350, then FM 1606 and FM 2085 west. Other nearby towns include Ira, Vincent, Big Spring, and Gail.

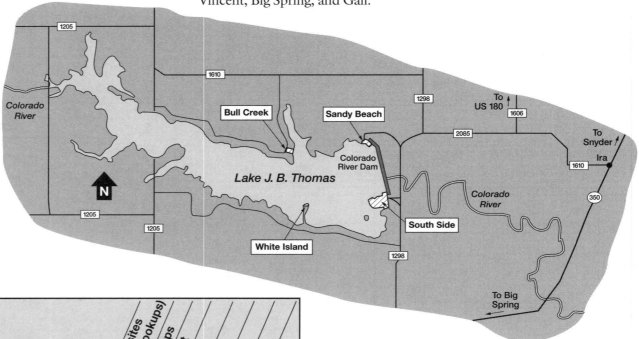

Parks	Total Number of Campsites (none have electrical hookups)	Camping Area for Groups	Toilets: F=flush; V=vault	Trailer Dump Station	Picnic Sites	Group Picnic Areas	Boat Launching Ramp
Bull Creek	8		V		•		•
Sandy Beach	10		V		•		
South Side	35	•	F	•	•	•	•
White Island	5	•	V	•	•	•	•

Note:
Drinking water is not available, nor are there
designated swimming areas at any of the parks.

Another reason why boaters should
bring a buddy is to help load the boat.

LAKE MEREDITH NATIONAL RECREATION AREA

FOR INFORMATION

Lake Meredith National Recreation Area
P.O. Box 1460
Fritch, TX 79063
806/857-3151

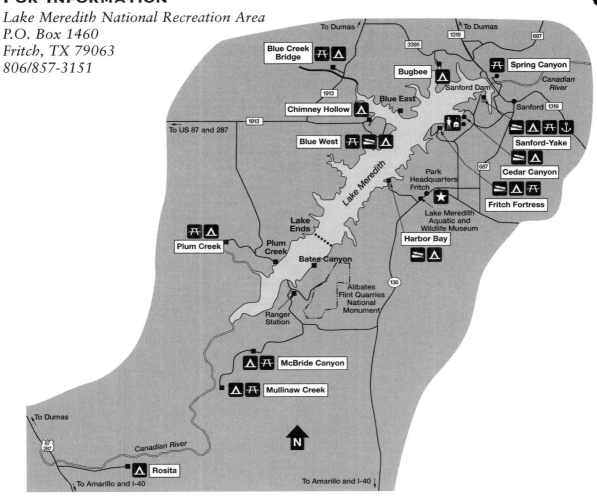

To Dumas
To Dumas
3395
1319
687

Blue Creek Bridge

Bugbee

Spring Canyon

Sanford Dam

Canadian River

1913

Blue East

Chimney Hollow

Sanford 1319

1913

To US 87 and 287

Blue West

Sanford-Yake

Lake Meredith

687

Cedar Canyon

Park Headquarters Fritch

Fritch Fortress

Lake Ends

Lake Meredith Aquatic and Wildlife Museum

Plum Creek

Plum Creek

Harbor Bay

Bates Canyon

136

Alibates Flint Quarries National Monument

Ranger Station

N

McBride Canyon

Mullinaw Creek

To Dumas

87 287

Canadian River

Rosita

To Amarillo and I-40

To Amarillo and I-40

FACILITIES & ACTIVITIES

approx. 300 RV & tent campsites at
   12 campgrounds
designated swimming area at Spring Canyon
waterskiing/sailing/sailboarding
fishing/indoor & outdoor fishing docks
marina/boating/5 boat ramps
limited groceries & fishing supplies
dryland boat storage
2 off-road vehicle-use areas
ranger-guided tours at Alibates Flint Quarries
museum/interpretive exhibits
amphitheater

An amphitheater is located at the Fritch Fortress campground.

Lake Meredith National Recreation Area (Continued)

Location

Lake Meredith National Recreation Area is located northeast of Amarillo. Formed by impoundment of the Canadian River, the 16,500-acre lake, with 100 miles of shoreline, provides the setting for numerous water-oriented activities. Alibates Flint Quarries National Monument adjoins the national recreation area; the quarries were a source of a high quality, rainbow-hued flint for Indians that roamed the plains.

Points of Interest

▲ Lake Meredith and the Canadian River offer refreshing waters to an otherwise arid windswept area; the flatlands are broken by canyons, buttes, and pinnacles.

▲ Cottonwoods and willows add a touch of green along the water; mesquite, prickly pear, and prairie grasses grow in drier regions.

▲ The Alibates Flint Quarries National Monument can be seen by free guided tours; tours are given by reservation only. Phone 806/857-3151.

▲ Lake Meredith Aquatic and Wildlife Museum provides lake-use information and features exhibits of area wildlife. The museum has five aquariums that display lake fish species.

General Information

▲ There are no entrance or camping fees; there are boating fees.

▲ Park headquarters and the museum are both located on TX 136 in Fritch.

▲ Campgrounds are open all year on a first-come, first-served basis; limit of stay is 14 days.

▲ There are 12 designated areas for camping; the number of campsites available varies when the lake level fluctuates. Camping areas include:
—canyon rim camping at Sanford-Yake, Fritch Fortress, and Blue West
—shoreline camping at Cedar Canyon, Harbor Bay, Chimney Hollow, and Bugbee.
—backcountry camping at McBride Canyon/Mullinaw Creek, Rosita, Plum Creek, and Blue Creek Bridge

Camping Areas	Drinking Water	Toilets; F=flush; C=chemical	Picnic Tables/ Shade Shelters	Dump Stations	Courtesy Docks	Boat Launch Ramps (water level at which usable, ft)
Blue Creek Bridge		C				
Blue West		C	•		•	70
Bugbee		C				
Cedar Canyon		C		•	•	69
Chimney Hollow		C				
Fritch Fortress	•	F	•	•	•	71
Harbor Bay		C			•	79–99
McBride Canyon		C				
Mullinaw Creek		C				
Plum Creek		C				
Rosita		C		•		
Sanford-Yake	•	F	•	•	•	*67

Notes:
*Sanford-Yake ramp remains usable the longest as lake level drops.
Spring Canyon is day use only.

▲ Sanford-Yake or Fritch Fortress campgrounds are recommended for those only planning a one-night stay as they are the most developed and provide a nice view of the lake. Sanford-Yake has 50 wheeled-camper or tent sites and Fritch Fortress has 10 sites.

▲ Sanford-Yake offers a marina, indoor and outdoor fishing docks, courtesy dock, public telephone, and limited groceries and fishing supplies.

▲ An amphitheater is located at Fritch Fortress.

▲ Off-road vehicle use areas are located at Blue Creek Bridge and Rosita.

▲ The only designated swimming area is located below the dam at Spring Canyon—a day-use only site.

▲ Good waterskiing areas are at Blue East, and Cedar Canyon.

▲ The 5 boat launch ramps are usable at various water levels.

LAKE NASWORTHY AND TWIN BUTTES RESERVOIR

FOR INFORMATION

Lake Nasworthy and Twin Buttes Reservoir
P.O. Box 1751
San Angelo, TX 76902-1751
325/657-4206

LOCATION

Lake Nasworthy is a 1,596-acre municipal lake that provides water supply, flood control and recreation for the San Angelo area; it is a companion to the larger Twin Buttes Reservoir. Twin Buttes Reservoir is an impoundment on the Middle and South Concho rivers. The lake is southwest of San Angelo, and is located between US 67 and US 277, as is Lake Nasworthy. Access to Twin Buttes Park is from US 67.

Parks	Number of Campsites with Electrical Hookups	Toilets: F=flush; V=vault	Showers	Trailer Dump Station	Picnic Sites	Boat Launching Ramp	Lake Swimming
Middle Concho	30	F		•		•	•
Spring Creek Marina	24	F	•	•		•	•
Twin Buttes	•	F			•	•	•

Notes:
Spring Creek Marina is operated by a concessionaire; it has 24 sites with full hookups.
All 3 parks have primitive tent areas available: Middle Concho, 25 acres; Spring Creek, 50 acres; and Twin Buttes, 200 acres.
Drinking water is not available at Middle Concho.

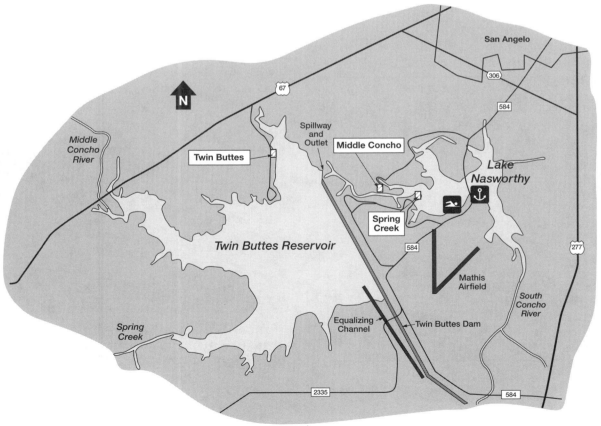

MONAHANS SANDHILLS STATE PARK

FOR INFORMATION

Monahans Sandhills State Park
P.O. Box 1738
Monahans, TX 79756
915/943-2092

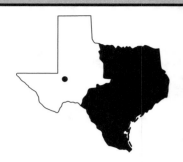

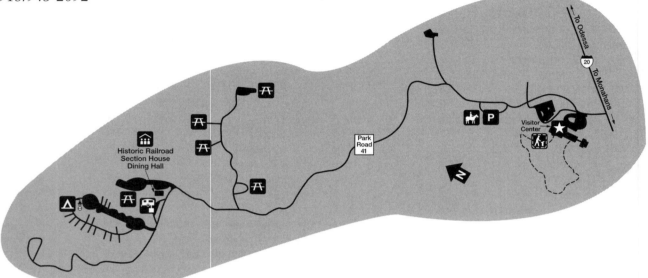

LOCATION

This state park is located 6 miles northeast of Monahans; take exit 86 off I-20 to Park Road 41. The park contains 3,840 acres of wild-sculptured sand dunes up to 70 feet high.

FACILITIES & ACTIVITIES

26 campsites with water/electricity

Historic Railroad Section House (group facility)

restrooms/showers

trailer dump station

picnicking

sandsurfing

rental boards & disks for sandsurfing

outdoor showers

¼-mile nature trail

hiking in sand dunes

equestrian area (600 acres)

interpretive center

park concession

TEXAS HIGHWAYS Magazine

Adults like to have fun too! There's something about making the first tracks of the day that brings joy to the heart.

O. H. Ivie Reservoir

For Information

O. H. Ivie Reservoir
Colorado River Municipal Water District
Box 869
Big Spring, TX 79721-0869
432/267-6341

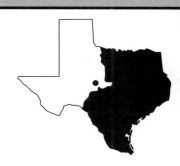

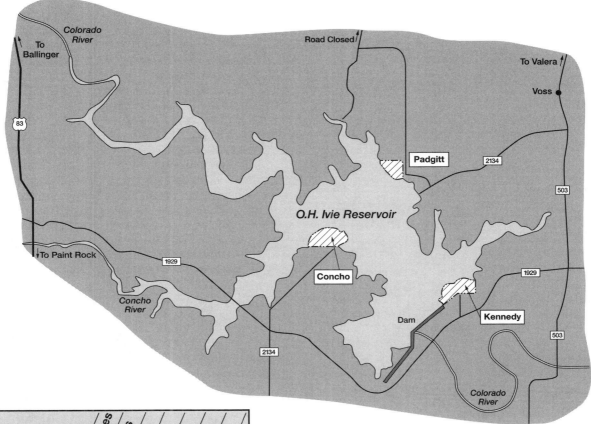

Recreation Areas	Total Number of Campsites	Camping Area for Groups	Toilets: F=flush; V=vault	Trailer Dump Station	Picnic Sites	Group Picnic Areas	Boat Launching Ramp
Concho	37	•	V	•	•	•	•
Kennedy	20	•	V	•	•	•	•
Padgitt	10		V		•		•

Notes:
Drinking water is not available, nor are there designated swimming areas at any of the recreation areas.
Concho & Kennedy have marinas; they are operated by concessionaires.
Concho & Kennedy marinas offer showers.
Full hookups: 30 at Concho; 12 at Kennedy.
Motel rooms: 30 at Kennedy; 15 at Concho.

Location

A 19,200-acre impoundment on the Colorado River, O.H. Ivie Reservoir was completed in 1952. Owned and operated by the Colorado River Municipal Water District, it was the first of three reservoirs constructed on the Colorado River to supply quality water to the citizens of West Texas. The lake is about 25 miles southeast of Ballinger; take US 83 south to FM 1929 and travel east. From Coleman, travel south on TX 206 to US 67 west, to FM 503 south. Other nearby towns include Coleman, Ballinger, Valera, Voss, and Paint Rock.

Palo Duro Canyon State Park

For Information

Palo Duro Canyon State Park
11450 Park Rd. 5
Canyon, TX 79015
806/488-2227

Location

Palo Duro Canyon State Park is located about 12 miles east of Canyon on TX 217. From Amarillo, it is south on RR 1541, then 8 miles east on TX 217. The Prairie Dog Town Fork of the Red River runs through this 18,438-acre park. The Pioneer Amphitheater, a 1,742-seat outdoor theater, is the site of summer performances of the outstanding musical drama "Texas Legacies."

TEXAS HIGHWAYS Magazine

Palo Duro Canyon has an extensive trail system for hikers, joggers, bikers, and equestrians. One 3-mile trail is for bikers only.

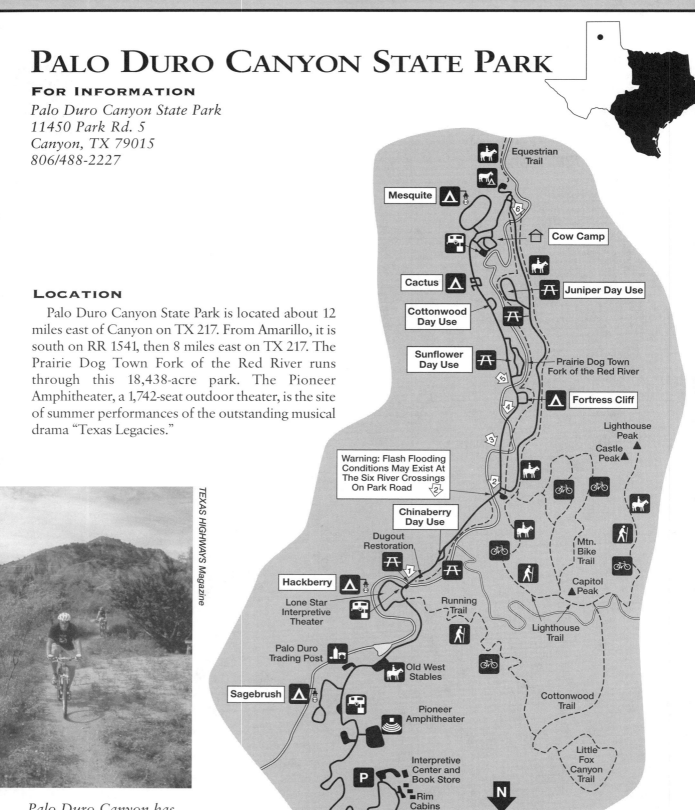

Equestrian Trail

Mesquite

Cow Camp

Cactus

Juniper Day Use

Cottonwood Day Use

Sunflower Day Use

Prairie Dog Town Fork of the Red River

Fortress Cliff

Lighthouse Peak

Castle Peak

Warning: Flash Flooding Conditions May Exist At The Six River Crossings On Park Road

Chinaberry Day Use

Dugout Restoration

Mtn. Bike Trail

Capitol Peak

Hackberry

Lone Star Interpretive Theater

Running Trail

Lighthouse Trail

Palo Duro Trading Post

Old West Stables

Sagebrush

Cottonwood Trail

Pioneer Amphitheater

Interpretive Center and Book Store

Little Fox Canyon Trail

N

Rim Cabins

Park Road 5

To Canyon and Amarillo

FACILITIES & ACTIVITIES

80 campsites with water/electricity

25 developed campsites with no utilities

10 hike-in primitive areas (½ mile to 2 miles)

10 equestrian campsites (½ mile to 2 miles)

restrooms/showers

3 trailer dump stations

3 cabins

4 mini-cabins

picnicking

playground

6-mile (round-trip) hiking/horseback/mountain bike trail to Lighthouse scenic overlook

3 miles of mountain bike only trails

18½ miles of multi-use trails (hiking/biking/running)

12½ miles of equestrian trails

9-mile (round-trip) running trail to Lighthouse

Old West riding stables: horse rentals available for guided trail rides (806/488-2180)

*Pioneer Amphitheater: outdoor theater for the musical drama "Texas Legacies"

Lone Star Interpretive Theater

visitor center/exhibits (open year-round)

Palo Duro Trading Post/park store

Texas Longhorn herd

scenic overlook & 6-mile drive

*For reservations for "Texas Legacies," phone 806/655-2181.

The Old West Stables, located inside the canyon, offers guided tours to Timber Creek Canyon and the famous Lighthouse formation.

SAN ANGELO STATE PARK

FOR INFORMATION

San Angelo State Park
3900-2 Mercedes Rd.
San Angelo, TX 76901-2630
325/949-4757

LOCATION

Located on the shores of 5,540-acre O.C. Fisher Lake, this state park is adjacent to the city of San Angelo. From US 87 or US 67, take FM 2288 to the park entrance. The O.C. Fisher Lake, built on the North Concho River, contains some 18,000 acres, most of which are undeveloped. In 1995, management of 7,677 acres of the property were transferred to the Texas Parks and Wildlife Department, and San Angelo State Park came into existence. Park redevelopment to its full recreational potential is expected to take several years.

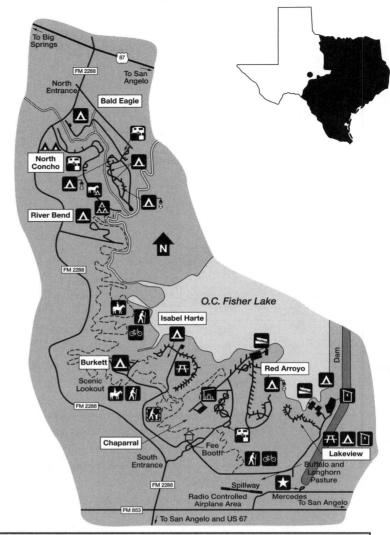

FACILITIES & ACTIVITIES

25 developed campsites at Lake View

40 campsites with water/electricity at Red Arroyo

3 developed campsites at Red Arroyo

30 developed campsites at Isabel Harte

3 developed campsites at Burkett

10 developed campsites at River Bend

10 campsites with water/electricity & horse pens at North Concho

13 developed campsites at North Concho

11 campsites with water/electricity at Bald Eagle

20 developed campsites at Bald Eagle

flush toilets/showers & vault toilets

trailer dump at Red Arroyo, Bald Eagle & North Concho

Chaparral Group Pavillion

20 sites with water/electricity surrounding Chaparral Group Pavillion

6 mini-cabins with AC/heat, RV hookup next to cabin near Group Pavillion

93 primitive campsites, scattered along the 15-mile trail

(accessible by foot, horseback & mountain bike)

equestrian camping

picnicking

group picnic pavillions

lake swimming

fishing

boating/waterskiing

2 high-level, 2 low-level boat ramps

nature trail

50 miles of hike/mountain bike/horse trails (some divided, some multi-use)

scheduled park tours

SEMINOLE CANYON STATE PARK & HISTORIC SITE

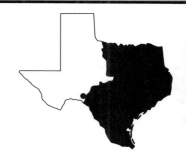

FOR INFORMATION

Seminole Canyon State Park & Historic Site
P.O. Box 820
Comstock, TX 78837
432/292-4464

LOCATION

Seminole Canyon State Park & Historic Site is located west of Comstock and east of Langtry off of US 90. From Comstock, travel 9 miles west to the park entrance; when approaching the park from the west, the entrance is just east of the high bridge across the Pecos River. In the canyon of this 2,172-acre park is Fate Bell Shelter, which contains some of North America's oldest pictographs, believed to have been painted as long as 4,000 years ago. Guided tours are conducted Wednesday through Sunday at 10 am and 3 pm to take visitors into the canyon to see these fine examples of rock art.

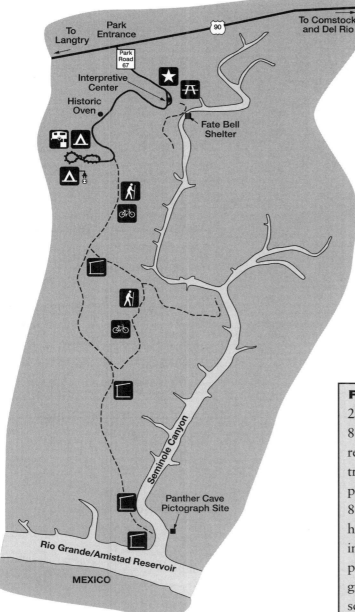

FACILITIES & ACTIVITIES

23 campsites with water/electricity
8 campsites with water only
restrooms/showers
trailer dump station
picnicking
8 miles of hiking/mountain bike trails
historical site
interpretive center/exhibits
park store
guided tour of Fate Bell Shelter (fee)
scenic overlooks

APPENDIX 1

FACILITIES AT A GLANCE FOR STATE PARKS

State Parks with Swimming Pools

Abilene, 157
Balmorhea, 158
Bastrop, 70
Choke Canyon (Calliham), 119
Goliad, 128
Lake Livingston, 88
Lockhart, 146

Notes:
Pools usually open last Friday in May and close the day after Labor Day; all pools charge a fee.
Balmorhea pool is open year-round on a swim-at-your-own-risk basis.

State Parks with Lakes Suitable for Waterskiing

Atlanta, 15
Caddo Lake, 19
Cedar Hill, 21
Choke Canyon, 119
Cooper Lake, 23
Eisenhower, 27
Fairfield Lake, 28
Falcon, 126
Inks Lake, 133
Lake Arrowhead, 33
Lake Bob Sandlin, 34
Lake Brownwood, 176
Lake Casa Blanca, 142
Lake Colorado City, 177
Lake Corpus Christi, 143
Lake Livingston, 88
Lake Somerville, 103
Lake Tawakoni, 38
Lake Texana, 144
Lake Whitney, 42
Martin Creek Lake, 49
Martin Dies, Jr., 91
Matagorda Island, 148
Possum Kingdom, 53
Ray Roberts Lake, 56
San Angelo, 23

State Parks with Mountain Bike Trails/Areas

Big Bend Ranch, 162
Bonham, 18

Brazos Bend, 76
Caprock Canyons, 165
Caprock Canyons Trailway, 165
Cedar Hill, 21
Choke Canyon (North Shore Area), 24
Cleburne, 22
Colorado Bend, 122
Cooper Lake, 23
Copper Breaks, 167
Davis Mountains, 168
Devils River, 123
Dinosaur Valley, 26
Eisenhower, 27
Fairfield Lake, 28
Falcon, 126
Fort Parker, 80
Fort Richardson, 29
Franklin Mountains, 171
Galveston Island, 81
Guadalupe River, 130
Hill Country, 131
Huntsville, 83
Lake Arrowhead, 18
Lake Bob Sandlin, 34
Lake Casa Blanca, 142
Lake Houston, 87
Lake Livingston, 88
Lake Mineral Wells, 36
Lake Mineral Wells Trailway, 36
Lake Somerville, 89
Lake Somerville Trailway, 89
Lake Texana, 144
Lake Whitney, 42
Lost Creek Reservoir State Trailway, 15
Martin Creek Lake, 49
Martin Dies, Jr., 91
Matagorda Island, 148
McKinney Falls, 149
Mustang Island, 150
Palo Duro Canyon, 18
Pedernales Falls, 154
Ray Roberts Lake, 56
Ray Roberts Greenbelt, 56
San Angelo, 186
Sea Rim, 102
Seminole Canyon, 187
South Llano River, 155
Tyler, 60
Village Creek, 110

State Parks with Surfaced Bicycle Trails

Bastrop, 70
Brazos Bend, 76
Buescher, 77
Garner, 127
Goose Island, 129
Huntsville, 83
Lake Mineral Wells Trailway, 36
Lake Livingston, 88
McKinney Falls, 149
Meridian, 50
Ray Roberts Lake, 56

State Parks with Golf Courses

Bastrop (18-hole), 70
Inks Lake (9-hole), 133
Lockhart (9-hole), 146
Stephen F. Austin (18-hole), 105

State Parks with Texas Longhorns

Abilene, 157
Big Bend Ranch, 162
Copper Breaks, 167
Fort Griffin, 170
Palo Duro Canyon, 184
Possum Kingdom, 34
San Angelo, 186

State Parks with Rock Climbing

Enchanted Rock, 125
Franklin Mountains, 171
Hueco Tanks, 175
Lake Mineral Wells, 36

State Parks with Equestrian Trails/Areas

Big Bend Ranch, 162
Caprock Canyons, 165
Caprock Canyons Trailway, 165
Choke Canyon (North Shore Area), 120
Cooper Lake (South Sulphur), 24
Copper Breaks, 167
Davis Mountains, 168
Dinosaur Valley, 26

Fairfield Lake, 28
Fort Griffin, 170
Fort Richardson, 29
Franklin Mountains, 171
Guadalupe River, 130
Hill Country, 131
Huntsville, 83
Lake Arrowhead, 33
Lake Houston, 87
Lake Livingston, 88
Lake Mineral Wells, 36
Lake Mineral Wells Trailway, 36
Lake Somerville Trailway, 89
Lost Creek Reservoir Trailway, 29
Monahans, 182
Palo Duro Canyon, 184
Pedernales Falls, 154
Ray Roberts Greenbelt, 56
Ray Roberts Lake (Isle du Bois), 56
San Angelo, 186

Notes:
Equestrian trails at Lake Livingston & Huntsville are
available for use ONLY for guided trail rides from
nearby stables.
Palo Duro Canyon has rental horses available for
individual & group trail rides.
Caprock Canyons State Park and Hill Country have
rental horses available near the park.

State Parks with Primitive Camping Areas for Backpackers

Bastrop, 70
Big Bend Ranch, 162
Caprock Canyons, 165
Caprock Canyons Trailway, 165
Choke Canyon (North Shore), 120
Colorado Bend, 122
Davis Mountains, 168
Devils River, 123
Dinosaur Valley, 26
Enchanted Rock, 125
Fairfield Lake, 28
Hill Country, 131
Inks Lake, 133
Lake Mineral Wells, 36
Lake Somerville Trailway, 89
Lost Maples, 147
Palo Duro Canyon, 184
Pedernales Falls, 154
San Angelo, 186

State Parks with Walk-In Campsites

Bastrop, 70
Bentsen-Rio Grande Valley, 115
Big Bend Ranch, 162
Buescher, 77
Caprock Canyons, 165
Cedar Hill, 21
Choke Canyon, 119
Colorado Bend, 122

Cooper Lake (South Sulphur), 24
Devils River, 123
Enchanted Rock, 125
Fort Griffin, 170
Fort Richardson, 29
Franklin Mountains, 171
Guadalupe River, 130
Hill Country, 131
Inks Lake, 133
Lake Bob Sandlin, 34
Lake Houston, 87
Martin Creek Lake, 49
Matagorda Island, 148
McKinney Falls, 149
Mother Neff, 93
Mustang Island, 150
Palo Duro, 184
Possum Kingdom, 53
Purtis Creek, 55
Ray Roberts Lake, 56
San Angelo, 186
Sea Rim, 102
Village Creek, 110

State Parks with Rental Cabins (#)

Bastrop (12), 70
Caddo Lake (9), 19
Cooper Lake (South Sulphur) (14), 24
Daingerfield (3), 25
Garner (17), 127
Lake Brownwood (16), 176
Lake Colorado City (11), 177
Martin Creek Lake (2), 49
Martin Dies, Jr. (2), 91
Palo Duro (3), 184
Possum Kingdom (7), 53

State Parks with Screened Shelters (#)

Abilene (8), 157
Blanco (7), 116
Brazos Bend (14), 76
Buescher (4), 77
Caddo Lake (9), 19
Choke Canyon (Calliham)(20), 119
Cleburne (6), 22
Cooper Lake (5 & 19), 23
Eisenhower (35), 27
Falcon (12), 126
Fort Parker (10), 80
Fort Richardson (11), 29
Galveston Island (10), 81
Garner (37), 127
Goliad (5), 128
Huntsville (30), 83
Lake Bob Sandlin (12), 34
Lake Brownwood (10), 176
Lake Corpus Christi (25), 143
Lake Livingston (10), 88
Lake Mineral Wells (15), 36

Lake Whitney (21), 42
Martin Creek Lake (19), 49
Martin Dies, Jr. (20 & 24), 91
McKinney Falls (6), 149
Meridian (11), 50
Stephen F. Austin (20), 105
Tyler (35), 60

State Parks with Group Trailer Areas

Abilene (36), 157
Buescher (14), 77
Eisenhower (37), 27
Falcon (31), 126
Galveston Island (20), 81
Lake Casa Blanca (18), 142
Lake Somerville (Birch Creek) (14), 89
Rusk-Palestine (Rusk) (23), 58
San Angelo (23), 186
Tyler (30), 60

Note:
*Eisenhower has full hookups; all other parks have
water/electricity.

State Parks with Full Hookups

Abilene, 157
Atlanta, 15
Bastrop, 70
Blanco, 116
Caddo Lake, 19
Cleburne, 22
Daingerfield, 25
Davis Mountains, 168
Eisenhower, 27
Falcon, 126
Goliad, 128
Lake Brownwood, 176
Lake Corpus Christi, 143
Lake Livingston, 88
Lake Whitney, 42
Lockhart, 146
Meridian, 31
Mission Tejas, 92
Rusk/Palestine, 58
Stephen F. Austin, 28

State Parks with Mini-Cabins (#)

Buescher (3), 77
Fort Griffin (1), 170
Inks Lake (22), 133
Palo Duro Canyon (4), 184
San Angelo (6), 186

State Parks with Cottages (#)

Cooper Lake (2 & 2), 23
Falcon (12), 126
Lake Bob Sandlin (8), 34
Martin Creek Lake (2), 49

APPENDIX 2

RESOURCES FOR FURTHER INFORMATION

National Forests & Grasslands in Texas
415 S. First St., Ste.110
Lufkin, TX 75910-3088
936/639-8501
www.southernregion.fs.fed.us/texas

National Park Service
Southwest Region
P.O. Box 728
Santa Fe, NM 87504
www.nps.gov

National Wildlife Refuges, Southwest Region
P.O. Box 1306
Albuquerque, NM 87103
www.fws.gov/southwest/refuges

Texas Parks and Wildlife Department
4200 Smith School Road
Austin, TX 78744-3291
512/389-8950
1-800-792-1112 (For Information Only)
www.tpwd.state.tx.us

U.S. Army Corps of Engineers
Federal Building
819 Taylor Street
P.O. Box 17300
Fort Worth, TX 76102-0300
817/334-2705
www.swf-wc.usace.army.mil

Guadalupe-Blanco River Authority
www.gbra.org

Lavaca-Navidad River Authority
www.lnra.org

Lone Star Trail Hiking Club Trail
www.lshtclub.com

Lower Colorado River Authority
www.lcra.org/index.html

Recreational Opportunities on Federal Lands
www.recreation.gov

Sabine River Authority
www.sra.dst.tx.us

Texas Department of Transportation
1-800-452-9292 (Travel Information)
www.dot.state.tx.us
www.traveltex.com

Trinity River Authority
www.trinityra.org

RESERVATION SYSTEMS

For Texas State Parks
Central Reservation System (CRS)
Texas Parks and Wildlife Department
Reservations may be made by e-mail, Internet,
   fax, or phone
Reservations and cancellations: 512/389-8900
www.tpwd.state.tx.us/park

For several LCRA park: Lake Bastrop, Lake, Fayette, and Black Rock Park at Lake Buchanan
Reservations available through the CRS of the TPWD
   (see above)

For select parks at the Army Corps of Engineers' lakes, National Park Service, and the USDA Forest Service recreation areas (Double Lake in the Sam Houston National Forest)
Reservations available through the National
   Recreation Reservation Service (NRRS) by toll-free
   telephone (1/877-444-6777) or by Internet.
   www.reserveusa.com

INDEX

ABOUT THE AUTHOR

 **Mickey Little, Ed.D.,** is professor emeritus of health and physical education at Texas A&M University, where she was founder and director of the Outdoor Education Institute. An avid camper, backpacker, and outdoor photographer, Dr. Little is the author of more than a dozen camping and hiking guides. She lives in the Hill Country near Johnson City, Texas, and continues to explore the outdoors.